The Question of Being

THE QUESTION OF BEING

East-West Perspectives

MERVYN SPRUNG
Editor

The Pennsylvania State University Press

University Park and London

Editorial Note

Each chapter in this book (except the first) originated at a symposium arranged by the philosophy department of Brock University. The symposium was made possible by grants from The Canada Council and Brock University.

Editorial thanks are due Ilse Sprung for her work on the translation of H.G. Gadamer's chapter from the German.

Library of Congress Cataloging in Publication Data

Main entry under title:

The Question of Being.

Includes bibliographical references and index.
1. Ontology. 2. Western Perspectives. 3. Eastern Perspectives.
I. Sprung, Mervyn.
BD331.Q4 111 76-41846
ISBN 0-271-01242-0

Printed in the United States of America

Contents

MERVYN SPRUNG

The Question of Being as Comparative Philosophy

Why do titles of books so often outrun their contents? Is it perhaps that, if they did not, the reader could hardly grasp their purpose? This is so in the present case, certainly. *The Question of Being*, as title, is presumptuous in contrast with the divergent chapters it shelters. Yet, as title, it links them all to a central undertaking which lends something of its range and depth to each.

This was the intent of the symposium at which the original papers were read. The gathering helped launch, at Brock University, a graduate program in comparative philosophy whose initial theme was the question of being. Those invited to offer their scholarship and their views could speak for a range of traditions which, it was thought, would have most to say about the theme: the Greek, the Christian, the post-Nietzschean European, the Hindu, and the Buddhist.

The sharp, possibly irremovable opposition between many of the views bespeaks the vitality of the problem. Charles Kahn holds that the Greek sense of 'be' is close to Quine's phrase "what there is." H.G. Gadamer argues that Plato's *idea agathou*, the highest form, is unlike all other Platonic forms in defying every ontic determination, something, he thinks, which Heidegger undervalues. Joseph Owens follows Parmenides' understanding of being as the ultimate object of thought deep into the Christian tradition, whereas J.G. Arapura treats being, within the central Hindu tradition, rather as an indicator of the ultimate (*brahman*) than as itself the ultimate. The thought of Martin Heidegger was, of course, strongly present throughout the symposium, refracted differently by Gadamer, Robert C. Scharff, and Zygmunt Adamczewski. Wilhelm Halbfass and J.N. Mohanty have quite different things to say about the Indian realists, and Mohanty's epistemological interest in Vedānta and the Buddhist logicians contrasts with J.G. Arapura's approach through the tradition and with my treatment of the Buddhist middle way as an alternative to 'being.'

The theme, it is hoped, is alive and well, certainly not exhausted, possibly invigorated by the treatment given it in these papers. Indeed, after reading them, one feels that the investigation could—and should—now begin. Certainly the thought of Plato, Aristotle, Plotinus, and the medieval Christians has yet to be held up thematically against the great tradition of the Upaniṣads, against Indian realism and against the attacks of the Buddhists on the concept of being. And, of course, preceding that and along with it, the question must be raised and pursued: is there a common question in all traditions, or is it alone the term 'being' (*sat*, *to on*, *Sein*) which lends the appearance of a common question? The theme itself demands this.

This theme will not allow itself to be confined within the horizon of the Greek-European tradition. If the thinkers of the Indian and Chinese traditions have been humanly concerned, their thinking will be of concern to us insofar as we think as humans. The first academic probings into the vast and little-known forests of Indian and Chinese thought have acquired the label "comparative philosophy." Inadequate as it is we can expect to have the term with us until the catholic approach it fumblingly designates has been accepted as the only adequate approach of our time. Those indomitably insular spirits who insist that as philosophy must be "argument" it is peculiar to Europe are entangled in at least one error and one sectarian view: that argument is limited to Western philosophy is quaint aberration, that philosophy is limited to argument is sectarian. Those who have ventured tentatively into the Indian and Chinese depths are no longer in doubt about the need and gains of penetrating further and further into them. Enough has been learned to found the simple conviction that any philosophic theme which is grasped only within the limitations of any one tradition, is, as theme, improperly grasped. It is not merely inadequate or provisional, it fails to be *philosophical*. Only scholasticism can be insular.

The term "comparative philosophy" does not appear to have been used consistently before P. Masson-Oursel published a book by that name in the twenties. His understanding of the term was so rigidly positivistic that the methods he advocates have had few, if any, practitioners. Comparative philosophy, he proposed, was to be a social science bent on a universal comparative study of human mental structures. So the name was born, even if to foster parents, and is still with us. The key notion of Masson-Oursel, the universality of philosophy, soon found a home in the philosophy department of the University of Hawaii. In 1939 and again in 1949, 1959, 1964, and 1969 important conferences in "East-West" philosophy were organized there, each lasting several weeks.

The hope of those responsible for these conferences seems now to have been overdrawn. The purpose of the conferences was to study the possibility of a single, homogeneous world philosophy. The goal of the philosophers participating was the discovery of avenues of progress toward a synthesis of Oriental and Occidental thought.[1] If Masson-Oursel demanded too little of philosophy, the Hawaii proponents demanded too much. Openness of thought, the touchstone of philosophy, is hardly amenable to a synthesis of views. But the vitality of the Hawaii enterprise persisted and its influence spread. In the late sixties the Society for Asian and Comparative Philosophy was founded in the United States, linked with the journal *Philosophy East and West*. This society has held comparative symposia on such themes as "Time and History," "Causality," and "The Languages of Philosophy." The Department of Philosophy at the University of Hawaii has itself held a number of symposia on comparative themes, such as "Heidegger and Eastern Thought" and "Aesthetics." A conference held at Wooster College in 1965 with the theme "Problems of the Self" was perhaps the first explicitly comparative conference in philosophy held in North America.

Long before the term "comparative philosophy" came into use, the essential work had been going on, though not in Masson-Oursel's positivistic sense. C.G. Jung suggests, audaciously, that Europe was already reaching for fresh sustenance when, at the end of the eighteenth century, Anquetil du Perron was drawn to Persia in pursuit of Eastern languages and thought. Du Perron translated into Latin a volume of Upaniṣads, originating in the Sanskrit but available to him in Persian, and it was this work which had such impact on Arthur Schopenhauer that he could say the Upaniṣads had been the consolation of his life and would be the consolation of his death. It was a Schopenhauerian, Paul Deussen, who at the end of the nineteenth century became the first, and he is today still the foremost, comparative philosopher of Europe. He came to the Sanskrit tradition not merely as a historian or philologist but as a philosopher with problems bequeathed him but not solved by his own tradition. C.G. Jung was another European of stature, the greatest as yet (Nietzsche does not count here), who approached Eastern thought with the purpose of learning from it. Jung, though not a comparative philosopher in the strict sense, nonetheless inquired into Chinese and Indian thought and confirmed the universality of human concerns.

The great and varied scholarly initiatives in England, France, Germany, Poland, and Russia from the second half of the nineteenth century on were devoted primarily to language study, the translation of texts, and sectarian interests but were only rarely comparative philosophy in the thematic and full sense. Indian scholars and thinkers of recent time, the best known being Aurobindo, K.C. Bhattacarya, and S. Radhakrishnan, have attempted to bring their tradition and the Western tradition into fruitful interaction. Many Indian departments of philosophy are comparative in their programs and are, in this respect, a generation ahead of Western universities.

All philosophy, insofar as it is based on historical scholarship, is by nature comparative. The philosopher pursues a problem by drawing what help he can from others within his own effective horizon. This horizon may be for some British empiricism, for others modern French and German thought; some live within a horizon which embraces the Greeks; not many can bring all facets and branches of the Greek-European tradition into a genuinely open and free interplay: we are limited as analysts or phenomenologists, Thomists or Marxists, logicians or existentialists. Yet these very limitations—our historical and thematic horizons—emphasize the fact that philosophers normally *are* comparative, within their capacities. And each understands himself as being as broadly based as his interest demands; it is just that one's interest seldom forces one to include more than a portion of the Western tradition within one's comparative study.

Ours is a time of encounter and discovery between hitherto autonomous cultural traditions. The encounter and discovery are moving at a dizzying speed and across a range of concerns from industrial engineering to the concept of man. Philosophy is caught up in this crumbling of horizons, usually reluctantly. New reaches with new problems are opening out breathtakingly. The attempt to push the horizon of contemporary philosophy outward to include these is "comparative philosophy." It is an odd label certainly because it appropriates an integral aspect of all philosophy for what is merely a new and special application. All other labels suggested so far are at least as inapt: "universal" philosophy? "synoptic" philosophy? All such names sit uncomfortably because philosophy is by nature comparative, synoptic, universal. When this new horizon, embracing not less than the Chinese, Indian, and Greek-European philosophies, has become accepted beyond polemics, then such terms will wither away. Until this happens we will presumably continue to refer to the special concern to draw Chinese and Indian thought into one thematic horizon with Western thought as "comparative philosophy."

There are already varying concepts of ways of proceeding in comparative philosophy, not all of equal promise. It may help to distinguish the apologist from the zealot, and the parallelist from the thematist. The apologist tries to persuade us that Eastern philosophy has struggled with the same problems as have the Greek and European. He thinks he must vindicate Eastern philosophy by showing that, underneath some misleading surface oddities, it is essentially the *same* as Western philosophy. He wants to show that the Indians and the Chinese were profound *too*, and in our way.

There are those who hold that philosophy means what is practiced in the philosophy departments of North American universities at the present time and such philosophy, it is claimed, is found *also* in the Sanskrit tradition. One of them has written, "Western analytical philosophers who had supposed that their discipline was unknown in the East, are now becoming aware of the scientific method in much of Indian philosophy."[2] Even such a prodigious scholar as the Russian Th. Stcherbatsky is something of an apologist in his attempt to show that the distinction of the Buddhist logicians between the irreducible given of perception, which is the absolutely real, and the named content of the mind anticipated Immanuel Kant's distinction between sense intuition and the categories of the understanding. There have been other attempts by both Westerners and Easterners to show that Hegel is implicit in Vedānta, that Buddhism and Yoga are "existentialist," and that, wonder of wonders, the Vaiśeṣika school in India was concerned with being much as Aristotle had been, and without direct influence!

Against the apologist, who implies the primacy of Western thought, one recognizes his opposite, the partisan of Eastern thought; he tends to discern a crippling incompetence in the Greeks and Europeans which has fated them to remain on the lower slopes of philosophy. This kind of zealot usually faults the West for succumbing to the object world, to linear time, to the lure of overt action, and so on. He finds Western proofs of God's existence and the concept of immortality childish and blames the woes of a technologically hapless world on Western philosophy.

Then there are those who take the term "comparative" too literally: these are the parallelists. Often close to being apologists, they seize on specific or even partial problems in the work of one philosopher and demonstrate in detail just how it parallels a problem in the thought of a philosopher in another tradition. Kant's concept of freedom may be presented in parallel to freedom in the *Bhagavad Gītā*; Sartre's *en soi* and *pour soi* are paralleled with *puruṣa* and *prakṛti* in the Sāṁkhya system; "structures of existence" are discovered in Buddhism and Vedānta; Nietzsche's skepticism is held to parallel Nāgārjuna's attack on language as mere naming.

Interesting work has been and can be done in this way if good sense prevails; historical scholarship provides a basis of understanding for those not familiar with the relevant languages. Parallelism is not, nonetheless, comparative philosophy in the fullest sense. To abstract sharply delimited problems from the overarching concerns of their matrices, discussing similarities and differences in their internal structures and resolutions, is to cripple such problems philosophically. To do this is scholastic and may even be arbitrary. It can be an indispensable aid to comparative philosophy, so long as it does not think it is that. Halbfass says strongly in his chapter, "What comparative philosophy needs is not more and more juxtaposable data . . . but the courage to develop its own hermeneutics."

There is much left to be done when the apologists, the partisans, and the parallelists have done all they can. There is still the undertaking of comparative philosophy in its peculiar, special sense: thinking into the most acute problems of one's own time within the historical horizon of all known philosophical traditions. Such problems are not found entire and concrete *in* any one tradition; problems are fresh and unique in every age; to compare problems seized from history is to distort them and perhaps to deceive oneself. Living problems are not found in earlier thought, though they arise out of it. Living problems are by definition not the problems of any one tradition. What Sanskrit philosophers have meant by *mokṣa* (freedom) is a problem within Indian philosophy, it is not a living problem. "Freedom," however, is such and in pursuing it Indian thought concerning *mokṣa* will be (along with modern European "free will," the Taoist "true man," and so on) indispensable to penetrating into the problem.

It follows from this central position of the problem that the word "comparative" refers not so much to a method of comparison as it does to the problem itself, which is the beginning and the basis of the comparison. The aim of taking up a problem comparatively is not to compare philosophers or traditions with one another but to establish the problem on a universal, human basis and to pursue its mysteries in the light of the thought of all relevant traditions. The search for relevant, helpful work across the traditions may, at times, fail. Where this is so one critically refuses to draw in only apparently relevant thought. Where, however, a problem opens up both itself and the historical thought found relevant to it, then one might say, but in metaphor only, that the traditions were being "compared." It is clearer to say that the problem is comparative, or synoptic, or universal.

Does this book exemplify comparative philosophy? It may not be exemplary, yet in its form and by its interest it is comparative philosophy. Though only Scharff's chapter is explicitly comparative, the others constitute an experiment in comparative philosophy. The experiment is perforce halting. The theme dwarfs the attempt to close with it. The aspects explicitly treated do not form a continuous, embracing, well-woven comprehension of the reach of the problem in our own time. Perhaps this volume can throw the difficulties of comparative philosophy into relief, encouraging both caution and the will to return and persevere. Further work may interweave the most promising aspects of the theme more closely and fruitfully.

One question arises which blocks any thought of straightforward pursuit of the question of being in a comparative way. This question concerns the question of being itself, or, as Halbfass puts it, the "questionability of the question." The concern which gives pause is whether there is a theme, a problematic running through Greek, European, and Eastern thought identifiable by the name 'being.' Indeed we must query the assumption, commonly made, that the Greeks and the modern Europeans are concerned with the same problem. Can we move from Aristotle to Heidegger, from *to on hē on* to *Sein*, without questioning whether the philosophical problem is the same? Can we indeed move even from Parmenides to Plato, assuming that a similarity of language ensures an identity of problem? Are we not, then, making a gigantic assumption in comparing a Greek or a European thinker's concern with *to on* or *Sein* or being with the Indian thinker's *sat*?

Consider the shifting variegations of the term 'being' presented in this book. Owens states in his chapter on Parmenides, "whatever is known is known as a being." His exposition makes it crystal clear that "the first metaphysician" in Greek thought used the term 'being' as the self-evident way of referring to whatever can become an object of cognition. He writes of "the immediate experience that whatever is thought of is necessarily thought of and expressed in terms of being." This being according to Owens is that of the visible and tangible universe, a striking emphasis compared with the later very different concerns of Plato, Aristotle, and Plotinus.[3] Perhaps the primary point is Parmenides' conviction that the being of particular things was directly intuited "after the manner in which the ordinary mortal considers himself to be intuiting color or extension or movement." When we remind ourselves that this conviction was not shared by all Greeks, was indeed bluntly rejected by Plato and Plotinus and would have been regarded as a view arising from ignorance by the Vedantists and the Buddhists, we may wonder how many uses the term 'being' can have.

Charles Kahn approaches the problem of being in Greek thought through the uses of the verb *eimi*, 'be.' He finds that what he calls the veridical use was primary in determining the sense of being at which Parmenides, Plato, and Aristotle had arrived. Being, he finds, was for them a question of the structure of the reality in terms of which statements are true or false. For both Plato and Aristotle this became the object of inquiry, of scientific investigation, and the basis for the notion of truth; "in Greek ontology, from Parmenides on, the question of being is a question as to what reality must be like, or what the world must be like, in order for knowledge and true (or false) discourse to be possible." Kahn finds this to be, in effect, the first question Wittgenstein sets out to answer in the *Tractatus*, differing greatly from the topic pursued by Heidegger. The

One of Plotinus is clearly excluded from consideration by Kahn's formula; and of course Vedānta and Buddhism criticize the claims of cognition in such ways as to make it a forlorn approach to being.

In his chapter on Plato and Heidegger, Gadamer reinterprets Heidegger's position within Western thought. If the question of being is restricted to the problem of Plato's forms, then indeed being became lost to philosophy; and if Aristotle's criticism of Plato remains within the assumption that being is presented immediately as a determinable something, then being in our time had once more to be re-thought in its own nature. Gadamer calls this interpretation of Plato and Aristotle into question, suggesting that the *idea agathou*, Plato's late dialectic, and Aristotle's *nous* do not conceal being. This, which is at wide variance with Kahn's view, is offered as evidence for the persistent unity of the understanding of being in the West. Yet this very "persistence" makes it all the more clear that the non-Heideggerians of the intervening centuries demonstrate the many senses which being has had in the West.

Scharff's chapter on Heidegger and the Upaniṣads is the only explicit attempt at East-West thinking in this book, and the only attempt to set the problem squarely in our own time. He follows Heidegger's path of thinking from the inauthenticity of everyday man through the authentic awareness of time as finitude to the acceptance of the coming to pass of presence (*Ereignis*) where the limitations of the ordinary human are not operative. Scharff compares this path with the way of meditation in the *Māṇḍūkya Upaniṣad*. He finds there the same discontent with an everyday existence in which concern for objects dominates, and an analogous movement toward freedom from everyday limitations which is reached in the silent merging with *ātman* where all distinctions are absent. In this merging, he finds, one belongs to *brahman* even as one belongs to *Ereignis*. Whatever difficulties may arise in pursuing this comparison (and that of the timelessness of *brahman* will be one of these) it is a bold attempt. Is it significant that in it the question of being, or at least the term being, loses something of its primacy? For being does not embrace the *Ereignis* but is given in it.

Adamczewski pursues certain questions which arise within Heidegger's thought about being. He exposes the problem of the ontological difference in an original way, pointing out that such matters as truth, time, worldhood, speech, the fourfold, freedom, and homelessness are neither entities nor one with being. They are inseparable from man's being and are somehow positively related to his ability to participate in being though being itself withdraws beyond the reach of such metaphysical relationships. Adamczewski brings out the primacy of being in Heidegger's thought. "Because to speak of entities as such includes: to understand in advance entities as they are, i.e., in their being. . . . Man is one who says: yes and no." Adamczewski adds, "If there were not some understanding of what it means 'to be,' then human speech could not exist." The affinity of such thinking to Vedānta is striking: all things are an expression of but do not exhaust *brahman*. Buddhist opposition is no less striking: the everyday sense of being lends a false reality to things.

Halbfass opens up the difficulties, the bewildering variations, and something of the promise of treating the question of being comparatively. His views on the status of comparative philosophy are perhaps the clearest we have and can only be endorsed. He is certain that being never became a central theme of Indian philosophy as it did in the West following Aristotle. In the Vaiśeṣika school, to which Halbfass devotes himself especially, it was a horizon, a framework of the program of exhaustively classifying the totality of what there is. 'Beingness' (*sattā*) is simply the common denominator of what there is, the highest universal. In the complex history of the Vaiśeṣika school other terms made their appearance: *astitva*, isness, the objective basis for saying of something 'it is'; *svarūpa*, own being, the irreducible selfhood of anything. The relationships of these concepts to one another are clearly complex and open to endless debate. Though no tradition of ontology grew out of the Vaiśeṣika initiative, it demands that we ask ourselves if we know what many of the common terms of Western philosophy—existence, essence, being, nothingness—really mean. That Halbfass can make this statement so bluntly and so convincingly announces that comparative philosophy is with us.

Arapura emphasizes, in his study of Advaita Vedānta, the primacy of *brahman* and the derivative nature of being (*sat*). *Brahman* is objectively given through the authoritative scriptures, the Vedas and the Upaniṣads, as presence, and *sat* is interpreted in terms of this given presence. The essential definition of *brahman* comprises the three terms *sat* (being), *cit* (consciousness), and *ānanda* (bliss). These are of course not predicates but "indicators" of *brahman*. Being is the logical principle by which one grasps *brahman* intellectually; consciousness and bliss point to the concrete presence, the thisness, without which *brahman* would be an abstraction. This statement of the bearing of being (*sat*) within Advaita Vedānta forces a question on us: If being is so subordinated to something greater, *brahman*, is this the being of Aristotle, Heidegger, and the Vaiśesika? For all of these being was the end of thought, that which nothing else could throw light on. This is strikingly not so in Vedānta. It appears that we must say either that *sat* is cognate with *Sein* only terminologically, whereas *brahman* is the true cognate, or else that *brahman* overarches being. Plotinus should enter here, and the problem sprouts its comparative wings.

My own "Being and the Middle Way," interprets the Mādhyamika school of Buddhism in a radically counterontological way. Nāgārjuna and Candrakīrti, I argue, draw out the full significance of the Buddha's repudiation of the two "dogmas": that things are and that they are not. They take this to mean that the notion being is delusively applied both to the everyday world and to the "true" world, and that, in consequence, the philosophical quest for knowledge is doomed to failure, there being nothing capable of being known. They slip from the clutches of nihilism and skepticism by means of the theory of *prajñapti*, which holds that names are guides to action, i.e., ways of taking things, not referents to things. The way of the Buddhist wise man, the 'middle way,' on which things neither have nor do not have being, is the way on which things present themselves in their truth. 'Middle way' replaces 'being' as the end of philosophical thought.

Mohanty explicitly compares the thought of three Indian schools, the logical realists (Nyāya-Vaiśeṣika), the Buddhist logicians, and Advaita Vedānta. The Nyāya-Vaiśeṣika school gives a logical turn to the problem, asking how the universal term 'existence' is to be used in judgments. 'Existence' is the highest universal, yet, as according to Nyāya-Vaiśeṣika only substances, qualities, and motion exist in the full sense, it must be restricted to these. This leaves the status of universals and relations, which obviously are, to be understood in a weaker sense of existence, not an entirely satisfying outcome. The Buddhist logicians (not representative of middle way Buddhism) regard the universal term 'existence' as a mental construct and so strictly inapplicable to anything. The term 'being' is restricted to the unnameable, pre-perceptual base (*svalakṣaṇa*) of all language which is given in point-instants of experience without duration. No part of the linguistic world, not even the named percept, can be said to be. Vedantists likewise have a severe and discriminatory criterion of being: only what cannot possibly be negated truly is. This means that the *content* of any possible experience fails to qualify because the content of one experience is necessarily being overtaken and negated by subsequent experiences. Only the possibility of experience itself—self-shining and self-manifesting consciousness—can never be negated and so can be taken as being. That the particular contents of experience make a false claim to being is inevitable because of the primal ignorance of humans. It is only too clear from Mohanty's exposition that these three schools do not, in essential respects, share a common problem. The world of everyday objects —precisely what exists according to Nyāya-Vaiśeṣika—is denied the status of being by both Buddhists and Vedantists. Whether these differences are semantic or substantial, what remains of a single theme of being?

Thus—in moving variegation—the question of being from nine or ten vantage points. What generates the variegation? Is it a matter of technical terms: either that 'being' in semantic strictness means the same for different philosophers but is located differently in their fields of experience; or that 'being' has quite different meanings, so that under a single term quite different problems are concealed? Or, on the other hand and not as a matter of terminology, is it the diversity of human thought itself which generates the seeming cacophany? If human thinking has understood its primary concern differently in the different schools and traditions would this concern not take the form of differing central themes and questions ('being,' 'way,' 'truth')? Yet, might one not see through language and the limitations of tradition and relate the diverse themes to a pervasive concern of human thought? To raise this question implies the possibility that the Greek-European formulation of the theme of being would lose its primacy, its right to adjudicate the various concerns of the other traditions.

This volume provides considerable evidence that the differences arise essentially from terminology. Is the pre-perceptual, sub-linguistic being of the Buddhist logician not recognizably that of Heidegger's *Sein* in that both are the condition for language to have meaning? And surely Plato's *eidos* is the source of the meaning of statements, and the Vedantists' *brahman* as well? Perhaps being is one but is located differently in each school? But then the Buddhist middle way repudiates the notion of being as ultimate, as does Plotinus; and the *sattā*, beingness, of the Nyāya-Vaiśeṣika school is an ontological specific, not a concept of source in the sense found in Plato and the Vedānta. Parmenides' being, intuitable as the object of knowledge, is not one with either the Vedantic *brahman* or Heidegger's *Sein*. The term 'being' appears after all to have definably different meanings and not merely to be located differently for different philosophers.

Perhaps then there is one essential question of being though we must tolerate a variety of terms used to refer to it. The upaniṣadic *brahman* has the strongest family resemblance to Heidegger's *Sein*. Are Aristotle's *to on hē on* and Plato's *to ontōs on*, despite Heidegger's insistence on their limitations, not other terms for the quintessential meaning of being? Indeed, does Heidegger's philosophical undertaking not presuppose that (in the West?) the question of being is one, in whatever terms it is raised or concealed? Could even the Mādhyamika's middle way, despite its rejection of the terms being and non-being, be concerned, in its own idiosyncratic way, to speak about being? And yet doubts of this rise up in flocks: Parmenides' *einai* is what is known and so are Plato's *eidos* and Aristotle's *ousia*; being here cannot mean Heidegger's *Sein*, which is not less than the possibility of knowedge; no less can it be *brahman* or the middle way, both of which demote knowledge to a contextual phenomenon. Indeed what meaning can it have to speak of one question of being persisting through Western thought if, for its great part, that question is mistaken for a lesser question which merely resembles it?

Not much light comes to us from considering the variegation as a matter of terminology, it seems. Must we concede then that the theme is only apparently one, that the manifest differences reflect a genuine plurality of problems even though a fortuitous similarity of technical terms partially obscures this? This is clearly a possibility and might well be the outcome of a prolonged study. And yet there is still another possibility which we cannot exclude.

If the strong resonances which echo back and forth between the traditions indicate that something common binds them together, might it be not certain questions in their Greek-European form, but an underived, tacit concern for the *ultimate in sense* which can be reached by human thought—keeping open the possibility that 'sense' may go beyond 'thought'? If it were, would the Greek-European question of being not become one of several forms which this concern for the ultimate in sense may take? Vague and indigestible as such a prospect may appear to be, it at least keeps open the possibility of our finding the capacity to understand all the human traditions of thought as *human*, as speaking to a concern that arises from the vital center of human need and genius—if hitherto inexpressible in the language of any one tradition. In fact, is it so difficult for us to understand the upaniṣadic word, "There are two forms of *brahman*, the manifest and the unmanifest,"[4] even though one has been brought up on the difference between Plotinus' One and being, Plato's idea of the good and the Forms, Heidegger's *Sein* and *Seiendem*? Cannot we understand a thought even as different as the Buddhist middle way (or for that matter as the Chinese *Tao*) as an attempt to say the way things ultimately are, to say what in the end makes sense, to say what the human concern is?

This attempt would be abortive indeed if it were merely a formal, blanket covering for divergent traditions of thought not all of which qualify as philosophy. But it may be, it wants to be, more than this. It suggests, as an indefeasible challenge of our time, that we learn from the divergences, from the richness of the cacophony, that the concern of human thought is wider than we of the Greek-European tradition have suspected, that we learn, now, something new, something fresh about what the concern of human thought can be, that we continue our long effort to learn what the human concern is. Should this be more than empty rhetoric, then comparative philosophy is also more than an empty formula.

Notes

1. Charles A. Moore, *Essays in East-West Philosophy* (Honolulu: University Press of Hawaii, 1951), announcement on book cover.

2. This statement accompanies each number of the recently established (Oct. 1970) *Journal of Indian Philosophy*. The journal is in practice much more open-minded.

3. The sharp differences between Plotinus and both Parmenides (as interpreted by Joseph Owens) and Aristotle, and hence the reason why he deserves to be included in any discussion of the question of being, may be called to mind here. Consider the following passage from the *Enneads*:

> This produced reality is an Ideal-form—for certainly nothing springing from the Supreme can be less—and it is not a particular form but the form of all, beside which there is no other; it follows that The First must be without form, and, if without form, then it is no Being; Being must have some definition and therefore be limited; but the First cannot be thought of as having definition and limit, for thus it would be not the Source but the particular item indicated by the definition assigned to it. If all things belong to the produced, which of them can be thought of as the Supreme? Not included among them, this can be described only as transcending them: but they are Being and the Beings; it therefore transcends Being.
>
> Note that the phrase 'transcending Being' assigns no character, makes no assertion, allots no name, carries only the denial of particular being; and in this there is no attempt to circumscribe it: to seek to throw a line about that illimitable Nature would be folly, and anyone thinking to do so cuts himself off from any slightest and most momentary approach to its least vestige. [Plotinus, *Enneads*. Trans. Stephen MacKenna (London: Faber and Faber, 1969, p. 408]

4. *Bṛhadāraṇyaka Upaniṣad*, II. 3. 1.

Bibliography

Books

Masson-Oursel, P. *Comparative Philosophy*. Eng. trans. London: Kegan Paul, Trench, and Trübner, 1926.

Jung, C.G. *Gesammelte Werke*, vol. 11. *Zur Psychologie westlicher und östlicher Religionen*. Zurich: Rascher Verlag, 1963.

Deussen, Paul. *The Philosophy of the Upaniṣads*. Eng. trans., A.S. Geden. New York: Dover, 1966. (1st ed. 1906).

———. *The Philosophy of the Vedānta*. Eng. trans., G.A. Jacob. Calcutta: Susil Gupta, 1957.

Radhakrishnan, S. *Eastern Religions and Western Thought*. Oxford: Oxford University Press, 1939.

———, ed. *History of Philosophy Eastern and Western*. 2 vols. London: Allen and Unwin, 1953.

Raju, P.T. *Introduction to Comparative Philosophy*. Lincoln: University of Nebraska Press, 1962.

Raju, P.T., and Albury Castell, eds. *East-West Studies on the Problem of Self*. The Hague: Nijhoff, 1968.

Raju, P.T., and S. Radhakrishnan, eds. *The Concept of Man*. London: Allen and Unwin, 1960.

Singh, R.J., ed. *World Perspectives in Philosophy, Religion and Culture Essays presented to R. M. Datta*. Patna: Bharati Bhavan, 1968.

Moore, Charles A., ed. *Philosophy—East and West*. Honolulu: University Press of Hawaii, 1944.

———. *Essays in East-West Philosophy*. Honolulu: University Press of Hawaii, 1951.

———. *Philosophy and Culture, East and West*. Honolulu: University Press of Hawaii, 1962.

———. *The Status of the Individual in East and West*. Honolulu: University Press of Hawaii, 1967.

———. *The Indian Mind*. Honolulu: University Press of Hawaii, 1967.

———. *The Chinese Mind*. Honolulu: University Press of Hawaii, 1967.

———. *The Japanese Mind*. Honolulu: University Press of Hawaii, 1967.

Journals

Ānvīkṣikī. Center for the Advanced Study of Philosophy. Banaras: Hindu University.

Philosophy East and West. Honolulu: University Press of Hawaii.

Journal of Indian Philosophy. Dordrecht: D. Reidel.

Journal of Chinese Philosophy. Dordrecht: D. Reidel.

Some Western Perspectives

JOSEPH OWENS, C.Ss.R.

Being in Early Western Tradition

Genuine interest in the problem of being has been on the increase throughout the last few decades. Even those who wish to regard it as dead and buried acknowledge that at least its ghost keeps knocking at the door. Moreover, a much keener sense of the way the history of a philosophical problem bears upon its actual consideration and treatment seems alive in current discussions.[1] Further, the need of approaching a metaphysical problem not only in light of Western tradition but also in that of the various Eastern legacies has made itself felt with surprising force in recent years. For instance, the American Metaphysical Society, after seventeen years of more or less parochial confinement to Western thought, acknowledged, in a meeting at the Inter-American Congress of Philosophy at Quebec in 1967, that in isolation it was not attaining its proper objectives. The result was the organization of the First International Congress of Metaphysics, held at Varna in September 1973, with both East and West participating.[2] East-West colloquia and philosophical journals of professedly international scope likewise attest to this interest. A deep metaphysical problem, such as that of being, accordingly must be approached today against the background of long philosophical traditions both in the East and in the West.

The essays in this book bring together representatives of the different traditions in both East and West, presenting an exchange of insights and a constructive dialogue begun at a Brock University symposium. The first condition for dialogue of this kind is a clear understanding in depth of the respective views. As a contribution to the project this paper aims to examine the problem of being in its earliest appearance in Western thought, and then to show briefly how that early position of the problem exercised its influence through later Greek and medieval times down to early modern thought.

The problem of being was first posed in the West by the Greek Parmenides in the fifth century B.C. An effort has been made to show that an earlier philosopher, Anaximander, was the first Western metaphysician.[3] The notion of metaphysics, of course, has been understood in various ways, and in one or the other of its senses a case may be made for classing Anaximander as a metaphysician. But in the sense of an investigation of things from the viewpoint of their being, the sense that became standardized through Peripatetic tradition, it would be difficult to show that metaphysics takes its origin in Anaximander. Rather, the earliest surviving record of a philosophical study of things in the light of their being is to be found in the fragments of Parmenides' poem. The problem of being in Western tradition finds its starting point in these fragments.

Parmenides flourished in Elea, a Greek colony on the west coast of Italy, south of the Gulf of Salerno. The colony had been founded about 540 B.C. by Greeks from Ionia, who evidently brought with them the Ionian interest in the origin and development of the visible universe. At any rate, some fifty years after the foundation of the colony, a philosophical poem composed by Parmenides handed down the first recorded Western attempt to account for the universe in terms of being, instead of through the Ionian way of change and growth. This poem of Parmenides had far-reaching effects on subsequent philosophic development, as is amply attested in later Greek writings. It continued to be read for about a thousand years, and its tenets were discussed penetratingly by thinkers of the stature of Plato, Aristotle, and Plotinus. Its influence on the thought of lesser figures is apparent. By the time the last copy of the complete poem had disappeared it had been quoted so abundantly by other writers that the sections and verses copied allow the general structure of the poem to be reestablished and permit the characteristic tenets attributed in tradition to Parmenides to be studied in the fragments themselves.

The poem had three parts, which formed a unified whole. The fragments that remain show how the second part followed in express sequence upon the first, and the third in express sequence upon the second. The first part was an introduction or proem, the second dealt with being, and the third with the way things appear to men. The composition fits into a recognized literary genre of the time. Somewhat as in Hesiod's *Theogony* (1–108) the goddesses appear to the poet at the foot of their sacred mountain and impart to him the truth about the way the immortal gods came into being, so Parmenides in the proem of his work introduces himself as being borne along in a chariot guided by sun maidens who "leaving behind the dwellings of night, sped me toward light" (Fr. 1.9–10; DK, 28 B). There Parmenides is warmly welcomed by a goddess into her home. She tells him he is to learn from her "all things, both the unwavering heart of well-rounded truth, and the opinions of mortals, in which there is no true assurance."[4] The two other sections of the poem go on then to show him first what the truth is, and second how things appear as they do to mortal men.

The tenses used by Parmenides in the proem indicate clearly enough that he was describing a journey made regularly, quite as a philosopher repeatedly journeys into the regions of his thought.[5] In consequence the poem is meant to describe the travel of the philosopher in his own proper world. The road traveled is characterized as "far away from the wandering of men."[6] On it Parmenides is to learn first the truth about all things, and then how the contrasted appearances are able to penetrate all in a way that makes them so readily acceptable to human cognition.[7] The contrast is clear between truth and appearance. Things are considered to appear to men in a way radically different from what the truth about them reveals. In this framework the second section of the poem intends to explain the truth, while the third section will explain how things are able to appear to men in a way different from the truth about them. The proem envisages truth as something unwavering, something firm and stable. The way men ordinarily think is, on the contrary, "wandering," unstable. Appearance—the ordinary thinking of mortals—is in this manner sharply contrasted with the inspired teaching of the goddess.

The fragment accepted as second in order, listed immediately after the proem and consequently as the first statement in our record of the poem's section on being, states that only two ways of inquiry can be thought of. One is that (it) is and that (for it) not to be is impossible. This is the way that follows truth. The other is that (it) is not and that (for it) not to be is of necessity. This path offers no possibility whatever for inquiry, since non-being cannot possibly be known or expressed (Fr. 2). The fragment accepted as third then gives the reason in a rather cryptic statement that translated word for word reads "For the same thing is to think and to be" (Fr. 3).

These assertions maintain that being follows upon or accompanies truth. Truth, as envisaged in the proem, is accordingly to be given in terms of being. The stability or firmness required by the proem is here couched in the necessity involved by being. Being necessarily excludes non-being. No stronger type of stability could be found. This necessity is seen extended to everything that can be thought of or expressed. All that remains outside it is non-being, which likewise involves its own impossibility and in consequence is a path of inquiry that cannot even be entered. The basic reason given in the fragment is that non-being cannot possibly be known or expressed. If the third fragment followed immediately, it would confirm this reason with a positive statement: what is able to be known and what is able to be are the same thing.[8] That is the minimal bearing of the fragment, and seems entirely appropriate at this initial stage of the reasoning. So understood it appeals to an immediate evidence, namely, that whatever is known is known as a being. If you try to represent non-being you find it impossible.

Translated as "For thinking and being are the same," Fragment 3 gives a maximal sense that may well turn out to be in accord with Parmenides' overall thought. But can it be regarded as an immediate evidence? Is it not rather part of a conclusion that being is a whole and is identified with all things, including thought? If that is its meaning, should not the fragment be located later in the poem, and not at the beginning of the second section? Located immediately after Fragment 2, it should express a basic evidence that shows why the path of non-being cannot even be entered. This evidence is the immediate experience that whatever is thought of is necessarily thought of and expressed in terms of being. In consequence the alleged path of non-being cannot offer any possibility for inquiry.

However, mortals do in fact travel a path different from that of truth. It is readily observable. It seems to wander back and forth between being and non-being. It seems to assess them as the same yet not the same (Fr. 6). Ordinary custom is regarded as urging men toward it. Yet it as well as the path of non-being is forbidden to Parmenides. Instead, he is told by the goddess to judge by reason (*logos*) the controversial argument given in her words (Fr. 7). The way of being is then sketched (Fr. 8). It shows that what exists cannot be engendered or destroyed and that it cannot change or be subject to differentiation, for any of these would require the presence of non-being. Being is accordingly whole and entire, held firmly within its limits, neither more nor less in any direction. For it all things will be a name (or, in regard to it all things are named),[9] "whatever mortals have established believing that they are true, that they come to be and perish, that they are and are not, that they change in place and vary through range of bright color" (Fr. 8.39–41).

What is the notion of being that is offered under this rather difficult phrasing? It is something that necessarily excludes non-being from its range, and on the other hand includes everything that is or exists. Any distinction between "is" and "exists" is bound to prove futile in this context. There are only two sides to the division. One is utter nothingness, and cannot even be thought of. All else, whether expressed in terms of being or in terms of existence, falls on the other side.

But precisely what is it that is or exists? In most cases no subject at all is expressed in the Greek. In those cases in which it is expressed, the participial or infinitive form of the verb "to be" is used. Nothing other than being seems envisaged as the subject. The question accordingly returns to the original formulation: What is the notion of being that is intended in the phrases of Parmenides? Modern views differ widely.[10] However, the text does not give any subject other than being, and usually does not feel any necessity to express even that. This indicates plainly that Parmenides is seeing no distinction in fact between being and the subject that is or exists. They are regarded by him as one and the same. He writes as though this is a matter of immediate intuition. If this analysis of the beginning of the section on being is correct, Parmenides is immediately intuiting being as something necessarily different from non-being. It is a matter of just looking and seeing. You see at once that you think in terms of being, and cannot think or express non-being. Under intense philosophical scrutiny, being seems intuited after the manner in which the ordinary mortal considers himself to be intuiting color or extension or movement.

But precisely what is this being that is so intuited? Is it something corporeal or something incorporeal, something ideal or something real? The historical background against which Parmenides did his thinking would tend to limit it to the corporeal and the real. The Ionian as well as the Pythagorean thought which Parmenides could be expected to have absorbed as he grew up could hardly have directed his attention to anything beyond the visible and extended world. It was that world that his predecessors had been striving to understand and explain. It is that world that Parmenides expressly endeavors to understand and explain in the final section of his poem. He offers, it is true, an unexpected and utterly original explanation of it. But nothing else in all the poem seems indicated as the object of his study. In the setting in which Parmenides thought and wrote, anything other than the visible and tangible universe would seem incongruous as a subject for philosophizing. In the composition of the poem, moreover, the proem envisages Parmenides as located in a world of change and highly differentiated objects, and using them as a means to rise to light. The starting point of the philosophical journey seems in this way to be represented as a world of plurality and change, a world already known in the opinions of mortals but now to be explained from the viewpoint of truth.

Can these indications or at least suggestions be at all substantiated from the actual text of the poem? After explaining why being is changeless, unique, and whole, the poem (Fr. 8.38–41) goes on to state that all things are a name for this sole being, or at least that all things are named in reference to it. The "all things" are the things that mortals have set up, believing that they are true. What is it that mortals have set up in this way? Fragment 8.51–61 and Fragment 9 describe the world of appearance as set up conventionally by mortals through the use of two basic and opposite forms. One of the forms is called light or fire, the other is designated as "unknowing night" (Fr. 8.59). Both are given equal force. Change and differentiation are accordingly able to appear in this world of human construction, and men are unhesitatingly convinced that the myriad objects composing it are true in the sense that things actually are as they appear in this universe. According to Fragment 16 this ever-changing object of ordinary human cognition appears to all and to each according to the individual's constitution at any given moment. This would allow for a common universe, with the differences of individual perception.[11] In this way, according to Fragment 19, a common universe of appearance can be known by all, and each thing in it given a distinguishing name.

But do these two forms, light and night, represent doxically the being and non-being of the section on truth? There are indications that they do. Light seems something, while darkness or night would seem to be its opposite, lack of light.[12] Each is represented as apart from the other (Fr. 8.57–58). According to what seems the more likely sense of Fragment 9.4, neither partakes of the other. The only reason found in the fragments for the unusual assertion that "all things are named light and night" (Fr. 9.1) would seem to be the observation in the section on truth (Fr. 8.40) that mortals believe all things both to be and not to be. Doxically men do not in fact name all things "light and night." But in the section on truth they were found to be convinced that all things in the universe they construct are composed of the two opposites.

At any rate, the statements (Frs. 6.8–9; 8.40) are clear that ordinary men mix being and non-being in their way of thinking, and that the things of their universe are composed of both. But what all these things name is being. Here at last is something that may be submitted to an obvious test. The way men thought at the time of Parmenides is well enough known to us through their literature and their historians. They spoke and thought as though Athens were different from Miletus, a spear different from a shield, a horse different from a chariot. In this respect their way of thinking was quite what it is with ordinary people today. In what sense do people then and now think that a thing is and is not? Certainly they do not think that a thing both is itself and is not itself. They do not think that a table is not a table. But they definitely do think that a table is not a chair. They think that each individual thing is itself and that it is not any other of the millions of things in the universe. In this way they do unite being and non-being in their conception of every single thing. This is the sense in which they think that each thing both is and is not. It is itself. It is not anything else.

The fact that men think in terms of both being and non-being is accordingly verifiable in actual life, but only in the way just described. Parmenides speaks as though he is expressing what is actually happening, and what is actually happening is found to be the above way of speaking in terms of being and non-being combined. But in fact only being is there to be named. All these constructs of appearance in human thinking can name only being.

The overall picture of Parmenides' thought now begins to take definite shape. Being is intuited as a thing that presents itself as any other thing, but which upon examination is seen to absorb everything else into itself and leave nothing outside itself except sheer non-being, which cannot be represented in thought or expressed in language. Whatever presents itself to human cognition is a being, whether it be a stone, a tree, a man, or Parmenides himself. In this way of thinking there is no difficulty in finding that everything in the universe, including Parmenides, his thought, and his poem, exists.[13] But the being seen in each of them is all-inclusive. It includes everything else in the universe. It is being that is whole and continuous, absolutely stable and undifferentiated. To understand that this being exists or is, is the way of truth. But to mix with it non-being and think that any one thing *is not* the other is to fall into the way of appearance, the *doxa*. It is to accept that thing in the way in which it appears, not in the way in which it is.

This will mean that what actually is, what constitutes the being that is described in the section on truth in Parmenides' poem, is the visible and tangible universe in which men live, work, love, and suffer. Parmenides gives no hint of knowing any other. He is insistent on showing how that universe really is, in contrast to the way it appears. According to the truth it is immobile and undifferentiated, but in appearance it is multiple and ever-changing. But under both ways of knowing it, it remains the same thing. This is what the fragments seem to show. This is the way Aristotle, writing at a time when the whole poem was still extant, understood its contents. What is one according to *logos* is multiple according to sensation (*Metaph.*, A5, 986b31–33), and Parmenides called being and non-being fire and earth (986b34–987a2; *GC*, I3, 318b6–7) and was among those who thought that "what is" is identical with the perceptible world (*Metaph.*, Gamma 5, 1010a1–3). So clear, in fact, is Aristotle's testimony in this regard that it must be radically discredited if one wishes to interpret Parmenides in any other sense.[14]

What Parmenides is explaining in his poem, then, is the perceptible universe. He is showing that the things in it are not what they seem to be—partial, differentiated, and changeable—but that each is being in its entirety, absolutely stable and whole. His motivation seems to be the pure metaphysical joy of understanding things as they really are, of knowing the truth just for the truth's sake. His teaching explains the changing universe in terms of being and non-being, and does not at all interfere with one's normal life within it. The poem, however, offers no reason why men should set up a second basic form and then proceed to the construction of a differentiated and changing universe. The fragments merely state the fact that men do so, and Aristotle found no better reason than that Parmenides was forced by the *phainomena*, the things that appeared, to posit a second basic principle in order to explain them. It looks as though Parmenides gave no reason for the transition from truth to *doxa*. Indeed, how could he have done so without raising the *doxa* to something that could be justified by reason? But that would be raising it to the level of truth, and destroying its very nature as *doxa*.

The cogency of Parmenides' reasoning about the characteristics that follow from the nature of being exercised a profound but partial influence upon his Greek successors. Empedocles and the Atomists accepted his conclusions about the impossibility of any generation or perishing. Nothing could come into being or pass out of being. But for them differentiation and local motion were too obvious to banish from truth in the realm of real existence. The compromise was the location of being in a multiplicity of basic particles that could be neither engendered nor destroyed, but which could move about freely and give rise to a truly mobile and differentiated universe. The notion of being as something radically unchangeable and permanent, however, continued under this guise, and stood out in contrast to becoming or change. For Gorgias being was in this sense ruled out of consideration as impossible, unknowable, and inexpressible, quite as non-being had been described by Parmenides. Plato, in strong reaction to the Sophistic world of *doxa* and subjectivity, located genuine being in a world of objective Ideas, separated from their changing and individuated instances, yet participated in by these instances in a way that failed to achieve satisfactory explanation. Parmenides had posed a tremendously profound problem of being. None of these Greek successors in the philosophical tradition could accept his conclusions on the unicity of being. Being had to be a plurality, according to all evidence, even though its nature demanded stability and permanence.

Aristotle faced the Parmenidean problem in a new way, by recognizing in the notion 'being' a number of different senses (*Metaph.*, N2, 1089a2–15). This meant that being could not be regarded, in Parmenidean fashion, as the object of a single intuition. It involved different concepts, those of substance, quantity, quality, relation, and so on. Yet it was a single notion that embraced all things, just as obviously for Aristotle as for Parmenides. Unity in it had to be established, in spite of all its differences. Aristotle achieved this unity by relating all the instances of being to a single primary instance, specified as substance. But his exact meaning in this regard was by no means clear, and remains controversial to the present day.[15] On the one hand, the nature (*physis*—*Metaph.*, Gamma 2, 1003a34) of being was located expressly in a definite instance, namely substance. But substance is itself a wide and multisignificant notion, embracing in its range the indefinite multiplicity of living and non-living material substances and extending to immaterial or separate substances. Even in the realm of separate substance it is at least open to a multiplicity. On the other hand, the Aristotelian notion of being functioned as a supergeneric concept, allowing its highest instance to be interpreted as merely one of its inferiors. This interpretation, though it does not seem to be present in the Greek commentators, has become widespread in modern times, allowing the view that in Aristotle there are in fact two different and radically contradictory notions of being.[16]

This difficulty goes back, undoubtedly, to the position of the problem of being by Parmenides. It arises naturally when being is regarded as the object of an immediate intuition in the manner in which other objects are intuited. In order to differentiate, the difference first has to be. But thereby a dilemma arises. According to Parmenides' reasoning, each differentia turns out to be already contained within being. Only non-being is left outside. Non-being is nothing, and accordingly cannot come in and function as a differentia. The result is that the whole nature of being is contained within a single instance, and nothing is left outside this one instance. Aristotle faced this difficulty in explicit terms: "But it is not possible for either 'unity' or 'being' to be a genus of things; for each differentia of any genus must *be* and also be *one*" (*Metaph.*, B3, 998b22–24, Apostle trans.; cf. 4, 1001a29–b1). If the notion of being is modeled after a generic notion, as it has to be in the setting of Parmenides, it will contain all its differentiae within itself. Its content will be all-embracing. But if, on the other hand, each differentia is allowed its own being, the differentia will absorb all the content, leaving only a blank or empty concept or unintelligible surd for the nature of being as such.[17]

It is hard to see any trace of this latter interpretation in Aristotle, even though he faced the problem of being as a genus. It has been read into Aristotle, but only much later. In Duns Scotus being was placed above its divisions into finite and infinite, created and uncreated. This followed through into Suarez and Wolff. Kant had little difficulty in showing that being when so understood lacked all content, and for Hegel it took on immediately the aspect of "just Nothing" (*Logik*, 87, Wallace trans.). Against this background the more recent controversies concerning being, whether or not it is a real predicate, and whether or not it has any content, have formulated the problem.

The stand that being has no content, however, cannot in any way be said to stem positively from Parmenides, even though it may have been occasioned remotely by his position on the problem. It is, rather, an extreme reaction against the consequences of his reasoning. If anything, being for Parmenides involves content, total content. This extreme reaction would avoid the consequences by denial of all content to Parmenides' starting point. The tradition that stems positively from Parmenides, on the other hand, strove to retain content in being while avoiding the Parmenidean consequences of unicity and absolute immobility. The tradition of the Greek commentators on Aristotle gave to separate substance intelligible but immobile content and allowed it to serve as the primary instance of being and as final cause for all mobile being. Plotinus likewise accepted being as a plurality with intelligible content, placing the unity of things in a principle above being. Early Christian Neoplatonism used Neoplatonic language in placing God above being, yet in a way that made him the being of all things.[18] The phraseology naming God the being of all things was carried over into early medieval language, but with the careful proviso that he was so through efficient causality, and not through anything like similarity of formal or material composition with creatures.[19]

It is in this last direction that the trend initiated by the magnificent vision of Parmenides reaches its high point with the thought of Thomas Aquinas in the mid-thirteenth century. In a radically new and quite startling noetic, Aquinas regards being as apprehended originally in sensible things, not through any conceptualization of a nature but through a judgment that can be expressed only in a proposition and sentence. This means that being, though immediately intuited, is not present as a nature in sensible things and accordingly is not immediately known as a nature. When the nature of being is reached as the result of a long reasoning process, it is shown to contain in itself all the perfections of things, quite as in Parmenides but now in infinite degree. This subsistent being is unique and immobile, again as with Parmenides, but is able to impart being to other natures provided the being does not enter into these natures or form any part of them. Yet their being remains primary to these natures, and in this sense most intimate to them. Accordingly the one subsistent being, operating most intimately within them in imparting to them their own being, through efficient causality, functions effectively as "the being of all things."[20]

It would be hard to conceive of a more ample fulfillment of the positive inspiration handed down from Parmenides' poem. The nature of being includes all things within itself. It is the being of everything. Back of all perceptible things is the nature of being, operating most intimately in them and accounting for their being. It is imperceptible but able to be known by reasoning. The world of appearance, Parmenides had shown, has its positive ground in a unique and immobile being. With Aquinas the type of causality had changed from formal to efficient. But in this more advanced framework the metaphysical inspiration of Parmenides continues to play its significant role.

The thinking of Parmenides is an event that took place over twenty-four hundred years ago. Yet its influence has continued down the centuries, as has just been noted, and reached a surprisingly high grade of development in medieval thought. It still stimulates inquiry, an inquiry perhaps more intensive today than at most times in the past, even though not so widespread. At any rate, the interest in Parmenides over the last few decades has been called in a recent monograph "immense" in its extrinsic and intrinsic considerations.[21] This is attested by the large number of recent studies on the Eleatic and his thought. These have done notable service in elucidating the text of the fragments and clarifying the issues in question. But on the main point involved—what Parmenides meant by being—the problem outlined by him remains open to intense study and invites further pursuit.

Why is this? The plain fact is that the problem of being, as presented by Parmenides at the beginning of Western metaphysics, still confronts the thinking man. In the nineteenth century Longfellow, in his *Psalm of Life*, wrote

> For the soul is dead that slumbers,
> And things are not what they seem.

For the person who is intellectually alert, who is not slumbering, the way things appear proves unsatisfactory. The way things are ordinarily accepted does not answer the questions that naturally arise. "All men by nature desire to know" was the observation with which Aristotle had commenced his *Metaphysics* (A1, 980a21). This attitude is basically the same today. Men wish to penetrate through the appearances and come to know what the reality is that sustains and authenticates them. The way to do this, Parmenides pointed out, is the way of being, a way that is still to be followed with profit.

Notes

1. E.g., "There can be no really worthwhile pursuit of philosophy apart from the history of philosophy, and little sense to any history of philosophy save in so far as it contributes to the current activity of philosophizing." Henry Veatch, "Reviews," *International Philosophical Quarterly* 13 (1973):447.

2. For an account of the Congress, see W. Norris Clarke, "Reflections on the XVth World Congress of Philosophy and the First International Congress of Metaphysics," *International Philosophical Quarterly* 14 (1974): 122–24. On the motivation, see address of Paul Weiss, "Announcements," *Review of Metaphysics* 22 (1968): 425–26.

3. See George Bosworth Burch, "Anaximander, the First Metaphysician," *Review of Metaphysics* 3 (1949): 137–60.

4. Fr. 1.28–30. See L. Taran, *Parmenides*, on the controversies about the meaning of these lines (Princeton: Princeton University Press), pp. 210–16.

5. See Taran, pp. 9–13.

6. Fr. 1.27; trans. Taran, p. 9; cf. p. 16.

7. Fr. 1.31–32. On the problems in these two lines, see Taran, pp. 211–15; and Alexander P.D. Mourelatos, *The Route of Parmenides* (New Haven: Yale University Press, 1970), pp. 194–219.

8. On the translations of the fragment, see Taran, pp. 41–44; also Mourelatos, pp. 165–80, on the parallel statement at Fr. 8.34–36.

9. See Leonard Woodbury, "Parmenides on Names," *Harvard Studies in Classical Philology* 63 (1958): 145–60; reprinted, with slight revisions, in *Essays in Ancient Greek Philosophy*, ed. John P. Anton and George L. Kustas (Albany: State University of New York Press, 1971), pp. 145–62. Taran's views are discussed in the revised version, p. 161, n. 29a; cf. p. 160, n. 18a. A coverage of the topic at about the same time may be found in Mourelatos, pp. 181–91.

10. For a survey and discussion, see Taran, pp. 33–36; Mourelatos, pp. 269–76; Leo Sweeney, *Infinity in the Presocratics* (The Hague: Nijhoff, 1973), pp. 93–110. In solidarity with proem, Charles H. Kahn, "The Thesis of Parmenides," *Review of Metaphysics* 22 (1969): 710, views the subject as "the knowable."

11. Fr. 16 has been discussed at great length. For literature and discussion, see Taran, pp. 169–70 and 253–68; Mourelatos, pp. 253–59.

12. So night is "unknowing" (Fr. 8.59), just as the way of non-being is a path "from which no tidings ever come" (Fr. 2.6, trans. Mourelatos, p. 23; cf. p. 24, n. 37), or, more strongly, "totally uninquiring." The obvious sense of Fr. 8.54 seems to be that only one of the two forms is justified. Yet, apparently on grounds of alleged philosophical requirements, the first half of line 54 has been read in at least three other ways; see Taran, pp. 217–25, for a survey.

13. Taran, on the contrary, continually interprets Parmenides' doctrine to mean that things like thought (p. 122) or the sensible world (p. 202) can have no existence at all.

14. E.g., by Taran, pp. 278–91; 299–302.

15. For a survey of the controversy see my monograph *The Doctrine of Being in the Aristotelian Metaphysics*, 2d ed. (Toronto: Pontifical Institute of Mediaeval Studies [PIMS], 1963), pp. 15–68; and a more recent study, Karl Barthlein, *Die Transzendentalienlehre der alten Ontologie*, vol. 1 (Berlin: de Gruyter, 1972), pp. 111–53. Barthlein's understanding of the overall Aristotelian doctrine differs about as far as is possible from mine. Though on systematic grounds he regards the controversy as closed, his coverage of it is interesting, informative, and up-to-date.

16. See Werner W. Jaeger, *Aristotle*, trans. Richard Robinson, 2d ed. (Oxford: Clarendon, 1948), pp. 218–22.

17. See above, n. 15, for references to surveys.

18. "The divinity above being is the being of all things"—Pseudo-Dionysius, *Caelest. Hierarch.*, c. IV; PG, III, 177D. "He himself is the being of the existents"—*De Div. Nom.*, c. V; *PG*, III, 817D. Translations, unless otherwise noted, are mine.

19. "Therefore their maker himself is the being—but causal, not material—of all things that are made." St. Bernard, *In IV super Cantica*, ed. Jean Leclerc, in *S. Bernardi Opera* (Rome: Cistercienses, 1957), I, 20.17–18. See also Gilbert of Poitiers, *In I de Trin.*, 52, ed. Nikolaus Haring (Toronto: PIMS, 1966), p. 89.5–6; Thierry of Chartres, *In Boeth. de Trin.*, II, 56, ed. Haring (Toronto: PIMS, 1971), p. 173.44, and *In de Hebd.*, 24, ed. Haring (Toronto: PIMS, 1971), p. 409.48–49.

20. See Aquinas, *In I Sent.*, d.8, q.1, a.2; ed. Mandonnet, I, 197–98. *SCG*, I, 26, is phrased to attack the interpretation of this tenet in the sense that God would be the formal being of all things, and the theme is not brought out again in express terms in Aquinas' later works. But the doctrine remains the same; cf. *In de Div. Nom.*, c. V, lect. 1, Pera no. 630; *De Pot.*, III, 7; *ST*, I,4,2,c. For a discussion of the theme in general, see Gerald B. Phelan, "The Being of Creatures," *Proceedings of the American Catholic Philosophical Association* 31 (1957): 118–25. In its weakest form of expression, this doctrine of Aquinas means that all finite being is the proper effect of the subsistent existence operating intimately (*ST*, I, 105,5,c) within every other existent.

21. See Mourelatos, p. xii. For a survey of the actual state of research on Parmenides, see Karl Bormann, *Parmenides* (Hamburg: Meiner, 1971), pp. 1–27, and bibliography, pp. 253–59.

Bibliography

On Parmenides

Jaeger, Werner W. *The Theology of the Early Greek Philosophers.* Oxford: Clarendon, 1947, chap. 6, "Parmenides' Mystery of Being," pp. 90–108.

Taran, Leonardo. *Parmenides: A Text with Translation, Commentary, and Critical Essays.* Princeton: Princeton University Press, 1965.

Mourelatos, Alexander P.D. *The Route of Parmenides: A Study of Word, Image, and Argument in the Fragments.* New Haven: Yale University Press, 1970.

Bormann, Karl. *Parmenides: Untersuchungen zu den Fragmenten.* Hamburg: Meiner, 1971.

On Later Greek Developments

Jaeger, Werner W. *Aristotle: Fundamentals of the History of His Development*, trans. Richard Robinson, 2d ed. Oxford: Clarendon, 1948.

Merlan, Philip. *From Platonism to Neoplatonism*, 2d ed. The Hague: Nijhoff, 1960.

Barthlein, Karl. *Die Transzendentalienlehre der alten Ontologie*, vol. 1, *Die Transcendentalienlehre im Corpus Aristotelicum*. Berlin: de Gruyter, 1972.

General

Gilson, Etienne. *Being and Some Philosophers*, 2d ed. Toronto: Pontifical Institute of Mediaeval Studies, 1961.
Owens, Joseph. "The Content of Existence," in *Logic and Ontology*, ed. Milton K. Munitz. New York: New York University Press, 1973, pp. 21–35.

CHARLES H. KAHN

Linguistic Relativism and the Greek Project of Ontology

Various answers have been given to the 'question' of 'being' in Western and Eastern philosophy. But is the question of being a valid one, to which answers may reasonably be given? I think we must begin by recognizing that the concept of being is itself problematical. By this I do not mean simply that the question of being is a question that admits of many answers. I mean that the question itself raises a meta-question: is the concept of being a clear and coherent concept, so that the question of being could be a legitimate philosophical question? If so, what is the question of being a question *about*? I take it for granted that clarity and coherence are among the primary philosophic virtues, and that if the concept of being is a legitimate topic in philosophy, it must admit of clarification.

In asking whether being is a legitimate concept, I do not intend to play the role of the old hard-nosed philosopher of the Vienna tradition, for whom all "metaphysical" questions were "cognitively meaningless." The meta-problem or meta-question of being is something much more limited and specific. It is to take a sober look at the charge of John Stuart Mill and many others who have claimed that "the frivolous speculations concerning the nature of being" were due to the erroneous assumption that the verb 'be' has a single meaning when used for existence, on the one hand, and for predication, on the other. Now linguists have been quick to point out that the existence of a verb 'be' with such diverse functions is a peculiarity of Indo-European languages and by no means a necessary or a universal feature of language.[1] So the question naturally arises, and must, I think, be taken seriously, whether in discussing the concept of being we are not discussing a pseudo-concept, an artificial, hybrid concept resting upon a confusion between such diverse notions as existence and predication, a confusion foisted upon philosophy by the structure of Indo-European languages and maintained by the sheer weight of the philosophic tradition.

The question of being is not limited to our Western tradition that descends from the philosophy of ancient Greece. But it is surely no accident that the Indian tradition, in which a question of being also arises, is founded upon texts in Sanskrit, a language whose grammar and vocabulary are cognate with Greek. The existence of two historically independent traditions concerned with being does not suffice to dispel the doubts of linguistic relativism about the Indo-European confusion that underlies this concept. For both of these traditions are originally Indo-European, and they have remained Indo-European for most of their creative development.

I am not myself a linguistic relativist. I want, in effect, to defend the concept of being against its modern detractors. What I hope to do in this paper is to show that when the Greek concept of being (as introduced by Parmenides and developed by Plato) is properly understood it represents a valid and indeed inevitable topic for philosophic inquiry. It turns out, in fact, to be fundamentally the same topic that is pursued in the modern ontological tradition of Frege, the early Wittgenstein, and Quine. And it also turns out to be very different from the questions of personal existence and the human condition which dominate that other school of modern ontology associated with the name of Heidegger.[2]

In order to meet the challenge of linguistic relativism, we must first give an adequate account of the linguistic functions of the verb 'be,' (*eimi* in ancient Greek), and then show that these functions provide the basis for a coherent concept and a clear philosophical question. Let me briefly indicate in advance what I take the solution to be. The concept of being in Greek philosophy refers to the nature of reality or the structure of the world, in the very general sense of 'the world,' which includes whatever we can know or investigate and whatever we can describe in true or false statements. The question of being is then: How must the world be structured in order for inquiry, knowledge, science, and true discourse or, for that matter, false discourse to be possible?

On this view of the concept of being, the key notion is that of truth—the goal of science and the aim of declarative speech. If the claims of linguistic relativism have seemed plausible in regard to the concept of being, that is due in part to the fact that they rely upon an inadequate account of the functions of the verb 'be,' an account in which the connections with truth and falsehood—what I call the 'veridical' uses of the verb—are generally overlooked. Once we put the notion of truth at the heart of the Greek concept of being, the internal coherence and general significance of this concept will become clear. I have argued elsewhere that this concept of being does not rest on an illegitimate confusion, since it brings together three distinct notions—existence, predication, and truth—which belong together in any ontology or in any metaphysical scheme.[3] At the same time it is important to recognize that these three notions *are* distinct, and that the distinction between them was not always clearly seen in Greek philosophy, precisely because the same verb *eimi*, and its participle *on*, was used to express all three. Here, as elsewhere, it is important to give the devil his due; if we do not, as the saying goes, he will take more than his share. In defending the concept of being against the charge of linguistic confusion, it is important to recognize the genuine possibilities for confusion that were latent in the multiple usage of the verb. If we bear in mind the distinctions between existence, predication, and truth, and recognize that these distinctions were often overlooked because of a single linguistic expression for all three, we will be in a better position to interpret a number of perplexing passages in Plato, Aristotle, and Parmenides, for we will be in a position to articulate some problems more clearly than the Greek philosophers were able to do. My guess is that the same may be true for Indian philosophy, for the basic functions of the verb *as* in Sanskrit seem to be very nearly the same as those of *eimi* in Greek. If my linguistic analysis of the verb 'be' is adequate for Greek, it (or a similar analysis) ought to be adequate for Sanskrit. And if the linguistic analysis of 'be' can shed useful light on the Greek concept of being, the same relation ought to hold between an analysis of the Sanskrit verb and the Indian concept of being.

Since I am not an Indologist, I offer this parallel only for what it may be worth, as a heuristic hypothesis and as a challenge to Sanskrit scholars and specialists in Indian philosophy. I shall limit myself to the Greek material, and proceed in two steps. First I shall report some of the results of the linguistic analysis of the Greek verb which I have published elsewhere. Then I shall apply this analysis to the interpretation of two key passages for the development of the terminology and concepts of Greek ontology. The first passage is from the poem of Parmenides, where the concept of being makes its first appearance in the philosophical tradition of the West. The second passage is Plato's initial exposition of the doctrine of Forms in the *Phaedo*, where we have the first full-scale statement of Plato's own ontology.

I begin, then, by summarizing some results of the linguistic analysis. One central feature of my account is the claim that the verb 'be' in Greek—and, I dare say, in Indo-European generally—is primarily and fundamentally a copula and not a verb of existence, as comparative linguists have usually held. There is no evidence for the traditional assumption that the verbal root *es* originally meant only existence (or the like) and gradually declined into the use as "mere copula." By claiming that the copula uses are primary I mean not only that they are factually (or statistically) predominant from the earliest texts, but also that they provide the only possible point of departure for a theoretic account of the whole system of uses for the verb. I do not claim that the copula uses are older than the others, but only that *if* we regard them as older we can understand how the other uses *could* have developed from them. Talk of "development" here is a mere theoretical convenience, like a myth of creation or an original social compact, a conceptual device that serves to clarify the relations of logical priority and dependence between different factors in a complex system.

From the point of view of the language, then, the primary or central use of the verb is as a copula.[4] By a copula use I mean an occurrence of the verb with a predicate adjective ("I am tall"), a predicate noun ("I am a man"), or a prepositional phrase ("I am in the conference room"). The copula use includes the so-called 'is' of identity: "I am C.K."; "I am the first speaker this afternoon." The verb 'be' as copula in Indo-European is characterized by two features which are important for the philosophical development. The first I call the *locative*, the second the *durative* aspect. By the locative feature I mean the fact that the verb serves for predication in general, not only with nominal predicates (predicate nouns and adjectives or participles) but specifically for statements of place, like "We are in this room." This locative use seems so essential to the meaning of the verb that we find Aristotle saying that most people believe that whatever is, is somewhere; what is nowhere is nothing: for Greek common sense, a thing cannot really *be* unless it is somewhere. Beginning with Plato, some philosophers will deny the necessity of this connection between being and being in some place. But it has a strong intuitive hold on the Greek feeling about "what is."

The second feature of the Indo-European copula, the durative aspect, is even more decisive for the Greek view of being. This is the aspect which contrasts 'be' with 'become,' *eimi* with *gignomai* as copula verb (and *as* with *bhū* in Sanskrit). What is at issue here is not simply the aspectual opposition familiar in comparative linguistics, where the present-imperfect stem is contrasted with aorist and perfect, but a more general linguistic contrast between being in a state or being in a place, on the one hand, and change of state or change of place on the other hand. This general aspectual contrast is best described as an opposition between *stative* and *mutative*, or *static* and *kinetic*. We can illustrate the opposition in English by contrasting "I am tired" with "I become tired," "I am tall" with "I grow tall," "I am in Canada" with "I go to Canada" or "I arrive in Canada." This aspectual contrast seems to be much more general than Indo-European, for it is founded in the nature of things, and there is likely to be some expression for it in every language. But it is characteristic of Indo-European that the root *es* is typically, and in Greek almost exclusively, used to express the stative aspect, whereas a variety of other copulas are used for predication with a mutative nuance (there is no *single* Indo-European word for 'become,' as there is a single root for 'be'). There is, in short, an essential connection in Indo-European between the idea of being and the idea of stability or remaining in the same state.

So far we have considered only the copula or predicative uses of 'be.' There are of course other, non-copulative uses, of which I will mention only two. One is the existential use, or rather the family of uses with an existential sense. As an example we may take the familiar Homeric verse, "There is a city Ephyre in the corner of horse-nourishing Argos." The connection of this existential use with the copula construction ("Ephyre is a city," "Ephyre is in Argos") is fairly obvious. Other existential uses are farther removed from the copula construction, but I shall not go into these complications here.

Finally we have what I call the veridical use, where 'be' expresses neither predication nor existence but the truth of a statement or a belief. The standard veridical construction is of the form "Things are as you say," *esti tauta houtō hōsper su legeis*, or for short, *esti tauta* or *esti houtō*. Curiously enough, the ancient veridical use has recently had a vigorous revival in colloquial English: "Tell it like it is." The distinctive features of the veridical construction are (1) that the verb is not construed with a predicate but with an implied or explicit comparison to a clause of saying or thinking ("it is . . . like you say"), and (2) that the underlying subject of the verb is a sentence or a sentential content—roughly speaking, a proposition: the 'it' refers to a sentence, expressed or understood. The importance of this veridical use in ancient Indo-European is reflected by the widespread use of the root *es*, and above all its participial derivatives (from *sant*), in the sense of 'truth': in Greek *ontōs*, *tōi onto*, 'truly'; *legein ta onta* 'state the facts'; in archaic English we find 'sooth' for 'truth'; and in Sanskrit there are the familiar derivatives of *sat* (e.g., *satya*) in the same sense.

So much for the linguistic preliminaries. We have first the copula uses with their locative connotation or locative application and their durative-stative aspect. We have next the existential uses; and, finally, the veridical construction with the related uses of the participial forms to mean 'truth.' Now my claim about the philosophic development of the Greek concept of being is roughly this: the last-named use must be placed first. The point of departure for the philosophers is the veridical use and the notion of truth. Philosophers are primarily concerned with knowledge or the search for knowledge, and hence with truth in speech and in thought. But as the veridical construction shows, the concept of truth involves some kind of correlation or 'fit' between what is said or thought, on one side, and what is, or what is the case, or the way things are, on the other side. Let us call this the correlation between assertion and reality, where 'assertion' is used neutrally both for *saying* that it is so and for *thinking* that it is so; and 'reality' is used simply as a convenient abbreviation for the fact that it is so or what happens to be the case. In saying that the concept of truth implies a correlation or a 'fit' in this sense between assertion and reality, I think we beg no metaphysical questions. We simply articulate the connection of ideas expressed in the Greek locutions *esti tauta* and *esti houtō*. And precisely the same connection is expressed in the modern locution "Tell it like it is."

So we see how the philosophers' interest in knowledge and truth, taken together with the use of 'be' and its participle to mean 'truth' or 'what is so,' immediately leads to the concept of being as reality. I repeat, I am using 'reality' here not in any large metaphysical sense but simply as a convenient term in the hermeneutical metalanguage: as a mere name or counter for the facts that make true statements true and false statements false, or for whatever it is "in the world" (for whatever "is the case") that makes some assertions and some judgments correct and others mistaken. If I assert—either in thought or in speech—that the sun is shining, and if what I assert is true, then the corresponding 'reality' is simply the fact that the sun is shining.

So far I have said nothing about 'be' as verb of existence or as copula. I have shown only that starting from the veridical locutions and the notion of being as truth we immediately get to the related notion of being as reality, in a suitably loose and generalized sense of 'reality.' I think that these two notions, together with the locative idea that whatever is, is somewhere, and with the durative-stative aspect of the verb, are all we require for interpreting Parmenides' notion of being. Of course, we can easily see how the existential and copula uses of 'be' will also turn up, if we think of the reality in question as expressed by a subject-predicate sentence—for instance, by the sentence "The sun is shining." For if this sentence is true, then its subject (the sun) must exist. And the sentence uses the copula verb 'is' to predicate something of this subject, namely that it is shining, or that its light reaches us. So when we are talking about truth and reality, the existential and copulative uses of 'be' are never far away. But I insist that if we *begin* to interpret the concept of being by looking for existential or copula uses of the verb, we will not only make unnecessary trouble for ourselves; we may miss the real point. We will not only play into the hands of the linguistic relativists; we will fail to grasp the essential features of the Greek concept of being.

Consider now what Parmenides says about being or what is, *to eon*. He introduces it as the object for knowledge and the territory or homeland of truth. "These are the only ways of inquiry there are for knowing [or 'for understanding,' *noēsai*]: the one, that it is . . . the other that it is not." The former he calls "the path of Persuasion, for she follows upon Truth"; in other words being, or what is, is what we can and should believe (be persuaded by), because it leads to (or is identical path ("that it is not") he rejects as "unheard of (*panapeuthes*) a way that cannot be trusted, "for you is not . . . nor can you point it out." Parmenides' explic rejecting what *is not* (*to mē eon*) is that it cannot be an obje (*gnonai*), a path for understanding (*noēsai*), or a topic o discourse (*phrazein*). Since in Greek the expressions *to mē on* an would normally designate the content of lies and false belief, it ious why these labels will not signify an object of knowledge or reliable information. The peculiarly Parmenidean touch is to identify "the thing that is not" as the content of falsehood and error, with *nothing* or nonentity, *mēden* (Parmenides 8.10; cf. 6.2).

I submit that the guiding thought at the outset of Parmenides' poem, the thought which motivates his articulation of the concept of being, is the idea of truth as the goal of knowledge and inquiry. But of course the being which is known and truly asserted must be a reality in the very general sense indicated earlier. So for Parmenides the veridical notion of being leads directly to the concept of reality as opposed to appearance or false seeming: being and truth—*to eon* and *alētheia*—are explicitly contrasted with the erroneous opinions (or seemings, *doxai*) of mortals. By setting this contrast between true reality and false or mistaken appearance at the center of his doctrine, Parmenides passes beyond the commonsense, pretheoretical notion of reality implied by the ancient locutions for truth, and articulates for the first time a metaphysical concept of being.

I cannot undertake a general interpretation of Parmenides here.[6] But let me point out that the stative or durative aspect of 'be' gets articulated in Parmenides' principal proof: that *what is* cannot be a subject of change, that it cannot come into being or cease to be, but it simply *is*, now and forever. The fundamental linguistic contrast between the stative and mutative aspects—between being and becoming—did not provide Parmenides with his arguments. These belong to philosophy proper and not to the linguistic substructure which I am exploring. But the essentially static connotations of the verb *eimi* probably contributed to the formation of Parmenides' metaphysical position, and they certainly helped to make his extraordinary conclusion plausible to speakers of Greek. That it did seem plausible is shown by the unanimity with which this conclusion is echoed by his predecessors: what truly is cannot be generated or destroyed; what appears as generation or destruction is simply the mixing and remixing of something real and eternal.[7]

Finally the locative associations of the verb 'be'—with their implication that whatever *is*, is *somewhere*—help to explain the otherwise perplexing fact that this extraordinarily 'metaphysical' being, accessible only to the intellectual apprehension of *noein*, with which it is apparently identified,[8] is nevertheless conceived of by Parmenides as a dense, symmetrical mass or body, "like to the bulk of a rounded sphere." Not until Plato does Greek philosophy succeed in separating the notion of being from being-in-a-place. For of course the Forms, although metaphorically situated in a *noētos topos*, or "intelligible region," are not literally *anywhere*. The nonspatial, nonlocalized being of the Forms is clearly indicated in the earliest statement of Plato's ontology, in the *Symposium*, where Beauty itself is said to be "not somewhere, not in something else" (211 A8–9). And this point is finally and fully spelled out in the *Timaeus*, with its basic division between the Forms, as true being, and Place (*chōra*) as "the Nurse of Becoming."

Location and bodily mass aside, the Eleatic attributes of being are all preserved in the ontology which Plato develops for the Forms in the middle dialogues. Let us look briefly at the first systematic statement of this doctrine in the *Phaedo*,[9] in order to see how the notions of truth, knowledge, and reality which we have discussed provide us with a more accurate guide to Plato's meaning that any notions based directly on the predicative or existential functions of the verb.

The expressions *ta onta*, *to on*, and *ousia* are used to refer to the Forms beginning at 65 C3–E1, where Socrates in his new *apologia* is explaining why a philosopher will not be grieved by the separation of soul and body at death. The immediately preceding context is: Will the body be of any use for the acquisition of wisdom (*phronēsis*)? Do sight and hearing possess any truth (*alētheia*)? No, these bodily perceptions are neither exact nor reliable. The soul will grasp truth only if it does not carry on its investigation together with the body. "Is it not in reasoning or calculation (*logizesthai*), if at all, that any of the *onta* will become clear to the soul?" Here, in the first ontological formula of the dialogue, *ta onta* are of course "the realities" as objects of knowledge. The connection with truth is obvious from the context, and in his commentary Burnet accurately paraphrases *ta onta* here by *ta alēthē*, "things true."[10] Throughout the following context the terms 'being' and 'truth' alternate as designations for the object of philosophic knowledge and inquiry (66 A3, A6, A8, B7, C2, etc.). What immediately follows the two passages cited, however, is a mention of "justice itself . . . the beautiful and the good," which introduces the first statement of the doctrine in its full generality: "I speak concerning all these, for instance concerning magnitude, and health and strength, and in a word concerning the being (*ousia*) of all the rest, what each one really is."[11] Socrates' immediate point here is that these entities are accessible to thought and reason alone, and not to bodily sensation. And my point is that being (*ousia*, *on*) as a designation for the Forms designates them precisely as realities which are the object of intellectual inquiry and knowledge and the content or correlate of truth.

One could reinforce this point by further citation, for example, from the even more Parmenidean passage in *Republic* V, where being (*on*) as stable object of knowledge is opposed to the many sensible particulars (*ta polla*) as object of *doxa* (pp. 478–80). But these brief remarks on the introductory statement of Plato's ontology in the *Phaedo* should suffice to establish what was perhaps never in doubt: The key to the concept of being in Plato, as in Parmenides, is provided by the notions of truth and knowledge, and by the very general concept of reality or *what is so* that is required by these two notions. In linguistic terms, the key to the philosophic use of *to on* and related terms in Plato, as in Paramenides, is provided by the veridical construction ("Things are as you say," or "It is as you suppose"), and *not* by the existential or the copula uses.

Of course, to say so much is scarcely to begin the analysis of Plato's philosophic use of the verb *to be*. To go further we would have to consider the existential and copula uses as well, and see how Plato relates these to the basic veridical sense that I have emphasized. The very passage cited from the *Phaedo* contains an important quasi-existential use of *einai*: "Do we say that justice itself is something (*ti*) or nothing (*ouden*)?"[12] And the phrase quoted about "the being of all the rest of the Forms, what each one really is" contains a copula construction ("What it really is") which returns repeatedly in the dialogue and finally acquires the status of a technical expression: "concerning all those things on which we set the seal of 'what it is.'"[13] Linguistically speaking, we can recognize *esti* in this crucial Platonic formula as simply the definitional copula (or the *is* of definitional identity) with a strong veridical overtone; "what the thing *really and truly* is."[14] Historically speaking, we can recognize this formula as a direct development from the Socratic question "What is *X* (really, essentially)?" in the search for definitions. To give any fuller conceptual account of these formulas would be to launch into a general philosophical analysis of Plato's concept of being, which cannot be done here. I offer the following brief and schematic program for such an analysis.

The general contours of Plato's concept of being are determined by the notions of truth, inquiry, and knowledge in the way indicated. That is to say, being for Plato is in the first instance characterized as the reality which is sought after in intellectual inquiry, apprehended in noetic cognition, and described or defined in true discourse. But when we pass from these general 'veridical' contours to a more detailed analysis, the copula construction emerges as the primary formula for the articulation of the concept of truth and its grounding in the reality of the Forms. Every truth for Plato can properly be expressed in the copula form '*X* is *Y*.' Even the existential proposition can be so expressed, as we have just seen: "Justice exists" is expressed as "Justice is something (*ti*)." Now the copula proposition in turn is to be interpreted ontologically in terms of participation:

'*X* is *Y*' is true only if and because *X* participates in *Y*-ness or in the *Y*. The special case where the predicate is 'being' or 'existence' may be slightly more complex. '*X* is' or '*X* exists' can be spelled out as '*X* is something,' and the truth conditions for the latter can be given either as *X participates in something* or *X participates in being*. Since anything which participates at all participates in being, and since being is something, these two conditions entail one another; but they are not identical. 'Participation in being' is a complex notion, whose full articulation would bring together the concepts of predication, truth, existence (as "being something") and reality (as being a Form, or sharing in a Form). In the last analysis, I suggest, Plato's concept of being is the being-of-a-Form, or the being-related-to-a-Form by way of participation. The concepts of truth and predication, which concern statement and knowledge, are grounded upon these more fundamental notions of being which concern the nature of things.

We began by asking the meta-question: What is the question of being a question about? We now have the answer: In Greek ontology, from Parmenides on, the question of being is a question as to what reality must be like—or what the world must be like—in order for knowledge and true (or false) discourse to be possible. It is, in effect, the first question which Wittgenstein set out to answer in the *Tractatus*: How must the world be structured if logic and scientific language are to be possible? Since for Plato knowledge is assimilated to discourse,[15] and discourse is analyzed in the predicative form '*X* is *Y*,' the problem of knowledge and true discourse becomes, in part at least, the problem of predication: What must reality be like if predications like '*X* is *Y*' are to be possible, and sometimes true? What will *X* be like? What will *Y* be like? And how can the two be related to one another? In Aristotle the concept of being becomes much more complex—too complex for treatment here. The doctrine of the categories and the discussion of being (*to on*) in *Metaphysics* Gamma, Epsilon, and Zeta do not lend themselves to summary statement. What is clear is that in Aristotle's work the theory of predication is for the first time developed systematically and explicitly. And to this extent the copula uses of 'be' tend to occupy the center of Aristotle's discussion of being, while the veridical notion becomes less conspicuous here than in Plato and Parmenides.[16] For simplicity, then, my conclusions will refer only to the original, pre-Aristotelian concept of being, as illustrated in the two passages quoted from Plato and Parmenides.

If we conclude, now, by glancing back at the linguistic considerations with which we began, we can answer the charge of linguistic relativism as follows. The concept of being in Plato and Parmenides cannot be regarded as an illegitimate confusion of existence and predication, since it does not rely initially and fundamentally on either notion, nor on their special connection in the uses of the Indo-European verb *to be*. Instead, the concept of being must be understood by beginning with the notion of truth and its correlate, the notion of knowledge or inquiry and its object. But the connection between these three notions—truth, knowledge, and reality in the general sense entailed by the other two—is in no way a peculiar feature of Indo-European. The connections here are firmly grounded in the logical structure of the concepts of truth and knowledge, and similar connections must turn up in every language where human beings try to acquire information or try to test the reliability of what is told them. If we leave aside the special complexities of theoretical cognition or science proper, and consider only the concepts of truth and reality as they will arise in any society, no matter how primitive, we see that every language must have some way to express the goal of inquiry, the commonplace notion of "the facts of the case" which is required, for example, in a judicial decision or arbitration of disputed claims, and in the most ordinary request for information. "How do I get to the next village?" "This is what I was told: is it right?" "How did the quarrel start? Who saw what happened? Is he reporting the facts as he knows them, or is he hiding the truth?" No language can do without these basic notions of truth, reality, and fact. The interesting peculiarity of Indo-European in this connection is to express these humble but necessary notions of truth and reality by nominal derivatives from the basic verb of predication. The philosophical result is to bring the theory of predication into a central position in Plato's account of reality, and to an even greater extent in Aristotle's. It seems to me that this was a philosophical advantage, and that the language spontaneously brought together concepts which genuinely belong together. Opinions will perhaps differ on this, and some may hold that the theory of predication was not the appropriate philosophical device for getting at the concepts of truth and reality. But I for one can see no evidence that this project of ontology rests in any essential way upon linguistic confusion. If the structure of Indo-European made Western ontology possible—and, perhaps, Indian ontology as well—that is not obviously a mark of discredit either for Indo-European or for ontology.

Let me conclude by restating the understanding of the relationship between being and knowledge which I have expressed in this paper. Being for the Greeks never *means* 'being knowable.' That would make knowledge logically prior, whereas the Greek view is that being or reality is logically prior. Knowledge is determined by its object, by what is there to be known. But being is 'encountered' as what is known or knowable: knowledge, or successful inquiry, is our mode of access to reality. Cognition and inquiry, together with the language which mirrors or articulates them, constitute the dimension within which being comes into view. Or perhaps we can say more precisely that, for the Greeks, the question of being is originally *asked* within the context of inquiry or search for knowledge of the truth. But it is eventually *answered* within the context of a theory of predication or *logos*, the expression of true cognition in rational discourse. A doctrine of being is a theory of what the world must be like for such inquiry, cognition, and discourse to be pursued with any chance of success.

Notes

1. See, e.g., Émile Benveniste, *Problèmes de linguistique générale* (Paris: Gallimard, 1966), pp. 70f., 151ff., 187ff.

2. I shall not dwell here upon the contrast between the Greek and the Heideggerian conceptions of Being. See my remarks on "static being and personal *Dasein*" in *The Verb 'Be' in Ancient Greek* (Dordrecht: Reidel, 1973), pp. 415–19.

3. In addition to Chapter 8 of *The Verb 'Be' in Ancient Greek*, see "On the Theory of the Verb 'to be,'" in *Logic and Ontology*, ed. Milton K. Munitz (New York: New York University Press, 1973), pp. 1–20. In these studies I was primarily concerned with the unity of the linguistic system of the verb as ordinarily used. By contrast, the present paper deals explicitly with the special quasi-technical use of the verb and its nominal derivatives (ὄν and οὐσία) to formulate the philosophic concept of Being. I thus return to the topic originally sketched in "The Greek Verb 'to be' and the Concept of Being," *Foundations of Language* 2 (1966): 245–65.

4. This linguistic claim that the copula uses are fundamental for the system of the verb as a whole is logically independent of my claim that, as a fact in the history of philosophy, the idea of truth (and falsehood) associated with the veridical uses is the primary notion for the development of the metaphysical concept of Being in Plato and Parmenides. Either claim might be in error without the other thesis being affected either way. But of course there is some connection between the function of copula and the veridical idea. See my remarks on the notion of truth-claim implicit in the copula use, *The Verb 'Be' in Ancient Greek*, pp. 186–91, 407f.

5. Cf. John Lyons, *Introduction to Theoretical Linguistics* (Cambridge: Cambridge University Press, 1968), pp. 397–99. I have applied Lyons' analysis to Greek in *The Verb 'Be' in Ancient Greek*, pp. 195f.

6. For a fuller statement see "The Thesis of Parmenides," *Review of Metaphysics* 22 (1969), 700–724.

7. Compare Anaxagoras Fr. 17, Empedocles Fr. 8–12, Democritus A.1 44 (Diels-Kranz II, p. 84, lines 11–12).

8. I think the identification of *νοεῖν* and *εἶναι* in Parmenides Fr. 3 must be taken at face value. (Compare 8.35–37 and, on my interpretation, 6.1 as well.) The parallel identification of *νόησις* with its object (*τὸ νοούμενον*) in Aristotle may help us to understand what Parmenides meant.

9. I assume that *Symposium* 211A–212A, which adapts the Eleatic ontology to the description of a *single* Form, the Beautiful, presented dogmatically as the object of a hieratic vision, was written for an audience that had not yet read the *Phaedo*, where the doctrine of Forms is developed as a generalized theory and supported both by careful argumentation and by a systematic statement of philosophic method (100A–101E). The ontological doctrines of the two works are substantially the same, but the mode of presentation in the *Symposium* is clearly that of revealing something *new* to an audience not fully prepared for what it is going to hear; whereas the exposition of the *Phaedo* is addressed to philosophic initiates. From the literary point of view, this means that the readers of the *Phaedo* are expected to know the ontological doctrine of the *Symposium* already (in addition to the pre-ontological preparation for this doctrine in the *Euthyphro*, *Meno*, *Lysis*, etc.). Like the *Phaedo* (65 D7, 78 D3, 100 B6, etc.) the *Cratylus* also begins its discussion of Forms by taking for granted a familiarity with the Beautiful itself (439 D3–6)—with precisely that Form which was revealed with such pomp and ceremony in the *Symposium*.

10. See Burnet's note to *Phaedo* 65 C3, where he observes, "The verb *εἶναι* often means 'to be true', especially in Herodotus and Thucydides (cp. L.S. *s.v.* *εἰμί* A.III)." This is of course my veridical use. Six lines later, at 65C9, where Socrates speaks of the soul as "reaching for Being" (*ὀρέγηται τοῦ ὄντος*), Burnet again correctly paraphrases "Being" as "the True" (*τοῦ ἀληθοῦς*).

11. 65 D13–E1: (*περὶ . . .*) *τῆς οὐσίας* (sc. *πάντων τῶν ἄλλων*) *ὃ τυγχάνει ἕκαστον ὄν*. This phrase is discussed in what follows.

12. 65 D4 *φαμέν τι εἶναι δίκαιον αὐτὸ ἢ οὐδέν*. The question is a standard one. See 74 A12: *φῶμέν τι εἶναι ἢ μηδέν*; in reference to *αὐτὸ τὸ ἴσον*. And compare *Protagoras* 330 C1: *ἡ δικαιοσύνη πρᾶγμά τί ἐστιν ἢ οὐδὲν πρᾶγμα*; D2 *οὐκοῦν καὶ ὁσιότητά τινά φατε εἶναι*; 332 A4: *ἀφροσύνην τι καλεῖς*; C3: *φέρε δή, ἦν δ' ἐγώ, ἔστιν τι καλόν*; C5: *τί δέ; ἔστιν τι ἀγαθόν*; etc. Settling the question *whether X exists* or (more literally) *whether X is something* is a methodical prerequisite to investigating *what it is*. Compare Aristotle's doctrine that one cannot know the *τί ἐστιν* of anything unless one knows *ὅτι ἔστιν* (*Post. An.* II.7).

13. *Phaedo* 75 D1: *περὶ ἁπάντων οἷς ἐπισφραγιζόμεθα τὸ "αὐτὸ ὃ ἔστι."* (So Burnet; the manuscripts have *τοῦτο ὅ ἐστι*; I suggest *τοῦτο τὸ ὅ ἐστι*. The strong accent of *ἔστι* here is modern and arbitrary: see *The Verb 'Be' in Ancient Greek*, p. 420 and n. 2.) Although the text is in doubt, there is no doubt of the general formula, introduced at 74 B2: "do we say that the Equal itself is something? And do we know *what it is*?" (*ἦ καὶ ἐπιστάμεθα αὐτὸ ὃ ἔστιν*;), and anticipated at 65 D13–E1, in the passage quoted in n. 11: "concerning the *οὐσία* of all the others (sc. Forms), *what each one really is*; is it through the body that the primary truth of them (*αὐτῶν τὸ ἀληθέστατον*) is beheld?" As these two passages make clear, the underlying syntax of *ὃ ἔστι* in the *τὸ ὃ ἔστι* phrase is simply that of a standard transform of the familiar definitional question *τί ἐστι*, after a verb of knowing or saying where the relative pronoun *ὅ* regularly replaces the interrogative form *τί*. The construction here is "to apprehend *X* (and know) what it is." But the syntax would be exactly the same for "to state *X* (and specify) what it is." So we may describe *ἐστί* here in the *τὸ ὃ ἔστι* formula as the definitional copula, the copula as used in definitions (or, if one prefers, the *is* of definitional identity) with the veridical nuance emphasized by the connection with a verb of knowing: to apprehend *what X most truly is* (*αὐτῶν τὸ ἀληθέστατον*,

Phaedo 65 E1). The concept of essence arises from reflection upon this notion of Socratic definition or Platonic dialectic, understood as seeking the intelligible in contrast to the sensible nature of a thing, the universal and essential or *per se* attributes in contrast to the particular and accidental, and (finally, for Aristotle) the necessary as opposed to the contingent properties.

14. The syntax is no longer transparent once the phrase gets used as a technical label (*αὐτὸ τὸ ὃ ἔστιν* at 74 D6, *ἐκείνου τοῦ ὃ ἔστιν ἴσον* at 75 B1–2); but the underlying structure will re-emerge whenever there is any direct connection with the idea of knowledge: 75 B5–6: *εἰληφότας ἐπιστήμην αὐτοῦ τοῦ ἴσου ὅτι ἔστιν* "having acquired knowledge of the Equal itself, [knowledge of] what it is." So far as I can see, the existential uses of *εἰμί* are strictly irrelevant for the understanding of this formulaic occurrence of the verb in Plato. What we have is the ordinary copula as used in definitions, with a heavy veridical nuance, just as in the Socratic *τί ἐστι* question: "What is *X*, truly?" or "What do you really mean by *X*?" The Forms "on which we set the seal of 'what it is'" are just those entities whose nature is under investigation when the *τί ἐστι* question is asked and whose definition is expected to be formulated in the answer to this question. It is the same question and the same syntax which underlies the use of the *finite* verb in Aristotle's technical expressions *τὸ τί ἐστι* and *τὸ τί ἦν εἶναι*. In the latter formula, the indirect question *τί ἦν* is simply *τί ἐστι* recast in the philosophical imperfect. But the use of the infinitive here (as in the simpler formula *τὸ ἀνθρώπῳ εἶναι*) seems to correspond to a conceptual innovation in Aristotle's view of essences. Aristotle may well have preferred the infinitival, and hence unmistakably verbal expression of *τὸ* (*τί ἦν* or *τινὶ*) *εἶναι* as indicating his own conception of forms as predicates or universals, in contrast to the thing-like or substantival connotations of the Platonic term *οὐσία* (which Aristotle then re-employs for his own concept of *substance*, as the solid furniture of the universe).

15. *Theaetetus* 189E–190A; *Sophist* 263E–264A.

16. But see Aristotle's remarks on Being as Truth (*τὸ ὡς ἀληθὲς ὄν*) in *Met.* Δ.7 (1017^{a}31), E.4, and Θ.10.

H.G. GADAMER

Plato and Heidegger

What we learned from Heidegger was above all the pervasive unity of the metaphysics originated by the Greeks and its continued validity under the subtly altered conditions of modern thought. The Aristotelian question concerning a primary science, which Aristotle himself expressly designates as the knowledge to be sought for, initiated the tradition of Western thought. In this tradition the question of the being of beings was posed in terms of the highest and most eminent of beings, namely, the divine. If Heidegger understood his own endeavor as a preparation for posing the question of being anew, then this assumed that the traditional metaphysics, since its beginning in Aristotle, had lost all explicit awareness of the questionableness of the sense of being. This was a challenge to self-understanding for a metaphysics which would not recognize itself in its own consequences: in the radical nominalism of the modern age, and in the transformation of the modern concept of science into an all-embracing technology. One of the concerns of *Sein und Zeit* was just this: to urge a recognition. At the same time Heidegger's destruction of metaphysics gave rise to the question of the beginnings of Greek thought, beginnings which preceded the development of the metaphysical question. It is well known that in this respect Heidegger, like Nietzsche, placed special emphasis on the origins of Greek thought. For Heidegger, Anaximander, Heraclitus, and Parmenides were not a preliminary phase of the metaphysical inquiry, but witnesses to the essential openness of the beginning—where *alētheia* had as yet nothing of the correctness of a statement, indeed not even of the revealedness of a being.

What of Plato in this matter? Did his thinking not stand in between the early thinkers and the scholastic form of metaphysics—a metaphysics which assumed its initial form in the teachings of Aristotle? Can we determine Plato's position? Heidegger's going back to a point before the question of metaphysics was posed, i.e., to the being of beings, was certainly not a presumptuous criticism of metaphysics from a superior standpoint. Heidegger never wanted to "overcome" metaphysics as an aberration of thought. He understood metaphysics as the historical course of the West, determining its destiny. Here destiny is that which has overtaken us and which has irrevocably determined our own position and all possible paths into the future. And so Heidegger most certainly attempted to find the way of his own questioning within the history of metaphysics and its internal tensions, and not apart from it. Aristotle was in many respects not only his opponent but also his ally. It was especially Aristotle's repudiation of Plato's idea of a universal good, based on the concept of analogy, and Aristotle's penetration of the nature of *physis*, particularly Book VI of the *Nichomachean Ethics* and Book II of the *Physics*, which Heidegger interpreted in a fruitful way. It is evident that it is precisely these two positive aspects of Aristotle's thought which are the most important documentation of Aristotle's criticism of Plato. In the first place, there is the severing of the question concerning the 'good,' as man must ask it for human *praxis*, from the theoretical posing of the question concerning universals generally. In the second place, there is the criticism of the Platonic theory of forms. This finds its expression in the ontological primacy of motion in Aristotle's concept of *physis* and claims to overcome the orientation toward the Pythagorean quantitative forms. Both point at Plato and in both respects Aristotle appears almost as a forerunner of Heideggerian thought. The doctrine of *phronēsis* as practical knowledge stands opposed to all objectifying tendencies of science, and in the concept of *physis* and its ontological primacy there is at least a hint of a dimension of givenness which is superior to any subject-object opposition.

This was certainly Heidegger's own fruitful "recollection" and not mere influence. In describing the role which Franz Brentano's treatise on the various significances of being in Aristotle had played for him, Heidegger himself has told us what Aristotle meant to him as an initial inspiration. Brentano's careful delineation of the variety of meanings which lie in Aristotle's concept of being led Heidegger to be seized by the question of what might be concealed behind this variety. In any case, a critical position vis-à-vis Plato's theory of forms was implicit in the question.

But then, opening *Sein und Zeit*, we find right on the first page the famous quotation from the *Sophist* concerning the question of being, which has always been posed and always in vain. It is true that this quotation contains no detailed articulation of the way in which the question of being is posed. Furthermore, the overcoming of the Eleatic concept of being which commences with the *Sophist* points in an entirely different direction from that of the question concerning the hidden unity of the various meanings of being which had aroused the young Heidegger. There is still another passage in the *Sophist* which Heidegger does not quote, although he refers to it, and which actually, even though only in a merely formal way, implies the continuing predicament concerning being. The predicament was the same in the fourth century before Christ as in our twentieth century. The stranger from Elea expounds the two basic modes of manifestation of beings as motion and rest. These are two mutually exclusive modes of being, but they appear to exhaust completely the possibilities of the manifestation of being. If one does not wish to conceive of the state of rest, one must conceive of motion, and vice-versa. Where should one look if one does not wish to catch sight of the one or the other but of being? There appears to be no possibility whatsoever of open questioning. It is clearly not the intention of the Eleatic stranger to understand being as the universal genus which differentiates itself into these two aspects of being. What Plato has in mind, rather, is that in speaking about being a differentiation is implicit which does not distinguish different realms of being but rather suggests an inner structuredness of being itself. Selfness or identity as well as otherness or difference are essential to all discourse about being. These two aspects, far from being mutually exclusive, are rather mutually determining. Whatever is identical with itself is thereby different from everything else. Insofar as it is what it is, it is not everything else. Being and non-being are inextricably intertwined. Indeed, it appears to be precisely the mark of a philosopher as against the sham logic of the Sophists that it is the togetherness of being—the affirmation, and of non-being, the negation—which constitutes the nature of beings.

Now it is precisely at this point that the later Heidegger takes up the question: the determinate nature of beings, whose relation to being constitutes the entire truth of being, prevented any posing of the question concerning the sense of being. Heidegger, in fact, describes the history of metaphysics as the growing forgetfulness of the question concerning being. The revealedness of beings—the self-manifestation of the *eidos* in its unchangeable form—amounts to the abandonment of the question concerning the sense of being. What is manifest as *eidos*, i.e., as unchangeable and immovable presence, determines as well the meaning of unconcealedness, that is, truth, and establishes the criterion of right or wrong for every assertion about beings. Theatetus cannot fly. In this way, by his reinterpretation of the Eleatic doctrine of being as the dialectic of being and non-being, Plato grounds the meaning of 'knowledge' in the *logos* which allows assertions about the beingness of beings, that is, about *what* they are. In so doing, Plato predetermines the way the question will be put in the Aristotelian doctrine of the *logos* of the *ousia*, the core of his metaphysics. In this sense the distortion of the question of being begins with Plato, and the criticism which Aristotle brings against the Platonic doctrine of forms does not change the fact that the science of being which Aristotle sought remains within this prior determination and does not attempt to question behind it.

It is not appropriate to develop at this point the problematic of modern philosophy to which Heidegger's critical return to Greek metaphysics is a response. It will suffice to recall the way Heidegger defined the task of "destroying" the basic concepts of modern philosophy, especially the concepts subjectivity and consciousness. Above all, the impressive way in which Husserl, in inexhaustible variations, attempted to determine the constitution of self-consciousness as temporal consciousness was a determining factor in Heidegger's own way of taking up the problem of the temporal structure of *Dasein*. Certainly, Heidegger's familiarity with the Greek philosophical heritage stood him in good stead in critically distancing himself from Husserl's neo-Kantian, idealistic programing of phenomenology. In any case, it is a crass simplification to interpret Heidegger's accentuation of history and the historical as merely a thematic turn which separates him from Husserl's thinking. Not only the controversy between Husserl and Dilthey but especially the unpublished second volume of the *Ideas* are evidence against any doubt of Husserl's concern with the question of history and the historical. Indeed they confirm the attempt to accommodate Heidegger's *Sein und Zeit* within the Husserlian phenomenology, as Oskar Becker unhappily attempted to do in the Husserl *Festschrift*. There is no doubt that it was clear to Husserl from the beginning that the "mortal danger" of skepticism, which he took historical relativism to be, could not be averted without clarifying the constitution of the historical structure of human social life. Nevertheless, what Heidegger undertook in *Sein und Zeit* was not only a deepening of the foundations of a transcendental phenomenology, it was also a preparation for a radical change which would bring the collapse of the entire concept of the constitution of all conceivable meanings in the transcendental ego, and above all of the concept of the self-constitution of the ego itself. In analyzing the temporal nature of the stream of consciousness, Husserl conceived of the self-manifestation of the stream, that is, the nonmediated presence, as the ultimate factor in the ego to which we can descend. He did not regard the detailed structure which becomes evident in the self-constitution of the ego in any way as an *aporia*, but claimed it as a positive description. This meant that, basically, he did not go beyond the Hegelian idea of the perfect self-transparency of absolute knowledge. Heidegger does not merely oppose the unpredictability of existence to this ideal, as the Young Hegelians and Kierkegaard had already done in a variety of ways. That is not what is truly novel about his endeavor. If it were, he would have remained in fact dialectically dependent, caught in a hegelianizing anti-Hegelianism.

It is odd to note that Adorno, in his "negative dialectic," never realized how close he comes to Heidegger, if one only sees Heidegger in this way. The truth is that Heidegger, as a student of early Greek thought and as one who also entered into dialogue with it, posed the problem of facticity in a more radical and original sense. Because metaphysics in its beginnings undertook to question the unconcealedness of beings through *logos* and its presence and preservation in thought and speech, the authentic dimension of the temporality and historicalness of being fell into a deep and lengthy shadow. Heidegger questioned behind the beginning of metaphysics and sought to open up a dimension in which, as in "historicism," historicalness is no longer opposed to the philosophers' claim of absoluteness and no longer is insisted on as a limiting hindrance to truth and the objectivity of knowledge. Nor can this be understood as a *coup de main* which attempts to solve the problem of historical relativism by radicalizing it. It seems to me significant that the later Heidegger, in his self-interpretation, no longer takes the problem of historicism seriously (see "*Mein Weg in die Phänomenologie*"). Historicalness is for Heidegger the ontological structure of the "temporalizing" of *Dasein* in self-projection and thrownness, in the clearing and withdrawal of being. It is a realm behind all questioning concerning beings. It is possible to recognize, as Heidegger does, this dimension of the question of being in the riddle of Anaximander, in the monumental singleness of Parmenides' truth and in Heraclitus' "one and only wise man." But one can raise the question whether the beginning of metaphysical thinking does not itself give evidence of this dimension and whether, in the *logos* of the Platonic dialectic or in Aristotle's analysis of *nous*, which perceives essence and determines it as what it is, the realm in which all questioning and speech find their field of activity does not also become visible. Does the initial question of metaphysics concerning the "what" of beings really obstruct the question of being totally, as without doubt do the modes of speech developed in the sciences which logic makes into its analytical theme?

Heidegger, as is well known, saw in Plato's doctrine of forms the first step in the transformation of truth from unconcealedness to the appropriateness and correctness of statements. That this is one-sided he himself later conceded, but his self-correction amounts merely to saying that Plato was the first to experience *alētheia* as the correctness of representation and statement but that it was experienced from the beginning and only as *orthotēs*. I would like to raise the question, contrary to this, whether Plato himself did not attempt to think the realm of unconcealedness, at least in the idea of the good, and not merely because of certain complications and internal difficulties in the doctrine of forms; but rather whether from the very beginning he had not questioned behind this doctrine and thereby behind *alētheia* as correctness. It seems to me that something can be said for this, only, of course, if one does not read Plato's works through the eyes of Aristotle's critique.

This critique aims relentlessly at the refutation of the *chorismos* of the ideas, a point to which Aristotle always returns and which he developed into the essential difference between the definitional questions of Socrates and Plato. In fact, this thesis of Aristotle's suffers from a weakness which was made into an accusation, especially by Hegel and the Marburg neo-

Kantians, that Plato himself in his dialectical dialogues of the later period dealt with *chorismos* in a radical way and critically rejected it. One feels driven to the conclusion that the genuine depth of the Platonic dialectic is its claim to show the way out of this dilemma of *chorismos* and participation by lessening the importance of the separation between what partakes and that in which it partakes.

That that is not merely a later development of Platonic thinking becomes clear, in my view, if one considers the exceptional role which the idea of the good played in Plato's works from early on. Because the idea of the good does not fit easily into the scheme of Aristotle's critique of *chorismos* and in fact, as could be shown, is only hesitantly and cautiously included in Aristotle's general critique of the ideas, the critique of the idea of the good is carried out from the practical point of view. The theoretical problem remains, however, that it is not merely chance equivocations which permit calling very different things "good," but that this conceals a genuine problem which Aristotle attempted to solve in his doctrine of *analogia entis*.

But let us turn to Plato himself. Initially we encounter the question concerning the good itself as the constant negative instance on which the collocutors understanding of *aretē* comes to grief. The underlying idea of knowledge, which is modeled on craft skill and whose meaning is the mastery of practical situations, proves to be inapplicable in the case of the idea of the good. It is obviously more than mere literary art when Plato's statements about the good in itself have a tendency to withdraw in a peculiar way into a realm beyond. In the *Republic* the special position of the idea of the good in contrast to the *aretē* concepts of definite content is insisted on so that it is only by means of a sense analogy, that of the sun, that the good is spoken of. It is decisive that the sun functions as the *bringer* of light and that it is light which makes the visible world visible to the seer. It is significant that the idea of the good, conforming to the frequently used analogy, is, so to speak, only indirectly visible. Within the whole of the thought of the *Republic* that means that the constitution of the soul, the state, and—in the *Timaeus*—the world is grounded in the One, that is, in the good, even as the sun is the ground of light that binds together everything. The good is that which bestows unity rather than that which is itself a one. It is, after all, beyond all being.

There can be no doubt that this superbeing should not be thought of, after the manner of neo-Platonism, as the source of a cosmic drama, nor is it the goal of a withdrawal and mystical union. It is true, however, that this one which is the good, is not, as the *Philebus* shows, comprehensible in any way as one but only as a trinity of measure, appropriateness, and "truth" as most suitably befits the nature of the beautiful. Does the good exist anywhere at all if not in the form of the beautiful? And does that not mean that it is not an existent particular, but is to be thought of as the unconcealedness of emergence into the field of vision (*to ekphanestaton*)?

Even Aristotle's interpretation of Plato takes account of this singular position of the good in an indirect way. As was mentioned earlier, Aristotle, in the context of practical philosophy, denied the idea of the good any relevance at all and, on the other hand, carries out his criticism of the doctrine of forms without regard for the idea of the good. But he sees the theoretical problem of the unity of the good so closely related to the problem of the unity of being that one is justified in distinguishing his methods of thinking, those of analogy and attribution, from his general approach to Plato's doctrine of forms. It can be shown from Aristotle's own work that he could indeed distinguish between the acceptance of the forms in general and their logical and ontological inadequacies which he pointed out, on the one hand, and the principle of this acceptance, on the other—which forms the topic of Book VI of the *Metaphysics*. In Aristotle's terms, that is, the good—and being likewise—is not one form among many but a beginning, an *archē*. It is not entirely clear if the good itself is the One which as *archē*, together with twoness, forms the basis of all determination of the forms, or whether perhaps the One is itself prior to this twoness of one and indefinite plurality. One thing, however, is definite: The One is as little a number as the idea of the good is a form in the sense of the *eidos* which Aristotle criticized as a vacuous duplication of the world.

The idea of the good is no longer spoken of in the later Plato when the central question of the dialectic, that is, the *logos ousias*, becomes thematic. That is true even of the *Philebus*, where the theme is explicitly the good, admittedly the good in the life of men. Here, however, the criterion of the good, which, as we saw, was defined as the form of the beautiful, cannot be left undiscussed. In the *Philebus* the fundamental discussion of the four categories is conducted without especially distinguishing the idea of the good. And in the *Sophist* and *Parmenides* the discussion of dialectic appears to be far beyond the doctrine of forms, and, indeed, these dialogues have been understood as the renunciation of the doctrine of forms. The doctrine of the *logos* of being which is developed in these dialectical dialogues is, in any case, as little subject to Aristotle's *chorismos* criticism as is the idea of the good. Platonic dogmatism, which Aristotle's criticism belabors, has no basis in these dialogues. On the contrary, the schema of the *dihairēsis* which Plato presents as his dialectical method in these dialogues has been for some time understood as a successful resolution of the *methexis* problem (Natorp, N. Hartmann, J. Stenzel), which invalidates Aristotle's criticism. It is noteworthy that the possibility of dialectic in the sense of *dihairēsis* cannot itself be justified by the dihairetic method. This theory of the highest categories wants to explain how the disjunction and synthesis of what belongs together is possible at all.

In this context the problem of error (*pseudos*) arises and plays a consistently disconcerting role. One may understand the problem to mean roughly that, if thinking is distinguishing, one is capable of distinguishing falsely. As the Platonic analogy has it: Mistaking the joints when carving the sacrificial animals, one proves that one is not master of the true dialectic and so, after the manner of the Sophists, one becomes prone to misconceptions of the *logos*. It remains unclear, however, how these misconceptions are possible if one understands the being of the forms as pure presence. So the question concerning error becomes hopelessly complicated in the *Theatetus*. The analogies of the wax tablet and the dovecote do not advance the argument a single step: In a case of error what can be meant by the presence of the erroneous, of the false? What is it that is present when a statement is false?

It is true that the *Sophist* attempts to advance this question toward a positive solution by means of the proof that non-being is and is indissolubly conjoined with being, as difference is with identity. If, however, non-being means nothing but difference which, along with identity, forms the basis of all differentiating speech, then it is indeed understandable how true speech is possible but not how error, falseness, and illusion are possible. The coexistence of the other (the different) with the identical is far from explaining the existence of something as what it is not, but explains it merely as what it is, that is to say, this and nothing else.

So a mere criticism of the Eleatic concept of being does not suffice to invalidate genuinely its basic assumption, the thinking of being as presence in *logos*. If even difference is a kind of visible, the *eidos* of non-being, then the question of error remains a puzzle. Insofar as the 'not' turns out to be the *eidos* of otherness, the erroneous (*pseudos*) conceals itself at the same time. At the most one can go on to say that one must accept a fundamental limitation in the way the 'not' presents itself; otherness turns up only intertwined with sameness, that is, with reference to something identifiable as the non-being of everything else. It appears entirely nonsensical to think of the totality of all differences, that is to say, the total presence of non-being as 'given'. The 'not' of otherness is, in this sense, a genuine 'not' of being. This is obviously what Plato had in mind when he posited the indeterminable twoness alongside the determining one. But if one accepts the 'not' of otherness and difference, the nothingness or nullity of error becomes harmless, and the concealment which began with the eleatic suppression of the 'not' is perpetuated. One might bear in mind as well that, in the production of the world according to the *Timaeus*, sameness and difference function as cosmological factors and constitute knowledge and opinion, of course, *alēthēs doxa*. An ontological foundation for *pseudēs doxa* is lacking.

We have assuredly arrived at the point where Heidegger discerned the limits of the concept of *alētheia*, that is to say, the beginning of the distortion of the question of being. One can, however, put the matter the other way around. As we become aware in Plato's thought of the insolubility of the question of error, we are forced toward a dimension in which non-being does not mean mere difference and being mere identifiability, but a dimension in which the One is more original, is prior to such a differentiation and at the same time makes it possible. The grand one-sidedness of the Parmenidean insistence on being in which there is no 'not,' no negation, brought the abyss of the 'not' to light. Plato's recognition of the 'not' in being cannot, in its turn, avoid bringing to light the nothingness of the 'not' as a problem. Even though he rendered the 'not' harmless, he nevertheless drew attention to the illusoriness and nullity of sophistry. And indeed that error (*pseudos*) is not merely mistake but comports the uncanniness of illusion is no longer discernible even in Aristotle's theory of *alētheia* and *pseudos* as given in Book IX of the *Metaphysics*. If one wants to think seriously about that aspect of illusion which is nothingness and about the way it belongs to being, and not make it out to be harmless, i.e., the mere confusion of a mistake, then one must either look back beyond Parmenides or forward beyond Hegel. Heidegger attempted to take the step backward and in so doing to take the step forward as well, a step which would allow modern civilization to realize the limits of Greek thought, of *alētheia* and its formative power. It may be that by virtue of this a dialogue has become possible with philosophical traditions which have developed outside these limits, if they learn to free themselves from any tendency to parallel Western thought.

ZYGMUNT ADAMCZEWSKI

Questions in Heidegger's Thought about Being

Throughout history different thinkers have needed and received varying treatment with regard to their thought: explication, commentary, criticism, defense, transformation. Along with these and no less appropriate would appear to be the raising of questions which emerge in a thinker's endeavor. This is especially proper in a genuine concern with a thinker who wrote early in his development: "Any research in this field where 'the matter itself is profoundly enshrouded' will beware of overestimating its own results. Because such asking always strives by itself toward the possibility of disclosing an ever more universal horizon, from which the answer could be drawn to the question: what does 'being' mean?" (*Sein und Zeit*, pp. 26–27). The unity of Martin Heidegger's thought is provided by his continual striving to ask about the enshrouded matter of being. That is why, from the myriad of questions that could be provoked by thought of such world-opening importance, I have selected three, all pertinent to the thread of that thought as involved in being. I raise no claim to their exhaustive character but regard them as of fundamental and pervasive consequence. They concern being and nothing, being and entities or beings, and being and man. Yet even before approaching these questions, I wish to stress the peculiarly weak significance of the *and* in all such references where no contraposition is intended or proper. This has to be stressed to remain true to the insight of the man who, writing about humanism and against existentialism, said: "Il y a principalement l'Etre [in principle there is being]" (*Wegmarken*, p. 165), and who devoted such a large part of his *Introduction to Metaphysics* to a very critical consideration of any limitation (*Beschränkung*, *Eingrenzung*) against being. Thus to say "being and . . . " could imply some overcoming of it, as if something could be set over and outside it—which cannot be granted. Therefore, when, for simplicity's sake, I use the word 'and,' I have in mind something like: being toward, as it concerns, with regard to . . . ; the German word might be *angesichts*. I shall reiterate this understanding further on.

Being and nothing: What must be thought about their relation in Heidegger

—if that expression is legitimate? At any rate, the *and* cannot be taken literally, since there is no possibility of setting or posing nothing as an addition to being. But then? In the text of his inaugural lecture, *What is Metaphysics?* (which is explicitly concerned with the question about nothing), Heidegger affirms the correctness of Hegel's statement: "Pure being and pure nothing is therefore the same" (*Wegmarken*, p. 17). This admission of sameness is at least at first bewildering. Is it unique? In the *Origin of the Work of Art* we find these words: "Does truth then emerge from nothing? Indeed it does"; while on the other hand in uncounted instances Heidegger speaks of truth as emerging from being: Does it mean the same? And yet, the same sentence continues: "wherever 'nothing' means only no-thing, not-a-being, and where a being is represented as that usually available . . . " (*Holzwege*, p. 59). One point may be remarked, then: Being and nothing are the same in that neither can be thought of as a being, an entity; rather, it, or they, can provide for the emergence of truth as well as of entities; in Heideggerian language, they belong together beyond the level of the ontological difference.

Another angle of approach offers itself in consideration of the principle of sufficient ground. There Heidegger cites it in the usual form: "Nothing is without a ground" (*Der Satz vom Grund*, p. 75), and this can point to a kinship with his often-expressed characterization of being as without a ground, a no-ground, an abyss (*Abgrund*). Sameness again? Not quite, because his text proceeds, with the aid of italics, to change the emphasis from: "*Nothing* is *without* a ground" to: "Nothing *is* without a *ground*." Would the distance consist then only of a change of emphasis? No, even though it should be remembered that in speech emphasis signifies force, vigor, prominence. But his further conclusion from its emphatically changed form is that the principle refers to all that is: "The 'is' names, although quite indeterminately, the being of any entities. . . . The principle of the ground speaks of being" (ibid., p. 90). In other words, it is to being that the character of the ground appertains, with all entities grounded in it, as they can hardly be grounded in nothing.

What has been called the distance of being with respect to nothing is also alluded to in *What is Metaphysics?* In the postscript is found the sentence: "Nothing as the other than beings is the veil of being" (*Wegmarken*, p. 107). Thus while its assignment to the other 'side' of the ontological difference is reaffirmed, such assignment is not a sign of equivalence with being. An equivalence or coincidence is denied explicitly in the lecture itself, just after the reference to Hegel. And on the same page it is said: "Nothing does not stay as the indeterminate 'against' toward entities, but uncovers itself as belonging [*zugehörig*] to the being of entities" (ibid., pp. 16–17); thus no *nihil negativum*.

The question of belonging: in the words just quoted a subordination is implied, but not always. In places Heidegger clearly rejects understanding of 'sameness' as coincidence, indifferent likeness (*Gleichgültigkeit*, *Einerlei*), and intimates instead a sense of belonging together, sometimes expressly on the ground of unity—and it was shown above that ground pertains to being rather than nothing. Such a sense of belonging he calls "the right conception of identity" (Schelling's *Abhandlung*, pp. 94–95). In the *Principle of Identity* he so interprets the belonging together (Parmenidean) of being and awareness and also, interestingly, of being and man. But the asymmetry therein is not unvaryingly stressed; it is when the Parmenidean sameness is understood, as, e.g., "Awareness [*Vernehmung*] happens for the sake of being" (*Einführung in die Metaphysik*, p. 106). Again, while the sameness is taken as belonging together, within it awareness or thought is subordinated to being.

In passing, this question may be asked: In what other way could sameness or identity pertain to being? The concept is applied without difficulty, perhaps with necessity, to all entities we encounter. But is it advantageous to ask whether being is identical with itself? Would such a question offer any grasp if all identification procedures applicable to entities must fail here? And, in particular, would it be appropriate for the Heideggerian thought about being, which understands it as nonstatic, as viewed on the horizon of time, as yielding and withholding itself varyingly through the epochs of its history? Yet if self-sameness fails to hold it, does this make it evanescent—like nothing?

The remembrance of Parmenides is fuller in the *Introduction to Metaphysics*; it also brings into light questions of the human attitude toward being and nothing. Commenting on the Parmenidean ways for man to travel, Heidegger underlines first the way to being, second the way to not-being; the latter "cannot be traveled" yet precisely as such must be brought into attention. He adds that here is the "oldest document in philosophy concerning this, that together with the way of being the way of nothing must be *thought about* on its own" (ibid., p. 85). Two ways then, thinkable for man and divided by a distance incomparable to any other. Also a reiteration: "That nothing is not a being by no means precludes that in its own mode it belongs to being" (ibid.). But it is this way, this mode, that challenges asking.

In the passage taking very seriously the evanescent indeterminacy of being for the ordinary human understanding, Heidegger asserts no less seriously its indispensability for man as he is. If there were not some understanding of what it means 'to be,' then human speech could not exist. "Because to speak of entities as such includes: to understand in advance entities as they are, i.e. their being. . . . To be human means: to be a speaker. Man is one who says: yes and no" (ibid., p. 62). The last phrase is telling, because in question is not the possible presence or absence of a word in a language. Rather, the power of speech is here referred to the ability to say yes and no—without which any language structure is indeed hardly imaginable—and these little everyday words mean: 'it is so' and 'it is not.' The implication therefore is of crucial import. As a speaker and a yes-and-no sayer the human being somehow, to some extent, always understands the distance between 'to be' and 'not to be,' which stretches toward being and nothing. As in *Being and Time*, speech and understanding are introduced as coequal existential features of man's way to be.

There is in the same work an even sharper expression of man's ontological reach. The question which circumscribes all that is: "Why are there entities at all rather than nothing?" This is addressed to the contingency of all beings including the human, their continuing exposure to the possibility that they might not be. Man alone asks this question, but he can do so not with just an intellectual demand for an available explanation. More than this is involved. "A ground is sought that is to establish [*begründen*] the dominance of entities as an overcoming of nothing. The ground asked for is now asked as the ground of decision for entities against nothing" (ibid., p. 22). As earlier a discrimination between Parmenides' ways was suggested, so here in full explicitness the stance of man is expressed: this involves not only thought and speech but decision: against nothing and in favor of entities in their being. Still, to decide, the human being must ask in open awareness; his stance must seek and reach that distance between being and nothing, which is perhaps no distance, since it must not preclude the relation whereby nothing belongs to being—a relation for which Heidegger has no name?

A passage toward the end of one of his many encounters with Nietzsche (*Nietzsche*, vol. 2, p. 253) says: "Being is at once the emptiest and the richest . . . the most understandable and resisting of all conceptions . . . the most reliable and the most abysmal." And the text suggests that too often human attitudes are one-sided in focusing on the negative aspects of being, taking it as empty, inconceivable, abysmal; this indeed would be the essence of contemporary nihilism. If the passage cited perhaps suggests bridging the distance mentioned, its direction is clearly opposite: not to think of being as nothing but to think of nothing as a mode, an aspect, a veil of being—truly abysmal and thereby no less questionable (*fragwürdig*).

Being and entities or beings: another controversial matter, perhaps even more specifically Heideggerian, since he insists in various references that its disregard deprives traditional ontology of its ground. Possibly for this reason Heidegger gradually comes to avoid identification of his thought as ontological. But its intent remains unaltered in the differentiation of all that is and its being, a difference within which man alone dwells, however improperly and forgetfully: the ontological difference. "If otherwise the distinctiveness of the human being [*Dasein*] consists in that it relates itself to entities while understanding being, then the ability to differentiate, in which the ontological difference becomes fact, must have struck the root of its own possibility in the ground of the way to be [*Wesen*] of the human being" ("Vom Wesen des Grundes," *Wegmarken*, p. 31). Here is a statement of the ontological difference and of its foundational character in Heidegger's approach to man. But two points may be noted: (1) the ontological difference is not made up by man but rather rooted in the ground of his existence; it makes up the phenomena of such existence, enabling him to differentiate, i.e., to take in the dimension between entities that are and their being; and (2) the use of the word *and* is again subject to caution, because there is no possibility of somehow counting entities over and above being. All that is is in being, and being lets it all be. The ontological difference is not a matter of extension or scope; this is what makes it so frustrating for logicians. Rather, if it may be put this way, it concerns depth: it is possible to experience and manipulate entities without sounding wherein they are grounded. Such a lack of depth tends toward what Heidegger attacks as forgetfulness of being; it does not, of course, do away with it. But even such human preoccupation with entities and forgetfulness of being cannot be complete or ultimate, if fundamentally some awareness of being—'ek-sistence'—is what determines the being of man (*Da-sein*).

That apart from being entities they could not be themselves, i.e., what they are, or even that, referring to the passage cited before, they could not be spoken of as entities, is inescapable in Heidegger's thought. Yet there seems to be also an asymmetry in the ontological difference. If it is one of depth, perhaps thought could dwell somehow in the greater and darker depth of being, apart from entities. On the one hand, there is an unmistakable early statement: "Being is ever being of an entity" (*Sein und Zeit*, p. 9). On the other hand, there is a much later statement which suggests a dual purpose: "My own thinking endeavor clearly knows in its way the difference between 'being' as 'being of entities' and 'being' as 'being' with regard to its own proper sense, i.e. its truth (clearing)" (*Unterwegs zur Sprache*, p. 110). This, to my knowledge, is never elaborated, yet it suggests that somehow thought could approach being while bypassing entities altogether. It could hardly be a different being—the thought of the sameness of being recurs—but even the notion of such an approach, so to speak, world-forgetting, is highly questionable. Is it not the case that the sense, truth, clearing of being yields itself only to the human being there in the world co-inhabited with other worldly beings? How else could man face being if not in so being there? What speculation with what sustenance could be expected in such a departure?

The fact of the ontological difference as it founds any determination of being human will not be disputed here. This acceptance does not, however, mean abrupt dismissal of questions which pertain to the outlines, the approaches and movements, within the dimension between being and entities. Thus, e.g., it is possible to ask in a quasi-logical manner whether *tertium non datur*? Is the dimension to be sounded here quite empty? Or to put it another way, what about any tangential connection on the lines of ontic versus ontological regards? Here is a rather definite expression: "Yet we speak of various 'entities' and in different senses. Everything is an entity, what we speak of, what we mean, what we adopt an attitude to; an entity is also what we are and how we are ourselves. Being lies in 'that it is' and in 'what it is,' in reality, availability, consistence, validity, in the human [*Dasein*], in 'there is' [*es gibt*]" (*Sein und Zeit*, pp. 6–7). To take this quite literally, excepting for a moment being and/or nothing, everything to be thought or spoken of pertains to entities, and these are considered in a variation of mode, status, area. But is this really sufficient? Does not Heidegger himself, and often, think and speak of that which is not synonymous with being, yet is hardly regarded as an entity? To begin with, that which has just been cited—sense, truth, clearing—are these terms ever used as names of entities? Hardly; rather, they are seen as ways in which being comes to entities, to let them show themselves as they are. Other examples: temporality in *Being and Time* temporalizes itself and 'is' not, consequently is not an entity. Then what about time, the horizon of being? Or, also in *Being and Time*, the world is mentioned as an entity, but not so its ontological structure of worldhood; and it could be argued that in some later texts the elaboration of the fourfold (*Geviert*) is intended as an explication of the proper understanding of the world, but not as an entity. To the list could be added references to what is of particular concern to man yet not under his sway. Speech, e.g., is said to hold man and not to be held by him; and in a telling phrase it is alluded to as the house of being. Care is determined as the being of man (*Dasein*); to whatever extent *Dasein* is an entity, its being need not be. And freedom? Seemingly a human possession, in Heideggerian thought it is the essence, or way to be, of truth; if truth is not an entity, the less so its way to be, prevailing throughout man's open 'ek-sistence.'

In the examples referred to, the leading thought is that standing in and expressing the ontological difference provokes a need to name whatever discloses itself therein. It is possible to insist that the above named are entities. But is it not also possible and advisable to think of them as 'data' or gifts of being, though not equivalent to it, or, to put it otherwise, to regard them as ontological powers yielding their influence on the ontic level? The dimension would then be not empty but enriched for that being whose character is a 'between,' man himself.

Another questionable point could be a rigid interpretation of an either-or in being versus entities. Already, from the early language of inauthentic against authentic existence, through various contexts the impression may arise that preoccupation with entities amounts to a deprivation of being, that to turn toward them is to turn away from it. This is indeed in the vein of Heidegger's criticism of metaphysics and his effort to transcend that. But it may be asked whether such an either-or is ubiquitously applicable. An important counterexample is provided with reference to art, for which no one has deeper respect than Heidegger. The situation described in *The Origin of the Work of Art* is such: "In great art, and we speak here of that alone, the artist, as opposed to his work, remains something indifferent, almost like a creatively self-annihilating transience aimed at the emergence of the work" (*Holzwege*, p. 29). In this case men, and not insignificant men, the great artists, voluntarily turn to and submerge themselves in entities, viz. their works. But is this improper, depriving, frustrating? Not at all: in Heidegger's view they bring it about that the truth of being happens and shines in those works, not only for the artist but for all men. At least in art, then, a turn to some entities is open re-turn to the discoveredness of being.

Art is unique in various respects; but is it here? To pursue and extend the asking, it is possible to consider other things and their place in the modern world. "Scientific knowledge, compelling in its own area, that of objects, has already annihilated things as things. . . . Thinghood of the thing stays covered, forgotten. The way to be of the thing never comes to the fore i.e. into speech. That is what is meant by speaking of the annihilation of the thing as thing" ("Das Ding," *Vorträge und Aufsätze*, II, p. 42). Heidegger develops a fuller description of what things of nature used to and could be; some might consider it overdeveloped. But is it not very characteristic that he speaks here of the forgottenness of things, and in the context of the scientific modern age wherein metaphysics terminates in nihilism—and this in turn signifies forgottenness of being? Even apart from his special regard for the thing, more transpires here: "Because the word 'thing' names, in the linguistic usage of Western metaphysics, that which is at all, anyhow, anything, therefore the meaning of the name 'thing' changes in accordance with the explication of that which is, i.e. of entities" (ibid., p. 49). By taking this statement with the preceding, it is possible to speak of the forgottenness of entities, of beings, of what is, so that all becomes evanescent. Yet such understanding must definitely be placed in a temporal framework. In consèquence, there are moving parallels in what happens about being, with its approach and withdrawal, and what happens about entities. Far from taking it as a fixed dimension between being and entities, is it not proper to think of the ontological difference as showing a history of its own? It would naturally belong to what Heidegger understands as the history of being, and, on the horizon of time, it would movingly determine the possibilities of the human stance and destiny, ever opening it to new questions.

Being and man: the initial access from *Being and Time* to Heidegger's whole thinking endeavor comprises this special relation, and unless the ontological weight in his determination of man's being there (*Da-sein*) is well understood, the integral intent of his thought must be missed. Man is throughout the locus and medium for being to yield and disclose itself. In this regard there is no such person as the early or the late Heidegger. This is not to say that there are no shifts of emphasis or angle of approach, in short, that there are no questions about this relation; nor would he wish to have none.

> First of all, the relation is not one, again, of a straightforward 'and.' We always say too little about 'being itself,' if we speak of 'being' so that we leave out its presence toward man's way to be [*Wesen*] and thus disregard that this way to be itself partakes in constituting 'being.' But we also say always too little about man, if we speak of 'being' (not the human being) so that we pose man for himself and only then go on to bring him, so posed, into a relation to 'being.' ("Zur Seinsfrage," *Wegmarken*, p. 235)

Once more, it is required to reiterate the principle, namely that there is being (*es gibt Sein*) of which man also partakes—as man—in a very distinctive way: being gives itself to him within and without, yet only he is open to the radiance of this gift, its guardian and shepherd. But taking the human being as, say, a part of being, it has to be noted that the relation is one not only of privilege but also of tension. This is nowhere more evident than in the passages of the *Introduction to Metaphysics* containing an exegesis of Sophoclean poetry. The picture that emerges there is one of confrontation between man and the rest of what is. Humans, described as strange, homeless, yet creative, do stand up against the overpowering order of nature in being, not to master it—the impression of lordship is only possible for man's attitude to particular entities—but rather to shatter against it. And still, this seemingly rebellious stand, this 'ek-sistence,' offers a break into being whereby it opens itself (cf. *Einführung*, pp. 123–24). A part arising against its wholeness? Strange indeed—and it must question an acceptance where naturally, with all the intimacy, man is at peace with being.

This can be pursued further by asking about man's home and homelessness. Again, an ambivalence shows itself in Heidegger's thought, perhaps intentional, perhaps inevitable. In *Being and Time*, the contrast is posed between inauthentic and authentic existence. The former is a failure of self, a disintegration, a loss among the contents of the world; and yet in its reliant and familiar movements through everyday life it provides at least superficially for a feeling at home. That which invades and removes man from such uses and contentments, along with the call of conscience, is the mood of anxiety in which his everyday world is devastated, reliance and familiarity are hollowed out, and the human being finds himself estranged and not at all at home (*unheimlich*). But anxiety is shown as an avenue toward authenticity, wherein man, instead of losing himself as one of many, can identify himself, i.e., can get more hold of being possible for him—it might perhaps be said, where he comes closer to being. Nevertheless, in his maybe too brief descriptions of authentic existence, Heidegger reiterates the availability of anxiety and man's need to be ready for it, which indicates that in coming to be himself man would not dwell at peace, unfamiliar with homelessness. This is disquieting, and it surely cannot be the whole story.

It is indeed supplemented. In later texts, in a varied perspective, Heidegger often turns to man's predicaments of this historical era, such as estrangement and uprooting, intimating—no more—prospects for their overcoming. So, e.g., in this passage:

> The authentic need of dwelling lies in that mortals ever search for the way to be of dwelling, that they *must first learn to dwell*. How would it be if the homelessness [*Heimatlosigkeit*] of man consisted in that man does not yet reflect on the *authentic* need of dwelling *as the* need? Yet as soon as man *reflects* on homelessness, it is no longer a misery. It is, rightly reflected on and well retained, the only call-up [*Zuspruch*] which *calls* mortals toward dwelling. ("Bauen Wohnen Denken," *Vortrage und Aufsatze*, II, p. 36)

These words seem to parallel the existential transformation toward authenticity—and go further. Particularly to be noted is the emphasis on the call of homelessness to be reflected on, which may correspond to the silent call of conscience to be heeded and accepted. In the passage just quoted, being authentic has or is a need: of homelessness to be accommodated, as in the earlier formulation of anxiety to be prepared for. Yet now a direction of the call is pointed to, assuaging the need, transcending anxiety and homelessness. These are not to be fled from into inauthenticity's pseudo-quiescence, but conscientiously reflected on in order to learn to dwell. There would be then a double sense of inhabiting the world as a home, separated by the phenomena of anxiety, conscience, reflection.

The easier and more common way is that of evasion, irresponsibility, thoughtlessness. The alternative dares to be aware of the risks of estrangement in existence yet learns to cope with them to achieve authentic dwelling in the world as man's home; it responds to the call of being, because "dwelling is a *ground feature of being* in accordance with which mortals are" (ibid., p. 35). How often, how likely, how soon that possibility of accordance awaits men?

Another question related to the possibilities and privileges of being human is in the ambiguity attaching to the key expression 'being there' (*Dasein*). In the analyses of *Being and Time* not only does this expression signify an entity, not only is it attributed as "ever respectively mine" (*Jemeinigkeit*) but also in the phenomena of depersonalization, of mood, of projecting ahead, it identifies this or that individual, me, you, him, her. Authentic or inauthentic, *Dasein* is man in his existential situation; although the choice of the term expressing 'being there' has wider grounds and connotations, particularly with regard to his awareness of what "to be there" does and can mean for him. But this avoidance of explicit synonymy leads in Heidegger's subsequent thought into a different level of application. "'Being there in man' is that way to be [*Wesen*] which belongs to being as such, but into which belongs man. . . . Man becomes his way to be in entering it as proper to him" (*Nietzsche*, II, p. 358). In this statement there is no legitimate admission of straightforward identity: though the indefinite article has not been used even earlier, now there is no imaginable usage of simply 'a man' instead of '*Dasein*.' To be sure, it must be kept in mind that from the beginning 'being there' pertains to entities with a very privileged relation to being; but now, instead of identifying such human entities, the phrase 'being there' is used for that relation alone. It used to be characterized by 'ek-sistence,' now it acquires equivalence to it. Does this not appear to be a change in thought as well as in emphasis? And further, the quoted statement speaks of entering such a human way to be—which leaves the disturbing prospect that not all men may be willing or able to enter it. 'Being there' for man has ever been described as determining possibilities, yet was it not intended also as the horizon of human actuality? Now *Dasein* itself becomes 'in man' a possibility, with the actuality left in the dark. From the Heideggerian standpoint, perhaps such a contrast in terms of possibility versus actuality is not the most adequate; yet how else to express this apparent differentiation? It seems to correspond to Heidegger's gradual lessening of interest in individuality, which itself may be a response to the early charges of subjectivism misdirected at him. Speaking of man as such, his possible belonging participation in being is not subject to doubt; yet the finding of 'being there' in an intermediary placement deserves reflective caution.

There is one other question which sometimes can be heard but whose consideration may well lead into a blind alley. It concerns the 'dependence' of man on being or of being on man; alternatively, it is sometimes with regard to human activity or passivity, the first referred particul to Heidegger's earlier utterances and the second to the later ones. But th whole phraseology is of dubious application. It is in doubt whether relations of dependence and independence, of activity and passivity can obtain in any but a causal framework which is binding only among entities. Is it not to treat being as another entity—which Heidegger rejects throughout—if being and man are visualized in a relation of relatives, of partners, or even of adversaries? It is quite true that in his earlier 'existential' phase Heidegger treats the human being as the discoverer, the beholder, the opener of the truth of being; but is it any less the case that even there being lets man occupy this ontological locus by yielding and disclosing its sense or truth to him? And in his more recent writing, when Heidegger criticizes nihilism and deplores the withdrawal of being, again it is quite true that he does not prescribe for human agency any mode of breaking out of this predicament. But counseling patient awaiting of a new dawn, of a re-turn and re-discoveredness of being also enjoins upon man a resolute preparedness for this. Is not a withdrawal of being also a withdrawal of man's proper way to be, and must not any new happening of the truth of being bring also a bearing upon man's 'being there'? In this regard, it would appear that a tendency to separate and strongly to contrapose being and man not only departs from Heidegger's intent but also moves in a direction which cannot be properly thought through, not to say resolved, in relation to his thought.

Only too briefly I have tried to ask about the question of being under its aspects confronting us in the work of Martin Heidegger. For purposes of explication I have held to three questions or themes for questions: being as it bears upon nothing, upon entities, upon man; though naturally even such themes are intertwined and hardly isolable: nothing appears as it exceeds the ontological difference with entities and the human being's stance toward it. These are offered for further reflection. But of course I am mindful of plenty of other, also essential questions latent in Heidegger's thought; they also could and should be asked sometime. Questions such as these: To what extent is *Being and Time*—which could be entitled *Existence and Temporality*—a preparation for thinking about being and time? How poetic or mythopoeic does Heidegger's expression sometimes become, e.g., with reference to the fourfold (*Geviert*)—and what does that signify? Can his late remarks about the end of philosophy be taken literally—and in that case would the contribution of his thought about being become nonphilosophical? Such questions, as well as those I have tried to pose, in order to be pursued require a history and a heritage. Responses or answers, if any, have to wait: to wait for quite a time.

Works of Heidegger Cited

Sein und Zeit, 8th ed. Tübingen: Niemeyer, 1957.
Nietzsche (2 vol.) Pfullingen: Neske, 1961.
Holzwege, 4th ed. Frankfort: Klostermann, 1963.
Der Satz vom Grund, 3d ed. Pfullingen: Neske, 1965.
Unterwegs zur Sprache, 3d ed. Pfullingen: Neske, 1965.
Einführung in die Metaphysik, 3d ed. Tübingen: Niemeyer, 1966.
Vorträge und Aufsätze (3 vol.), 3d ed. Pfullingen: Neske, 1967.
Wegmarken. Frankfort: Klostermann, 1967.
Schellings Abhandlung über das Wesen der menschlichen Freiheit. Tübingen: Niemeyer, 1971.

ROBERT C. SCHARFF

Heidegger's Path of Thinking and the Way of Meditation in the Early Upaniṣads

I will first consider Martin Heidegger's philosophy as a path that "begins" with an analysis of *Dasein* and "ends" with a thinking of the event (*Ereignis*) that clarifies man's relation to being but no longer regards either man or being as its primary subject. "Begins" and "ends" are set in quotes because, strictly speaking, a Heideggerian path of thinking can have no epistemological beginning or systematic results. However, Heidegger himself was a long time in recognizing the full import of this point. As I will try to show, in carrying out a *Daseins*analysis and planning a "dismantling" of the history of metaphysics, his earlier work so structured his thinking that only very recently has he found a fitting way to express the central "experience" that has animated his entire path.

In my opinion, re-thinking these themes not only marks out Heidegger's radical reconsideration of Western philosophizing but also points suggestively in the direction of the Indian tradition as well, especially the earlier Upaniṣads. Thus, in the second part of this paper, I will pursue the tendencies of my re-thinking into those early Indian writings and discuss briefly their alleged "practical-mindedness," the notion of four stages of awareness, and the famous "identification" of *ātman* and *brahman.* A few concluding remarks will raise the question of how seriously these dialogical efforts should be taken, in view of the "obvious" dissimilarities between Heideggerian thinking and the Indian concern for *mokṣa.*

In his continuing reconsiderations of the obscured and problematic relationship of man and being, Heidegger always felt that its surveillance from some external or third viewpoint is not just inappropriate but ultimately impossible. Thus, when *Being and Time* "raises again the question of being," it is with the disconcerting sense that we can be questioning only what we already, however vaguely and dissatisfyingly, "understand." Between this implicit, "preontological" understanding of being's meaning and the questioning which projects an explicit thinking of it, there is a kind of unavoidable "circularity." So, in *Being and Time*, philosophy—as "phenomenological ontology"—is that singular "interpretive" activity that arises out of the way man already "understands" both his own being and that of other beings as well.

However, this *Dasein*—this understanding of being that is man—is a problem. Even though man "exists"—that is, even though everything he says and does carries with it an interpretation of the understanding he already has—he is neither in touch with this understanding nor, upon reflection, does he find its interpretations satisfying. At first, then, philosophy seems to be *caught* in its circle. It never starts from scratch, but always interprets out of an implicit but unsatisfying understanding. Of course, if there were only that actual understanding which now seems to possess us, the best we could do would be to resign ourselves explicitly to our interpretive fate. But Heidegger suggests that our very dissatisfaction provides a clue for penetrating the closed circle of ordinary understanding and interpretation. It is a dissatisfaction with the way "something" is being slighted ontologically. At first, this something appears to be man's own way of being, i.e., his *Existenz*. *Being and Time*'s Division One analyzes the way everyday life is possessed by an "inauthentic" understanding that permits the interpretation of particular beings as either useful or objective but blocks an adequate interpretation of *Existenz* itself. Division Two seeks that "authentic" understanding from which genuine interpretation of *Existenz* can spring. Because this latter interpretation "bears the message and brings a name [*hermeneuein*]" to something previously hidden, it deserves the special title of "hermeneutic."[1] Because this hermeneutic uncovers the way of being of that being (man) through which every particular sort of being gets ontologically interpreted, it deserves to be called hermeneutic in the "philosophically primary" sense. Finally, as this hermeneutic of *Existenz* develops, it begins to appear that our dissatisfaction involves not just the usual interpretation of man's being but ultimately the whole Western treatment of being. An unpublished third division was to have explored this problem to see how the authentic understanding which makes the hermeneutic of *Existenz* possible might somehow also facilitate an interpretation of being generally, i.e., a hermeneutic in the "primordial" sense. In short, according to the whole plan of *Being and Time*'s Part One, clarification of the being-question is made dependent upon turning the seemingly closed and unreflective circularity of everyday understanding and interpretation into a radically deepened sense of *hermeneutical circularity*, using our initial ontological dissatisfaction as the clue. In its beginningless (i.e., circularly situated) beginning (i.e., point of departure), philosophy turns toward a "hermeneutic of *Dasein*."

The Preparatory Analysis of *Dasein*

In Division One's existential (*existenzial*) inquiry, the most obvious fact about everyday life—our encountering of a world full of tools and objects (i.e., "things," generally)—gives Heidegger an initial glimpse of *Existenz* as "being-in-the-world." Although we usually become aware first of these things, then of their totality, and finally of "our" encountering them, Heidegger points out that these things catch our attention in the first place only because we are always already informed as to their being, viz., their readiness-at-hand (*Zuhandensein*) or presence-on-hand (*Vorhandensein*), on the basis of a "situated understanding" through which they get interpreted and expressed in speech (*Rede*). Situationality (*Befindlichkeit*) constitutes the "thrownness" of ordinary *Dasein*; understanding, its "projectedness" toward encountered things. This thrown-projectivity Heidegger calls the "fore-structure" of situated understanding—a global and advance "fore-having," in terms of which it is "fore-seen" how things yet to be experienced are to be "fore-conceived." The "practical" understanding of readiness-at-hand, not the proto-theoretical understanding of presence-on-hand, is ordinary *Dasein*'s most basic world disclosure; and involvement in routine activities carries with it an implicit form of self-understanding, that of ourselves as "users" of practical things, in the company of others. However, since we normally do not know all this, when we try to make ourselves an explicit theme, we tend to do so in the same way we usually make practical things explicit themes, that is, by letting them emerge from their practicality so as to consider them as "objects" for thoughtful inspection. Just as things are what everybody uses or thinks about, a self is merely "the one" (*das Man*) who does the using or thinking. Secure within the circularity of everyday life, common sense takes it as obvious that people "are" the way they practice and think. However, as Heidegger points out, in thus taking for granted the all-too-familiar fact that "there are" things and people, we inevitably frustrate any attempt to articulate a more genuine sense of selfhood. In the commonsense attitude of everyday life, Heidegger detects a continuous tendency to "fall away" from any self-interpretation that is out of the ordinary and "into" a common, publicly regarded world "one" shares with others.

But Division One does not end with this serial analysis of situationality, understanding, and fallenness. Instead, Heidegger goes on to argue that thrown, determinate situationality (i.e., "facticity") and projective understanding (i.e., "existentiality") are always found together as a "factual existentiality" which at the same time "discloses" things as they are interpreted to "be." He calls this factual, existential disclosiveness "caring" (*Sorge*), in order to capture the way everyday life is both a concernful illumination of practical and objective things and at the same time an implicit regard for "oneself" as the being which has all these concerns. Finally, Heidegger calls this ordinary caring "inauthentic," because it is ontologically naive, i.e., uninformed both about its understanding of things as ready-at-hand and present-on-hand but also, and more important, ignorant of its way of leveling off man's self as a "one."

Thus the preparatory analysis confirms the fact that even in everyday affairs (and even without the monitoring of a reflective consciousness), the understanding and interpreting of beings in their being already belongs essentially to man. But Division One also shows that the closed circularity of ordinary understanding and interpreting is not a fatal trap. The all-too-obvious appearance of tools, objects, and people has been penetrated. Consequently, Division Two, while remaining within the beginningless circularity of man's ordinary relation to being, can nevertheless move one level deeper, so to speak, than common sense—by analyzing precisely that predominant and inauthentic mode of caring which is usually hidden from us, and by inquiring further into the dissatisfaction its picture of one's "self" has evoked.[2]

The Primary Hermeneutic of *Dasein*

The circularity of philosophizing now appears in the form, "Every interpretation is based on some prior understanding." Unfortunately, that mode of understanding which ordinarily dominates our interpretations cannot yield a hermeneutic of *Dasein*. Therefore, in Division Two Heidegger sets out to discover a more fundamental mode of understanding—one that permits *Dasein*'s "wholeness" and "authenticity" to be satisfactorily interpreted and allows the total care-structure to be appropriately conceptualized as "temporality."

"Anticipation" and "resolve" are the names Heidegger gives to care's existentiality and facticity, respectively, when they have been reconsidered in such a way that *Dasein*'s "wholeness" and "authenticity" are clarified. Anticipation emerges from the serious thinking-through of death; and resolve, from the analysis of conscience. If death is considered, not as an occurrence to be witnessed eventually by others but as my *own* ultimate and inescapable possibility, existentiality no longer appears to me only as the "always already ahead of itself" it seems to be when analyzed in terms of everyday activities. By "running ahead" toward my own inescapable end in "anticipation," I find I am "rounding off" my life directly and ontologically, i.e., in terms of existentiality itself rather than in terms of my unfinished dealings with more ordinary things. Similarly, a meditation on conscience exploits the contrast between ordinary and extraordinary possibilities by "calling" upon me to acknowledge that I need not be merely the "one" who always cares for the usual things. "Resolute" acceptance of this call counteracts my tendency to interpret "already being in the world" wholly in terms of everyday options and holds open a direct and ontologically perceptive view of facticity as the determinate ground of *all* my possibilities, not just ordinary ones. When facticity is no longer regarded as merely the common circumstances (*allgemeine Lage*) one shares with everbody else, existentiality appears to originate in a much richer and more open-textured "situation"—one that leaves me as free to bear witness (*bezeugen*) to the anticipated possibility of being whole as to fall away from it and lose myself in more obvious opportunities (*Gelegenheiten*). Without ever "leaving" the closed circle of ordinary life, Heidegger thus moves beneath it to discover that Dasein is "'essentially' *Dasein* in that authentic *Existenz* which constitutes itself as anticipatory resolve."[3] The "one" whose understanding springs from the "common circumstances" of everyday existence interprets things as practical and objective; but because the "self"—whose understanding springs from factual existence held open as my "situation"—directly interprets *Dasein*'s caring, its situation deserves to be called genuinely "hermeneutical."

Two-thirds of the fore-structure of authentic understanding has thus been uncovered: in anticipation, we *have* the wholeness of the care-structure before us; in resolve, we *see* in advance how existence offers up both authentic and inauthentic possibilities. Next, Heidegger analyzes the *way of conceiving* the care-structure "presupposed" by this fore-having and foresight, i.e., how anticipatory resolve discloses *Dasein* "as" being. In other words, he shows that "temporality" is the meaning (*Sinn*) of care in terms of which *Dasein* is authentically interpreted.

As Heidegger sees it, anticipation reveals primarily the *futurity*, and resolve, the *having-been* of *Dasein*; and together, they permit us to come back from the future and into our situation so that whatever we ordinarily encounter is "rendered-present" (*gegenwärtigen*) to us. In short, it is possible to conceive here, in a "moment of insightful penetration" (*Augenblick*), a temporality which—as it operates in everyday life—"has the unity of a future which renders-present in the process of having been." In the interplay of its three "ecstases," Heidegger finds the underlying meaning of the whole structure of ordinary caring. However, we do not normally recognize this "temporalizing." Instead, we think of time as that in which we "now" experience something in place of what we "no longer (now)" experience, and in which we will experience something else "not yet (now)" before us. To show that he is not merely announcing a dogmatic counterpreference, Heidegger attempts to *confirm* temporality's primacy by arguing that "now-time" originates in and is derived (*abkünften*) from it, under the ontologically naive conditions of commonsense life.

In the first part of this confirmation, Heidegger shows: (1) that in the rendering of useful things present, there is always a hidden movement of projective awaiting (*gewärtigen*) that is also a self-forgetful retaining (*behalten*) of a sense of other things to be dealt with; and (2) that in the shift to prototheoretical disclosure, rendering-present is transformed into a "re-presentation" (*Vergegenwärtigung*) of objects which carries with it a more deliberately reflective (*überlegende*) awaiting and retaining.[4] In these two modes of inauthentic temporalization, familiar things get taken as *being* ready-at-hand and present-on-hand "presently." Hence, temporality is that *primordial* time which grounds the twin meanings of being (in all their variations) in ordinary caring.

In the second part of the confirmation, Heidegger shows how the common concept of "now-time" arises from the way one usually regards things as "within-time." In the welter of complex phenomenological moves through which Heidegger traces the genesis of now-time, the single guiding thread is "being-within-time" (*Innerzeitigkeit*). Through this *sense of time*, inauthentic *Dasein* expresses its fundamental temporality in turning toward everyday affairs. It is that *in terms of which* inauthentic temporalizing differentiates itself into those twin modes of ordinary understanding which disclose practical and objective being.

Most important, however, is Heidegger's implicit extension of the coverage of being-within-time *to the whole metaphysical tradition.* For in discovering the relation between this sense of time and now-time, he claims he is brought to the threshold of an "existential-ontological interpretation" of Aristotle's definition of time as "that which is counted in movement with respect to before and after."[5] We need not analyze this claim in detail to see its profound implication. For if Aristotle's definition, too, bases itself on the "natural" way of understanding whose temporalization process has just been traced, and if "all subsequent discussions of the concept of time have clung in principle to the Aristotelian definition," then Heidegger has found—in the primordial temporalization of being-within-time—the "principle of differentiation"[6] for the whole variety of meanings of being in the history of metaphysics as well as contemporary common sense. Does this mean that every Western interpretation of being suffers from an excessive fixation on the present?[7] As long as primordial time has received only a backhanded confirmation (i.e., in terms of its *inauthentic* expression) and "history" remains undiscussed, it is impossible to say.

Primordial Time and Historicity

The key to Heidegger's whole analysis of temporality as primordial time lies, in my opinion, in his distinction between the "moment of vision" and "rendering-present." For although the latter may be "included" along with futurity and having-been as the temporal basis of *inauthentic* caring, it is the moment of vision that belongs together with anticipated futurity and resolute having-been in any *authentic* caring.[8] However, if Heidegger has already suggested *that* (i.e., in a moment of vision) and *how* (i.e., in anticipatory resolve) we might project extraordinary possibilities, he has not explained *on what basis* this could be done. The two descriptions of *Dasein*'s facticity given thus far were merely part of the clarification of inauthentic caring: Division Two says that anticipation brings me back to the "common circumstances" of my thrownness; and *Being and Time*'s Introduction says that "not only is *Dasein* inclined to fall back upon the world in which it [ordinarily] is . . . but it also simultaneously falls under the spell of its . . . explicitly apprehended tradition" as well.[9] The first description places *Dasein*'s extended self-extension (*erstrecktes Sicherstrecken*) "between" birth and death (and situated in current circumstances); the second adds that *Dasein* is also "in" a history which is, so to speak, prenatal but somehow "connected" with contemporary life (i.e., as its "tradition"). But only a more 'concrete' analysis of *Dasein*'s "temporalizing in a fully historical way" (*geschehen*) can avoid the excessive contemporaneity of these formal descriptions.

The central point of Heidegger's analysis of *Dasein*'s "historicizing" is to show how the moment of vision can ready us (by "facing away," so to speak, from more renderings-present) for a full illumination of the finitude of *Existenz*, so that when *Dasein* is torn away from the endless multiplicity of familiar possibilities it is brought back, not just to its present-day facticity, but to a full awareness of its whole fate (*Schicksal*).[10] Concretely conceived, to exist in an authentically historical (not just temporal) way is to accept and take over this whole fate (not just one's common circumstances) in a resolute turning of tradition into a heritage (*Erbe*). And for *Dasein* to transmit, (*überliefern*) fatefully and explicitly, this whole heritage involves a repeating (*wiederholen*) of its possibilities in ways that need not be either ordinary or traditional.

It would seem, then, that the moment of vision allows *Dasein* to see itself temporalized in two directions: inauthentically, toward further renderings-present and re-presentations; and authentically, in the direction of repetition. Thus, in its inauthentic and authentic modalities, temporality appears to be *the principle of differentiation for all Dasein's ways of being related to being, generally*, in its interpretive dealings with all possible beings. Through this temporal differentiation, *Dasein* projectively *understands* the multiple meanings of being (readiness-at-hand, presence-on-hand, *Existenz*, etc.). Small wonder, then, that Heidegger should say that "laying out the horizon within which . . . being in general becomes intelligible is tantamount to clarifying the possibility of having any understanding of being at all—and this very understanding is *Dasein*'s essential disposition."[11] In envisaging this "universal" promise of primordial time as the locus for the differentiation of the meanings of being, generally, Heidegger seems to be preparing to turn the hermeneutic of *Dasein* into a primordial one.

Nevertheless, the question remains, does historicity as the genuine temporalization of time project in such a manner that it involves a *fundamental* meaning (or what Heidegger once calls "the idea") of being, viz., something like "being as being historical," instead of being as presence?[12] In the language of *Being and Time*'s unwritten Part One, Division Three: What, finally, is the relation between "[Primordial] Time and [the meaning of] Being," generally? Division Three was apparently going to indicate how primordial time can come to be regarded as the ontological horizon through which both a fundamental and the traditional idea of being originate. And Part Two, guided by the idea of being as presence, was going to dismantle (*destruieren*) the history of metaphysics as a series of forgetful, excessive fixations upon one temporal *ekstase*, viz., the present. But this dismantling, guided also by the fundamental idea of being that keeps thinking open to the full tri-dimensionality of time, would also facilitate an "overcoming" of metaphysical fixations that could express the original, authentically historical experience of being that grounds all Western philosophy.[13]

Heidegger later admitted that in projecting these tasks, his thinking overshot the situation actually prepared for it in *Being and Time*. The "distressing difficulty" which continued to haunt his thinking was an "unsuitably conceived relation of being and man's being."[14] Historicity and temporality, conceived from the side of a *Daseins*analysis, contributed centrally to the problem.

Historicity and Temporality Reconsidered

In retrospect, Heidegger's notion of historicity remains incurably problematic in two ways. First, the historicity of being and the historicity of man's thinking about being are never satisfactorily distinguished. True enough, the *Letter on Humanism* insists upon the priority of the former. *Being and Time*'s Division Two, while analyzing historicity to illuminate man's existential finitude, points primarily toward something like being's self-differentiation, so that man can take up only repetitively what is fatefully beyond his "control." And a series of works after *Being and Time* argues in principle against the sort of "onto–theo–logical" thinking that, if it acknowledges its own finitude at all, usurps the ontological initiative by thrusting being "out–side" of history in a misguided effort either to secure being's inexhaustibility and wholeness (as in "metaphysical" theology) or to reject it entirely (as in "humanistic" atheism). Nevertheless, in *Being and Time*'s Introduction (par. 6), this same historicity is characterized as having emerged *within the history of man's thinking about being.* How can a notion which comes into play only out of twentieth-century man's dissatisfaction with metaphysics ever be more than yet another alleged root-concept—arrogantly elevated, like all the others, to "supra-historical" significance? Moreover, the projection of *the* fundamental idea of being in *Being and Time* only increases suspicion; and in subsequent "recollections" of metaphysics, Heideggerian thinking at least gives the appearance of equipping itself with *the* idea of being (now in the form of its fundamental and forgotten "truth") which has so far only secretly and one-dimensionally come-to-pass in a misunderstood "history of being." Does this thinking not appear to position itself polemically beyond the reach of metaphysics—"overcoming" it while simultaneously possessing the principle of differentiation for an ontological "science" of being's possible meanings? But a "scientist" of being does not listen to being's "self-differentiation."

In the second place, because *Being and Time*'s analysis of historicity is set out *in opposition to ordinary and traditional ways of thinking*, it is never entirely freed from the implication that inauthentic (and essentially "unhistorical") ways of thinking are inferior to authentic (and genuinely historical) thinking. Again, we seem to be on the threshold of a self-possessed "science" of being—and one with a bias for "historical" thinking, at that. Why, then, does historicity remain problematic and repeatedly appear as something Heidegger does not intend it to be? In my opinion, the answer lies in the way *Dasein*'s "priority" was first treated, and thus in the way time's primordiality was established.

In spite of Heidegger's disclaimer that, as a fundamental "existential," temporality is not a "concept" to be "applied" once its full meaning is cognized in advance, the fact is that when he takes up authentic temporality in order to excavate the temporal meaning of readiness-at-hand and presence-on-hand, it is very much like a fixed "transcendental" that he handles it. Now within the context of Division Two and as long as Heidegger is simply relating inauthentic and authentic modes of man's being to each other, this procedure may look harmless. But when he tries to turn this transcendentally conceived primordial time into the concrete principle of being's own self-differentiation, certain subject-ist and relativist implications of this "horizonal" thinking come out. For if utility and objectivity *depend* upon man's forgetful temporalizing, how is one to avoid the implication that the meaning of being generally *depends* upon man's historicity? Heidegger's assertion that *Dasein*'s historicity is not the historicity of being is insufficient. Historicity remains under the shadow of *Being and Time*'s "phenomenological" transcendentalism and the "horizonal" thinking produced through it.[15] So, for example, when Heidegger struggles in subsequent writings to work out a less anthropological notion of the "forgottenness" *of being*, he carries with him the only model of oblivion he had systematically worked out: *man's* forgetfulness. As a result, just as "nothing" had been said to lie behind the beings of everyday thinking, so later being itself is said to recede as merely the "abysmal ground" of metaphysical man's forgetful articulations of truth.[16] True enough, Heidegger had only intended for "fundamental ontology" to make *Dasein* "ontologically prior" temporarily and in relation to other beings; but even in the later turning (*Kehre*) toward being, echoes of the earlier preoccupation with *Dasein* remain—precisely in the effort to *grant* priority to being, to approach it *through* man's forgetfulness, and to think it *in terms of* the history and ground of metaphysics. Thus it was not enough for Heidegger to refrain from any "Promethean" dismantling of traditional doctrines. The whole struggle to "overcome" metaphysical tendencies by "going back" to rediscover being's fundamental truth remains too self-conscious an effort to approach being through *a* being, namely, man.

Nevertheless, these remarks carry us much too close to the familiar excess of many Heidegger commentaries, a preoccupation with the *structure* of his thinking at the expense of the *experience* that continued to guide it. To see how he could have stayed with the "matter for thought"—which even *Being and Time* knew was neither man nor being as opposed to men, but rather their relationship—we must pay more attention to that path from which Heidegger could make these self-criticisms. For help here, I turn to the lecture *Time and Being*, which not only tries to prepare the way for that experience which permits a "thinking of being without regard to beings [even man]," but does so in the very context of a late reappraisal of *Being and Time* and its unwritten Part One, Division Three.[17]

Time and Being

Following out the experience already at work in *Being and Time*, this lecture explains that the idea of a fundamental ontology had to be dropped because it incurably says something misleading: that such a discipline would be "the foundation for ontology itself which is still lacking but is to be based upon it."[18] No ontological science standing outside the (metaphysical) history of being is possible. Moreover, the whole "questioning" stance, which placed the author of *Being and Time* before "being itself" as "something" to investigate, partakes of precisely that metaphysically forgetful tendency about which he was already expressing dissatisfaction. "Questioning" seems to push thinking in the direction of "doing something" about its forgetfulness, of "seeking" its ground and "overcoming" its past.[19] Nevertheless, the fact that the author of *Being and Time* was already asking about the "*meaning* of being" is evidence of a more basic countertendency. In spite of the lingering epistemological and historicist echoes of the term 'meaning,' linking it up—however tentatively—with something like primordial time shows a predominant concern for being's *manner of occurrence*, rather than for any particular concept, old or new. To be sure, primordial time remained "tied up" with man; but even the author of *Being and Time* could have said that this "time is not the product of man [and] man is not the product of time."[20] But here the lecture takes a crucial step: the present task, says Heidegger, is not to correct an earlier alleged granting of priority to man by now granting priority to being. The task, instead, is to think being and time *together*. "From the dawn of Western-European thinking until today, being means the same as presencing [*Anwesen*]." Thus, somehow, he puzzles, "being is determined, as presence, by time. That this is so could in itself . . . introduce a relentless disquiet into thinking. This disquiet increases as soon as we set out to think through in what respect there is such a determination of being by time."[21] In my opinion, this is a thorough restatement of the ill-fated intention of *Being and Time*—one that includes everything its author has since learned.

Time and Being, it seems to me, is a very careful continuation of that hermeneutical path whose beginningless beginnings we have traced to *Being and Time*. Even if, as Heidegger explains in *On the Way to Language*, the terminology of "hermeneutic" and "circularity" was finally abandoned because it speaks too much from the outside of what thinking must place itself "within," these words retain a ring of truth which "phenomenology" and "transcendental philosophy" do not, because they speak of the *path* of thinking, not of the epistemological *structure* that path must have. Thus, the "hermeneutical situation" of Heidegger's thinking, whose forty-five year transformation I have been tracing, is precisely the "familiarity" with which the lecture begins. And this beginningless beginning proceeds, as always, with a carefully formulated "dissatisfaction," that is, the "disquiet" that comes when Heidegger tries to think being as somehow determined in its presencing by time, after having learned that time cannot be regarded most basically as the structure of human understanding. The Promethean language of "overcoming," "grounding," and "setting out toward" a quarry is gone—as are all the more implicit semi-metaphysical aspects of *Being and Time*'s *Dasein*-centeredness. But just as was his announced intention all along, Heidegger now moves within the circle of familiarity and dissatisfaction—a movement that forty-five years ago he called "repetition," and, in the very "raising again" (*Wiederholung*) of the question of being's meaning, set the tone for all his thinking. Along with other beings, man—with all his questioning and conceiving—has really disappeared, not just in name but for the sake of thinking.

But now what of Heidegger's thinking of being and time together? To do so, he says provocatively, is to think toward the "and," the relatedness of being and time. In this way, we might come to think being as determined as presence by time and time as "remaining" in the occurrence of presencing. In the expression "*es gibt Sein, es gibt Zeit,*" Heidegger finds a double way of thinking this reciprocal determination: taken first to say, "there is being, there is time," this expression turns thought away from metaphysical *representations* of their relationship—by reminding us not to think being and time as things or the ground of things, or as something static that happens or dialectically unfolds. But then, taken to say "It gives being, it gives time," this expression turns thought toward a cautious *meditation* upon the "it" which gives by letting being be brought into the unconcealedness of presence. Through this double translation, a way now lies open to meditate on presencing, without reducing thought to an ontological science of the varieties of presence that is conceptually guided by their "principle" of differentiation.[22] To think this doubly translated phrase is to meditate upon being and time as the two interrelated aspects of presencing.

1. To avoid thinking of being as something conceived or as something grounded in something else, Heidegger suggests we say being is sent (*geschickt*). This tells us *how* being occurs, namely, as presencing. Furthermore, this occurrence is not something that happens once and for all. It happens in a process of sending (*Schicken*) which Heidegger calls the being-sent (destiny, *Geschick*) of being. Although it normally appears to us as a sequence of overlapping epochs (i.e., a 'history' of metaphysical transformations of being), this epoch-like character of destiny should be thought as a holding-back (*epoché*), that is, a holding-back of both the sending process and the "it" which sends. However, precisely because we normally attend to entities, *how* they are *present* and how this presencing *takes place* remain unthought. Before anything more can be said of the "it" that sends, the "present" (and time, generally) must be discussed.

2. In a "repetition" of *Being and Time*, Heidegger reminds us that the present must be thought as the all-too-obvious center of a tri-dimensional temporal presencing. Cleansed of the existential tendency to attribute this time to *Dasein*'s understanding, at least we can say that even though man "always remains approached continually by the presencing of something actually present without explicitly heeding the presencing itself" (i.e., tends to be naively entity-centered), the "absence" in this approach of what is not yet and what is no longer present (*Gegenwart*) shows that presencing implicates the future and the past as well as the present in a "unified" interplay that proves to be the true extending (*das eigentliche Reichen*) that is peculiarly characteristic of time.[23] To think this extending (rather than *Dasein*'s *self*-extending) is to become aware that the unique interplay of dimensions which belongs to time comes to light (*lichten*) in this extending. There occurs, in this extending, an opening-up of openness

(*Lichtung des Offenen*) which is brought in the present mutual interplaying of future and past. What occurs in this openness ("brought" there, not *by Dasein* but *in* the extending) is precisely being as presence.

3. Moreover, "sending" as presence and "extending" as opening-up are not accomplished by being and time. Sending and extending are rather the manner in which being and time *are given*. If thinking does not remain beings or *Dasein*-oriented, this sending-extending might be thought as *Ereignis*—the "event" which gives, not itself, but being in a destiny of presencing, and which does so by simultaneously opening-up the open field (*Bereich*) of presencing. "The giving in 'It gives being' has turned out to be a sending and a being-sent of presencing in its epoch-like transformations. The giving in 'It gives time' has proved to bring to light the extending of an . . . open field."[24] This twofold giving lets presencing come-to-pass (*ereignen*) precisely by withdrawing and preserving itself as event. It is always difficult for thought to abandon its preoccupation with entities; but more difficult still is the thinking that does not "search" for *Ereignis* as something "behind" or grounding being and time. Heidegger suggests that we think of Its giving as a kind of "yielding of fitting conditions" (*enteignen*), through which the event undergoes no metamorphosis but remains truly (*bewahrt*) what it is.

Finally, remembering that the lecture's title recalls *Being and Time* in a transformed way, Heidegger suggests that "in being as presence there is manifest an ongoing arrival [*Angang*] which so concerns [*angehen*] us as humans that in growing aware and accepting [*übernehmen*] this arrival, we attain the distinguishing mark of human being."[25] To accept (not "take over," which is much too willful) this arrival is to stand within (not just "understand") the open field of giving, so that the interplaying dimensionality of genuine time reaches us (only then to be "temporalized"). And because being and time are only there and given in *Ereignis* (not in *Dasein*'s being-there), it is this event that brings man into his own as that being which "grows aware of being by standing in genuine time" (not: "asks about being by resolutely taking temporality into its self-interpretation").

To sum up, in the meditative thinking which prepares for an experience that is no longer 'about' any beings, being can still have a history, but it cannot be reduced to the history it happens to have. And man, standing in the arrival of presencing and in genuine time, can continue to acknowledge his historicity, but he cannot reduce himself to what he happens to understand. At the same time, *Ereignis* is nothing historical, and meditative thinking cannot abandon its path in a self-possessive historical understanding. To put the matter otherwise, in Heidegger's late meditations, everything (about how to treat our *disquietude*) has changed, but everything (that Heidegger has made *familiar* by following out the experience of his thought) remains. Meditative thinking is genuinely hermeneutical.

Now it seems to me that, standing within the "situation" of the sort of Heideggerian path of thinking outlined above, certain central teachings of the early Upaniṣads open up suggestively. In what follows, my intention is to contribute to a growing dialogue between two "situated" traditions which are no longer able to disregard each other, even as they simultaneously re-think themselves.[26] And it seems to me that the early Upaniṣads —in their so-called practical-mindedness, in their meditative marking out of four states of awareness, and in their enigmatic identification of *ātman* and *brahman*—strike responsive chords within the Western situation interpreted by Heidegger.

Practical-Mindedness

Familiarity with Western pragmatism has prompted many objections to the characterization of Indian thinking as "practical-minded." However, if we look for the intention of this phrase in a less provincial direction, we might tentatively adopt the suggestion that the central attitude of Indian thinking "springs from the practical interest of leading man out of *duḥkha* into a state of bliss, from inauthentic to authentic existence, from absorption in the object to self-realization. The concepts of *duḥkha* and *Sorge*, as also those of *saṁsāra* and *Geworfenheit*, are closely allied."[27] Leaving aside for the moment the all too obviously un-Heideggerian goal this "practical interest" projects, something can be made of both the path in terms of which it expresses itself and also the dissatisfaction, expressed through it, over everyday life. Like *Being and Time*'s hermeneutical path, the early Upaniṣads speak of a way in which ordinary experience and its attendant sense of self are to be undercut. This way, too, affirms no universally valid "method" and demands no initial acceptance or rejection of principles or assumptions. It, too, sees only the possibility of a beginningless beginning, in the form of a "thrown fallenness," which, if the term can be heard without its transmigratory implications, one might call *saṁsāra*. It is everyday life, a kind of existence in which, "according as one acts, according as one conducts himself, so does he become."[28] Just as ordinary *Dasein* understands its own being in terms of the beings to which it attends, the bondage of *ātman* is determined by its absorption, through action, into the objects of everyday reality. And, as is the case with Heidegger's preparatory analytic, the early Upaniṣads teach that the ordinary condition of the self cannot be changed by further actions or by their attendant thinking, but only through a fundamental alteration of attitude that facilitates awareness of *how it is* with everyday life. Man's ordinary ignorance (nescience, *avidyā*) is, like "inauthenticity," that pervasive ontological *Stimmung* that never gets past the unsatisfying point of defining one's self in terms of the worldly matters that usually take up our lives, i.e., as *jīva*. And the way to turn ignorance into a beginningless beginning, as all the early Upaniṣads agree, is the way of meditative "knowledge." Knowledge here is not yet anything fixed and technical; it is a knowledge, now often defended with self-conscious exasperation, that never tires of changing its language. Just like Heidegger's transformed repetition of *Being and Time*'s Division One in *Time and Being*, which is a thinking that avoids familiar existentialist and traditional ontotheological conceptions, early upaniṣadic meditation moves away from Vedic hymns and the symbolizing conceptions of the *Āraṇyakas* and listens directly to what is essential in the nescient play of ordinary life.

However, even if Heidegger's path of thinking and the upaniṣadic way of meditation have strikingly similar beginningless beginnings and at least superficially related dissatisfactions with ordinary existence, what about the dissimilarity of their projected goals? To prepare for a reply to this question, I turn first to one of the upaniṣadic path's most famous forms.

The Four States of Awareness

As the traversal of these states is described in the *Māṇḍūkya Upaniṣad*, meditation leads through wakefulness, dreaming, dreamless sleep, and mystic realization; and layers of misunderstanding give way until *ātman* is realized.[29] Of the many things that could be said about the waking state, two seem to have special importance: the constant attention to external objects, and the awareness that is at least latent in it. This state, "common to all," is said to be the first way in which the self comes to know itself: by understanding itself in terms of its active engagement with desired objects. To elaborate, we might say the self 'is' its continual preoccupation with them. I 'am' *the way* I desire them, and my desiring bodily self is understood as the experiencer of all this. But ceaseless desiring is suffering, as even the ignorant know when they sleep and dream. In the dreaming state, one pulls away from the sphere of external sensuality and inner objects appear. There is "perception without sensation," and the dreamer experiences the creative power of private enjoyment. And yet, still more satisfying is the deep sleep in which one experiences neither desires nor the sometime restlessness of dreaming. Who could long endure a life in which desires and dreams never ceased?

These brief descriptions of three states known to all are neither speculative nor technically explanatory. They are neither impressionistic nor random; nor do they, like "empirical" descriptions, trace the "facts" of life back to organic "functions." Nor, it seems to me, do they constitute even a rudimentary "phenomenology of consciousness."[30] They are descriptions of man's ordinary *condition of being*, of 'how' rather than 'what' he is. They describe man's existential state, which remains as it is, even if no consciousness monitors it. Like *Being and Time*'s preparatory analyses, these descriptions are non-theoretical and pre-scientific efforts to glimpse the ontological meaning of ordinary life. Heidegger's second thoughts about the technical apparatus of his early analyses only make the parallel more apparent.

However, in the *Māṇḍūkya Upaniṣad*, no "Division Two" explains that its way to *brahman* must be through an explicit recapturing of man's temporal-historical existence. For these ancient descriptions, there are no received metaphysical or scientific theories to work back through, and no twentieth-century sophistication to strip away. Because a readership "fitted" to hear these teachings is assumed, there is not even any lengthy "preparatory" nescient struggle but merely the simple reminder that, even if the common waking state is "first" in human awareness, it is not ultimately the most "basic."[31] Thus, without a word of transition, dreamless sleep is said to be not just the witness of dreaming and desiring but that "unified" and blissful condition which is undisturbed by any plurality of inner and outer psychic moments. Dreaming is thus "intermediate," pointing beyond itself toward dreamless bliss at the same time that it manifests its own "superiority" (*utkarṣa*) over entity-oriented, egoistic wakefulness.[32] No mere shadow of wakefulness, dreaming is the doorway to complete self-realization. No mere mindlessness, dreamlessness is that state of purely potential knowledge (*prājña*) out of which comes the "erecting" of the world and the "immerging" in it of dreaming and wakefulness themselves.[33] But finally, in its meditative turning toward the mystical fourth state, the *Māṇḍūkya Upaniṣad*'s language becomes negative: This state, it is said, does not know the external or internal, or both, or merely neither; indeed, it is neither knowledge or its opposite. No words used to conceive anything else apply to it. And yet it is also said, more positively, that he who "knows" all this, merges his self with *ātman*.

Now when I hear of this silent merging with *ātman*, which occurs in the sounding of the mystic syllable *AUM* and cannot be described in any language of wakefulness or dreaming, I return—hesitantly—to that Heideggerian thinking that leads from *Dasein*analysis to *Ereignis*. For this thinking, too, first reviewed its familiar preoccupations with beings (and the "oneself" that is thus preoccupied) and discovered that in the very illumination of these activities it was no longer possessed by them. Like the upaniṣadic meditation that first relies heavily upon concepts arising from nescient activity but "knows" it is moving away from it precisely in becoming aware of the way it "is," Heidegger's preparatory account of inauthenticity stays with the "ontic" concerns of everyday life, but only to unearth it as an implicitly "understood" condition. In the long struggle that follows, in which Heideggerian thinking frees itself from meta-metaphysical polemics against inauthenticity, metaphysical language is used, and negative conceptions that try not to be conceptions abound. So when I hear of the fourth state that is *not* any of the things which have so far been said along the meditative path that gradually reveals it, I am encouraged to follow Heidegger in cleansing hermeneutical thinking of its transcendental-phenomenological trappings and its "questioning" of being, so that there remains only a voiceless voice that tells thinking it is *not* the various dealings with beings of which it has been reminded. Moreover, when I hear it said, more positively now, that in this fourth silent awareness *ātman* "is," and that its four states are recapitulated in and beyond the *AUM*, I recall that Heideggerian thinking "repeated" the path of its emergence precisely by not trying to take possession of itself. It is said that only as *ātman* is there no temptation to fall back into what is uttered in the *AUM*, because each state is now "known" as a state, and not merely conceived through those particular experiences that permitted its initial realization. Is this not true also for Heidegger, whose late thinking has come to "stand in the approach of presence" and give up its attentive regard for "itself" as the thinking that lingered for so long within the fields of presencing? May I permit myself to hear—in the "mystical" merging of self with *ātman*, and in the meditative thinking which frees itself from the "stages" on the path of its emergence—the echo of a profound kinship?

But now I come to a matter in which 'hesitation' may already be too confident a mood. For in its introductory passages, the *Māṇḍūkya Upaniṣad* says that "everything here" is *brahman*. Is there anything in Heidegger's thinking which could carry me toward this *brahman* (that is also "not-different" from *ātman*)?

Ātman and *Brahman*

Indeed, I am told, the whole world, past, present, and future, and also what is beyond or transcends this threefold time, is in the *AUM*. And "everything here" is *brahman*.[34] In the true sounding of the mystic *AUM*, *brahman*, world, and time belong together, and yet *brahman*, "the unmanifest," disappears beyond the latter two.[35] How can this be? How can *brahman* permit both the whole world and time to be what they are, and yet only by not becoming them? What can thus transcend the world and time—without being thought cosmically as a "first cause" or theistically as the eternal Deity?[36] Can I hear in all this the echo of an *Ereignis* that gives being (i.e., the "whole" world) in its unconcealed presence, but only by withdrawing in the very sending of this presence? Do the Indian systems constitute what may be to Western eyes an unexpected and unthought "destiny" of presencing?[37] It seems to me I have learned that all of this "is," in "thinking"—that ultimately non-representative meditation that belongs to no one but is everyone's possibility. Is this thinking not-different from *ātman*—that silent self which is no longer anyone's self but, in its "identity" with *brahman*, "that art thou"?[38] If so, then the "suffering" that leads the self to *brahman* and the "dissatisfaction" that leads thinking to *Ereignis* open up paths of such striking similarity that hemispheric differences cannot entirely obscure it.

However, should I not remind myself forcefully that Western philosophers began in worldly wonder and Indian seers in the quest for *mokṣa*? Are not Western and Indian thinking, therefore, so differently "situated" that their respective dissociations from disquieting "appearances" necessarily remain worlds apart? How can I ignore the radical dissimilarity between the Western history of creatively metaphysical responses to being and the Indian tradition's self-effacing struggle to reinterpret anew the timeless message of what lies beyond the worldly? Perhaps the most I might be permitted to say is that Heidegger, in rediscovering for the West man's belongingness to *Ereignis*—in a thinking which undercuts the identification of thought and being—is carried toward the early upaniṣadic teaching which says that, in the meditative sounding of *AUM*, man belongs to *brahman*. But even then, is not Heidegger's acceptance of thinking as a "standing in the arrival of presence" inevitably more "worldly" than the achievement of *mokṣa*? Must I not conclude that my "comparisons" are premature and ungrounded? Is not the obvious point forced upon me, that whatever may be the affinities of language and conception, and however striking may be the similar placement of *Ereignis* in Heideggerian thinking and *brahman* in Indian meditation, Heidegger's "experience" and that of the ancient Indian seers are simply "different"? And must I not, then, make the only real (and worldly) "choice" open to me as a Westerner?

But there is something peculiar about these questions. In the first place, they seem so thoroughly wedded to the idea of the hemispheric isolation of thinking (and "objective" differences in geography and doctrines?) that all comparison gets ruled out in principle. For my part, I wish neither to deny the "differences" between Heidegger's thinking and upaniṣadic meditation nor to array all their "similarities" before me. I do indeed see dangers in merely assuming the studied neutrality of "comparative" analysis, or responding to the pressing political and spiritual demands of the age, or succumbing to the ready attractiveness of another tradition as a source of "new answers." I agree with Heidegger that thinking can only prepare itself for the acceptance of the event of presencing —no matter what one suspects this "includes" or "leaves out" as we begin. Otherwise, thinking gets more and more deeply entangled in its own history, making increasingly self-possessed attempts to "settle the matter" until its appeals to pure logic, rational insight, objectivity, and moral need push it over the brink into the twin frustrations of "democratic" relativism and totalitarian propaganda.[39] Heideggerian thinking takes finitude seriously. But this finitude is not, in my opinion, a sign of man's fallenness or his imperfect rationality, nor a flaw within being. Still less is it a merely hemispheric phenomenon. Rather, it involves *Ereignis* and its manner of giving and withdrawing. Thus, in an autobiographical retrospect with which I agree, Heidegger says of the thinking which truly opens upon this event: "One had to *be there* if one was called . . . but to *call oneself* was the greatest perversity one could be capable of."[40]

All this, I believe, leaves me at least without any desire to promote a hemispherically chauvinistic "choice." But I wonder if it leaves me "situated" in such a way that I must be speechless before the Upaniṣads' mysteries. Suppose there is a genuine kinship in the true saying of "*Brahman* is both unmanifest and manifesting" and "*Ereignis* is both withdrawal and sending." Then could it not be so that, whether the thinking that arises out of the contemporary global situation experiences the "Europeanization of the earth" from within or without, one might truly come to say—and mean—that the ancient Indian seers now appear to have penetrated too quickly to "unmanifest" *brahman*, and the first philosophers now appear to have been overawed by the "gift" of *Ereignis*? And finally, when questioning has been subdued in the interest of thinking, I am moved to say: There is possible a true thinking, which becomes more than historical (in the Western sense) *only by remaining worldly* (i.e., by letting itself stand in the arriving concern of presence), and there is in this thinking an acknowledgment of the withdrawal of *Ereignis* (or "unmanifest" *brahman*?), which remains beyond history (in the Indian sense) *only in having one* (i.e., one which has been "cyclical" in its manner of approach and "linear" in its accepting responses).[41] Most important of all, for this thinking there can be only a path; and any effort to settle in advance its shape or its subject matter, its situation, or its central experience, what concerns fall inside its boundaries and what outside—all are futile attempts to abandon the path instead of entering into its beginningless beginning and listening to the dissatisfactions that stir there.

Notes

1. *Sein und Zeit*, pp. 37–38 (English translation page numbers omitted; German pagination is found in the margins). Hereafter *SZ*. Cf. *Unterwegs zur Sprache*, p. 150; also pp. 97–98, 121–22 (Eng. trans. p. 51; also pp. 11, 29).

2. A careful reading of Division Two's much neglected introduction (par. 45), in which the "universal ontological" intentions for the primary hermeneutic of *Dasein* are emphasized, is necessary if "existentialist" misinterpretations of *Dasein*'s prominence are to be avoided. See my "On 'Existentialist' Readings of Heidegger," *Southwestern Journal of Philosophy* 2 (1971): 13–15, 19–20.

3. *SZ*, p. 323.

4. Heidegger goes on to say that even when this proto-theoretical disclosure is raised to the level of a "mathematical projection of Nature," it awaits and retains a subject matter which has already been disclosively thematized as present-on-hand. *SZ*, pp. 362–64. But this does not mean that there are no essential differences between what is envisaged as present-on-hand and the "things of Nature." That is why I refer to the concern that first arises out of practice as "proto-theoretical."

5. *SZ*, p. 421; and Aristotle's *Physics*, IV. 11, 219b 1ff. See also his suggestion that already in Plato's definition of time as "the moving image of eternity" there is an implicit dependency upon the concept of the arising and passing away of nows. If the nows come and go, the now-*character* of all experience can still be interpreted as itself *permanently present* throughout their uninterrupted flow, and the presence of what is *really* "in" time can then be regarded as unchangingly constant throughout its merely "apparent" changes. *SZ*, p. 423.

6. The phrase is Otto Pöggeler's, not Heidegger's. See "Heidegger's Topology of Being," in *On Heidegger and Language*, Joseph J. Kockelmans, ed. and trans. (Evanston: Northwestern University Press, 1972), p. 122n.

7. Indeed, Heidegger says as much at *SZ*, pp. 25–26. Already here he regards this fixation on the present as facilitating the interpretation of the meaning of being generally as presence (*Anwesenheit*).

8. *SZ*, p. 328. Heidegger says that *Dasein* "is all the more authentically 'there'" in the moment of vision.

9. *SZ*, p. 21. That we might come to terms with this tradition is evidence of *Dasein*'s historicality (*Historizität*); but that this can be done or left undone depends upon *Dasein*'s more fundamental historicity (*Geschichtlichkeit*). Clarification of the former requires prior analysis of the latter. *SZ*, pp. 20, 392–96.

10. *SZ*, pp. 383–86. Strictly speaking, since fate is not just "mine" but "ours," it is properly called destiny (*Geschick*), i.e., "the historicizing of the community, of a people." *SZ*, p. 384. Nevertheless, it is "*Schicksal*" that Heidegger continues to use. The seeds of a difficult problem lie here: "Who" inherits the Western tradition? A person, a generation, a people, an age? All these questions, Heidegger will eventually conclude, attach too much significance to man's taking up of destiny and too little to being's sending of itself. Cf. *Vorträge und Aufsätze*, pp. 144–46, 171, 174, *et passim*; and Pöggeler, "Historicity in Heidegger's Late Work," *Southwestern Journal of Philosophy* 4 (1973): 68–70, *et passim*; and "Heidegger Today," *Southern Journal of Philiosophy* 7 (1970): 304–8.

11. *SZ*, p. 231. Cf. Pöggeler, "Heidegger Today," p. 119.

12. See Pöggeler, "Heidegger's Topology," p. 121; and "Heidegger Today," pp. 297–99. The phrase, "idea of being," appears in *SZ*, p. 333.

13. *SZ*, par. 6, esp. pp. 25–26. Here, it seems to me, is the point where one has to distinguish commentary (however speculative in itself) from creative response to Heidegger. For the original intentions of *SZ* are explicitly closed off "with the task of interpreting the basis of ancient ontology in light of the problematic of temporality." *SZ*, pp. 25, 40. The whole question of how something like a fateful transmission of our heritage might repeat its possibilities non-meta-physically lies on the far side of the experience out of which *SZ* takes its rise. Cf. *SZ*, p. 26. I would suggest that this remains true of Heidegger's thought as a whole. Even if, as he cautiously indicates in his dialogue with a Japanese in *On the Way to Language*, his thinking opens up surprising, non-Western possibilities;.and even if the experience of being as *Ereignis* might open up post-metaphysical possibilities, Heidegger himself is not, I believe, a party to them.

14. "*Zusatz*," in *Der Ursprung des Kunstwerkes*, p. 100 (Eng. trans., p. 87).

15. On Heidegger's relation to Husserl and phenomenology, see esp. "*Mein Weg in die Phänomenologie*," in *Zur Sache des Denkens*, p. 90 (Eng. trans., p. 82); and "Preface" to Wm. Richardson, *Heidegger: Through Phenomenology to Thought* (The Hague: Nijhoff, 1963), pp. x–xvii. For general discussion, cf. J.L. Mehta, *The Philosophy of Martin Heidegger* (Varanasi: Banares Hindu University Press, 1967), pp. 20–29, and citations given there.

16. And so for a time, it seemed possible to catch philosophical thinking before it could *forgetfully* bring being "under the yoke of Idea," just as in Division Two, ordinary *Dasein* was caught before it could, by falling, interpret everything as ready-at-hand and present-on-hand. Heidegger explicitly rejects this picture of a historical transformation of truth through Plato in "*Das Ende der Philosophie und die Aufgabe des Denkens*, in *Zur Sache des Denkens*, p. 78 (Eng. trans., p. 70).

17. This lecture, together with notes from a seminar on it, appears in *Zur Sache des Denkens*, pp. 1–25 (Eng. trans., pp. 1–24), and pp. 27–58 (Eng. trans., pp. 25–54). Hereafter, *ZS*.

18. *ZS*, p. 34 (Eng. trans., p. 31). If this language is taken seriously, it seems to make the relation of fundamental ontology to the clarification of being's meaning "analogous to the relation between fundamental theology and theological system." Did the author of *SZ* project Division Three in light of such an analogy?

19. *ZS*, pp. 31–32 (Eng. trans., pp. 29–30). Thus the experience that is to guide thinking was "at first necessarily bound up with the awakening *from* being's forgottenness *to* that forgottenness." *ZS*, p. 57 (Eng. trans., p. 53; emphasis supplied). In *On the Way to Language* Heidegger specifically repudiates "questioning" as the appropriate posture of thinking. Pp. 175, 179–80 (Eng. trans., pp. 172, 175–76).

20. *ZS*, p. 17 (Eng. trans., p. 16). Cf. *SZ*, pp. 227–28, 419.

21. *ZS*, p. 2 (Eng. trans., p. 2).

22. *ZS*, pp. 2–6, 39–40, 41–43 (Eng. trans., pp. 3–6, 36–37, 38–40). There follows a very suggestive and selective repetition of *SZ*'s Division One, in which Heidegger remarks that long before we become aware of the early Greek representation of being as presence, we experience presencing in the "simple and unpre-

judiced" regard for what is ready-at-hand and present-on-hand. *ZS*, p. 7 (Eng. trans., p. 7). I think his intention here is twofold: first, by recalling our naive regard for ordinary entities before mentioning the history of metaphysics, Heidegger reduces the temptation to consider the gift of being exclusively in terms of the official history of presencing. But second, and much more important, by recalling Division One and then moving directly to a review of the Western tradition's "transformations of presencing" *without referring to* Division Two, Heidegger finally succeeds in getting to a reassessment of the history of being without either seeing it in terms of man's metaphysical thinking or reducing being to something which (unhistorically) grounds that thinking. "The development of being's abundant transformations looks *at first* like a history of being. But being has no history the way a city or a people does. What is history-like in the history of being is . . . determined solely by the way it historically happens (*geschieht*) . . . and this means the way *It gives being*." *ZS*, pp. 7–8; also pp. 9–10 (Eng. trans., pp. 8; 9–10; emphasis supplied).

23. *ZS*, pp. 13–14, 16 (Eng. trans., pp. 12–13, 15). These pages contain a remarkable transformation of *SZ*'s "ecstatic temporality," in which the interplay of time's three dimensions is thought together without recourse to a "resolute" or "falling" projectivity that unifies them "out of the future." Thinking is thus shown to be primarily a responsive listening, not a willful questioning or "making." Cf. *ZS*, pp. 16–17 (Eng. trans., p. 16).

24. *ZS*, p. 17 (Eng. trans., p. 17). As Heidegger goes on to say, the "*es gibt* . . ." should be heard in the same way as "it is raining," which does not call for us to identify the "thing" which, in this grammatical form, is called "it." *ZS*, p. 18 (Eng. trans., pp. 17–18).

25. *ZS*, p. 23 (Eng. trans., p. 23). "*Angang*" can also be translated "concern."

26. For a few hints, see esp. Mehta, *The Philosophy of Martin Heidegger*, pp. 521–31; and also his "Heidegger and the Comparison of Indian and Western Philosophy," *Philosophy East and West* 20 (1970), 303–17. (This whole number reprints the papers from a symposium on "Heidegger and Eastern Thought" held at the University of Hawaii.)

27. Jitendra N. Mohanty, "Phenomenology and Existentialism: Encounter with Indian Philosophy," *International Philosophical Quarterly* 12 (1972): 501. I wish to acknowledge my gratitude to Professor Mohanty, both for his informed recommendations of reading material (which saved me from much fruitless wandering at a time when I could not have judged this for myself) and for his friendly discussions even in the face of my ignorance of Indian teachings. He is, of course, in no way responsible for the position I have taken here.

28. *Bṛhadāraṇyaka Up.* IV.4,5; trans. in *The Thirteen Principal Upaniṣads*, by R.E. Hume (London: Oxford University Press, 1931), p. 140. Hereafter, bracketed page nos. refer to Hume. On the early Upaniṣads generally, see R.D. Ranade, *A Constructive Survey of Upanishadic Philosophy* (Poona: Oriental Book Agency, 1926).

29. I select this depiction of the meditative path in light of the common claim that the early Upaniṣads are dominated by an "introspective" or "subjective" turn that is meditation—rather than action-oriented, non-theistic and a-cosmic, and is thus more precisely represented here than in the efforts to think brahman's

nature in light of worldly phenomena, or in the occasional meditations on the nature of meditation itself (e.g., *Chāndogya Up.* VII. 2–26). See Surendranath Dasgupta, *A History of Indian Philosophy*, Vol. 1 (Cambridge: The University Press, 1963), pp. 29, 31–33, 37, 42–48; and M. Hiriyanna, *Outlines of Indian Philosophy* (London: Allen and Unwin, 1932), pp. 48–49, 51–52, 54, 63. If this claim is accurate, then it seems to me the parallel with Heidegger's increasingly non-metaphysical and non-epistemological path becomes even closer. Also, cf. this introspective turn with Heidegger's suggestive claim that "as compared with realism, idealism, provided that it does not misunderstand itself as 'psychological' idealism, has an advantage in principle ... [because it] emphasizes that being and reality are only 'in consciousness,' [and] this expresses an understanding of the fact that *being cannot be explained through entities*.... If the idealist thesis is to be followed consistently, the ontological analysis of consciousness itself is ... *the inevitably prior task*." *SZ*, p. 207 (emphasis added).

30. Thus, in my opinion, the early Upaniṣads should not be taken to have either a Cartesian or Husserlian starting point, for they speak neither of absolute beginnings, nor of the self-sufficient power of reason, nor of consciousness in general, but rather of meditation that starts with ordinary life and the origin of suffering. If parallels can indeed be found between Western metaphysics and the later Indian systems, perhaps it is necessary to think back to what could "give" traditional thinking its self-assurance. Cf. Mehta, "Heidegger and the Comparison of Indian and Western Philosophy," p. 317.

31. It is as if the early Indian seers, by asserting no metaphysical or theological expertise, so increased the power of their message that even the millions who came to pay them no more than lip service could never find in the early sayings any "doctrines" to turn into dogmas, and also could never find in meditation any merely archaic "procedures" to universalize and make more rigorous.

32. *Māṇḍūkya Up.* X. When these familiar conditions of awareness are regarded through the mystic syllable *OM* (= *AUM*; see Hume, p. 393, n.1), meditation effects a "reversal" of their experienced relationship. As awareness withdraws from the "A" of wakefulness ("from *āpti*, obtaining, or from *ādimatvā*, being first"), through the semi-independent inwardness of the "U" of dreaming ("from *utkarṣa*, exaltation, or from *ubhayatvā*, intermediateness"), the "M" of dreamlessness appears ("from *miti*, erecting, or from *apīti*, immerging"), *Māṇḍūkya Up.* IX–XI [393]. The fully realized self that "knows" all this and is not swallowed up by that knowing, lies "silently" in and beyond the sounding of *AUM*. Cf. *Praśna Up.* V.1–7.

33. Cf. "If no *Dasein* exists, no world is 'there' either." *SZ*, p. 365. In light of Heidegger's later explanations of the true relation between man and being, and in light of the fact that a silent *ātman* yet lies "in" dreamlessness that is "identical" with *brahman*, must one interpret these statements of *Dasein*'s "existing" and the self's "erecting" in the vein of a subjective (or psychological) idealism?

34. *Māṇḍūkya Up.* I–II. Cf. *Taitirīya Up.* I.8; and *Katha Up.* II.16. For discussion of the early Upaniṣads' struggle to think (1) *brahman* as "beyond" any positive characterization and yet somehow the "subject" of meditation, and (2) the world as the "unfolding" of *brahman* and yet *brahman* as not thus "becoming" the world, see Dasgupta, pp. 48–51; Ranade, *passim*; and Hiriyanna, pp. 59–65.

35. *Maitri Up.* VI.18–19. "There are two *brahma[n]s* to be known: Sound-*brahma[n]*, and what is higher. Those people who sound-*brahma[n]* know, unto the higher *brahma[n]* go" [438].

36. For discussion of the early Upaniṣads' struggle against both cosmic-naturalistic and theistic conceptions of *brahman*—which I am thus assuming would not be appropriate here—see Hiriyanna, pp. 59–64, 81–83.

37. My suggestion is this: If Heidegger has found a way to re-think being's manner of being-sent which succeeds in undercutting the history of Western metaphysics (together with its "speculative" and "analytical" philosophies of history), then may not his thinking yet meet with an Indian meditation which, while having prematurely understood itself as supra-worldly (and thus placed itself in opposition to both "cyclical" and "linear" conceptions of cosmological and historical theory), at least remained attuned to "unmanifest" *brahman*'s "giving"?

38. "*Tat tvam asi.*" *Chāndogya Up.* VI.8 ff.

39. See, e.g., the suggestive comments in Pöggeler, "Heidegger Today," pp. 304–7.

40. Quoted from Hans Erich Nassack's *Impossible Trial*, *ZS*, p. 58.

41. "Granted that the discussion of *Ereignis* is the site of the departure from being and time, being and time still linger on in a certain way, as the gift of *Ereignis*." *ZS*, p. 58.

Heidegger: Selected Bibliography

Note: The following is a list of principal published works, arranged in approximate chronological order of first public presentation, and accompanied in each case by partial or complete English translations.

Sein und Zeit (1927). 10th ed. Tübingen: Niemeyer, 1963. Translation by John Macquarrie and Edward Robinson, *Being and Time*. New York: Harper and Row; London: SCM Press, 1962, with variations between earlier and later editions noted by the translators.

Kant und das Problem der Metaphysik (1927). 2d ed., with new "*Vorwort.*" Frankfort: Klostermann, 1951. Translation by James Churchill, *Kant and the Problem of Metaphysics*. Bloomington: Indiana University Press, 1962.

Vom Wesen des Grundes (1928). 3d ed., with added "*Vorwort.*" Frankfort: Klostermann, 1949. Translation by Terrance Malick, *The Essence of Reasons*. Bilingual ed. Evanston, Ill.: Northwestern University Press, 1969.

Was Ist Metaphysik? (1929). 5th ed. Frankfort: Klostermann, 1949. ("*Nachwort*" added to 4th ed., 1943; "*Einleitung*" added to 5th ed.) Translation of lecture and postscript by R.F.C. Hull and Alan Crick, "What is Metaphysics?" in Werner Brock, *Existence and Being*. London: Vision Press, 1949, pp. 355–92.

Translation of introduction by Walter Kaufmann, "The Way Back into the Ground of Metaphysics," in Kaufmann, *Existentialism from Dostoyevsky to Sartre*. New York: Meridian Books, 1957, pp. 206–21.

Vom Wesen der Wahrheit (1930–1943). 2d ed., with enlarged "*Schlussanmerkung*." Frankfort: Klostermann, 1949. Translation, with concluding note from the 1st ed., by R.F.C. Hull and Alan Crick, "On the Essence of Truth," in Werner Brock, *Existence and Being*. London: Vision Press, 1949, pp. 317–51.

Einfuhrung in die Metaphysik (1935). 1st ed. Tübingen: Niemeyer, 1953. Translation by Ralph Mannheim, *An Introduction to Metaphysics*. New Haven: Yale University Press, 1959.

Die Frage nach dem Ding (1935–1936) 1st ed. Tübingen: Niemeyer, 1962. Translation by W.B. Barton, Jr., and Vera Deutsch, *What Is a Thing?* Chicago: Regnery, 1968.

Erläuterungen zu Hölderlins Dichtung (1936–1944). 2d ed. Frankfort: Klostermann, 1951. Translation of the first two essays (pp. 7–30, 31–45) by Douglas Scott, "Remembrance of the Poet" and "Hölderlin and the Essence of Poetry," in Werner Brock, *Existence and Being*. London: Vision Press, 1949, pp. 251–90, 291–315.

Holzwege (1936–1946). 4th ed. Frankfort: Klostermann, 1963. Translation of first essay (pp. 7–68) by Albert Hofstadter, "The Origin of the Work of Art," in Hofstadter and Richard Kuhns, eds., *Philosophies of Art and Beauty*. New York: Random House (Modern Library Series), 1964, pp. 679–701. Separate publication of first essay, *Der Ursprung des Kunstwerkes*, with new "*Vorwort*" and "*Zusatz*," Stuttgart: Reclam, 1960. New translation, following Reclam ed., by Hofstadter, in Heidegger, *Poetry, Language, Thought*. New York: Harper and Row, 1971, pp. 17–87. Translation of second essay (pp. 69–104, without notes) by Marjorie Grene, "The Age of the World View," *Measure* 2 (1951): 269–84. Translation of third essay (pp. 105–92) by Kenley Royce Dove, *Hegel's Concept of Experience*. New York: Harper and Row, 1970. Translation of the fifth essay (pp. 248–95) by Hofstadter, "What Are Poets For?" in *Poetry, Language, Thought*, pp. 91–142.

Nietzsche. 2 vols. (vol. 1, 1936–1939; vol. 2, 1939–1946). 1st ed. Pfullingen: Neske, 1961. Translation of essays 7, 9, and 10 (vol. 2, pp. 399–457, 458–80, 481–90) by Joan Stambaugh, "Metaphysics as History of Being," "Sketches for a History of Being as Metaphysics," and "Recollection in Metaphysics," in *The End of Philosophy*. New York: Harper and Row, 1973, pp. 1–54, 55–74, 75–83.

Vorträge und Aufsätze (1936–1953). 1st ed. Pfullingen: Neske, 1954. Translation of the third essay (pp. 71–99) by Joan Stambaugh, "Overcoming Metaphysics," in Heidegger, *The End of Philosophy*, pp. 84–110. Translation of the fourth essay (pp. 101–26) by Bernd Magnus, "Who Is Nietzsche's Zarathustra?" in *Review of Metaphysics* 20 (1967), 411–31. Translation of the sixth, seventh, and eighth essays (pp. 145–62, 163–85, 187–204) by Hofstadter, "Building Dwelling Thinking," "The Thing," ". . . Poetically Man Dwells . . . ," in *Poetry, Language, Thought*, pp. 145–61, 165–86, 213–29.

Platons Lehre von der Wahrheit: Mit einem Brief über den "Humanismus" (1942, 1946). 2d ed. Bern: Francke, 1954. Translation by John Barlow, "Plato's Doctrine of Truth"; and by Edgar Lohner, "Letter on Humanism," both in William Barrett and Henry Aiken, eds., *Philosophy in the Twentieth Century*, vol. 3, New

York: Random House, 1962, pp. 251–302. Reprinted by Harper and Row (Torchbook Series), 1971. New translation (with extensive running commentary) of the "*Brief*" by R.H. Cousineau, in *Heidegger, Humanism, and Ethics: An Introduction to the Letter on Humanism.* New York: Humanities Press, 1972.

Gelassenheit (1944–1955). 1st ed. Pfullingen: Neske, 1959. Translation by John M. Anderson and E. Hans Freund, *Discourse on Thinking*. New York: Harper and Row, 1966.

Was Heisst Denken? (1951–1952) 1st ed. Tübingen: Niemeyer, 1954. Translation by Fred D. Wieck and J. Glenn Gray, *What Is Called Thinking?* New York: Harper and Row, 1968.

Zur Seinsfrage (1955). 1st ed. Frankfort: Klostermann, 1956. Existing translation, *The Question of Being*, not recommended.

Was ist das—die Philosophie? (1955). 1st ed. Pfullingen: Neske, 1956. Existing translation, *What Is Philosophy?* not recommended.

Der Satz vom Grund (1955–1956). 1st ed. Pfullingen: Neske, 1957.

Identität und Differenz (1957). 1st ed. Pfullingen: Neske, 1957. Translation by Joan Stambaugh, *Identity and Difference*. New York: Harper and Row, 1969. Earlier translation under the title *Essays in Metaphysics* not recommended.

Unterwegs zur Sprache (1950–1959). 1st ed. Pfullingen: Neske, 1959. Translation of the first essay by Hofstadter, "Language," in *Poetry, Language, Thought*, pp. 189–210. Translation of the remaining essays by Peter D. Hertz, *On the Way to Language*. New York: Harper and Row, 1971.

Zur Sache des Denkens (1961–1964). 1st ed. Tübingen: Niemeyer, 1969. Translation by Joan Stambaugh, *On Time and Being*. New York: Harper and Row, 1972.

Some Eastern Perspectives

WILHELM HALBFASS

On Being and What There Is: Indian Perspectives on the Question of Being

Comparative Philosophy

"What is being?" In the fourth-century B.C. Aristotle says about this question that it "was raised of old and is raised now and always, and is always the subject of inquiry," and he designs the classical and paradoxical idea of "a science which investigates being as being, and the attributes which belong to it according to its own nature."[1] More than 2,000 years later we may acknowledge that the question is still with us. Yet we are in doubt with regard not only to its answer, but also to its meaning and status as a question, and to its very questionability. In fact, we may say that one of the more remarkable ways in which the question of being persists today is the question: Is there a question?

"The question is: Is being a mere word and its meaning a vapor, or does what is designated by the word 'being' hold within it the historical destiny of the West?"[2] Whether it is the "historical destiny of the West" or only a symptomatically Western misunderstanding, it is obviously correct that the question of being, as an explicit theme and program, and as framework of a philosophical discipline, has been formulated only in the West, initially by the Greeks. Among those who emphasize this today, critical, and even reductionist, tendencies are prevailing. Very often the interest in the question is nothing more than an interest in relating it to the contingencies of its historical occurrence, and, more specifically, in revealing its linguistic relativity: The history of "ontology" is claimed as a test case for demonstrating the linguistic conditions of philosophical ideas and problems; the ambiguous grammar of the verb *to be*, with its confusion of existential and copula functions, appears as the source and real depth of the intricacies traditionally associated with the question of being. The study of language, both as structural and logical analysis and as empirical study of their actual variety, seems to be more fundamental than the study of being (understood as 'being') itself. J.W.M. Verhaar expresses his confidence that such an inventory of linguistic varieties "will provide some of the necessary foundational material for research in logic, the theory of knowledge, and ontology."[3] A.C. Graham, in a programmatic article reprinted in the same series, states: "The concept of Being is a good test for the thesis of Benjamin Whorf that the grammatical structure of language guides the formation of philosophical concepts." Like other writers in this field, Graham seems to envy the good fortune of the Chinese and others whose language prevented them from lapsing into some of the typical mistakes and confusions of Western ontology.[4]

Not only orthodox Heideggerians may feel inclined to associate the linguistic approach to the question of being with what has been called "forgetfulness of being." The very idea of coping with the theme of being by laying bare and making empirically and structurally available its alleged linguistic foundations is in itself a significant historical symptom; and for all its cross-cultural breadth, it remains strangely parochial in its historical setting. This, of course, does not at all imply that it is philosophically irrelevant. We can learn from it; we have to learn from it. To take notice of this approach and its findings, and of the story of success which it has produced, is simply a question of intellectual honesty and alertness.

Rather different possibilities of cross-examining our Western theme of being seem to be suggested by what is called—*faute de mieux*—"comparative philosophy"—a discipline which still has difficulties in establishing itself as a discipline, and which has not yet produced any "story of success." Its reputation is still rather questionable, and among its more characteristic features is the discrepancy between its pretensions and its actual results. An impatient search for results and achievements, however, may in itself be detrimental to the not yet fully developed spirit of comparative philosophy, which has still to learn to understand better its own possibilities and aspirations. It would certainly be naive and futile to expect any quintessential, all-comprehensive concept of being from a comparison and adjustment of different ways of thinking about, or of dispensing with, what we call 'being.'

Yet the basic stimulus of comparative philosophy, the postulate and actual prospect of a richer and wider context of philosophical and historical understanding and self-awareness, can no longer be put aside in our present situation. What comparative philosophy needs is courage, modesty, and patience; not the accumulation of more and more juxtaposable data, not the rash jumping to general conclusions concerning "essential" differences and "ultimate" identities, but the courage and patience to develop gradually its own hermeneutics, to adjust its means, methods, and expectations to its subject matter, and to grow into its own context of understanding and of being understood.

In reexamining ontological terms and questions in this new and developing context of comparative philosophy, the following, in particular, would be relevant: the question of being and the philosophical discipline of ontology, as we find them in the Western tradition, are not to be taken as definite achievements, which we simply may or may not find missing or less developed elsewhere. Trying to think about the question of being in a "comparative" context means to think about the questionability of this question, about its dignity or vacuity as a question, about possible roots and horizons of its being asked—as well as of its being passed over in silence—and to be ready to learn from its absences as well as from its more or less explicit presences. Nor would this mean merely relating the question to any linguistic raw materials or similar conditioning factors. Being, after all, *is* not in such a sense that we might say *what* it is. How, then, can we define ontology in terms of its subject matter? And are we sure of it as a historical phenomenon? Anybody who is only slightly familiar with the historical dimensions of the theme will be reluctant to accept allegedly up-to-date and quintessential definitions, such as Quine's reduction of the "ontological problem" to the "simplicity" of the "three Anglo-Saxon monosyllables: 'What is there?'[5] Such a definition or delimitation would, in fact, amount to disregarding what, for all its ambiguity and possible vacuity, remains crucial to any radical philosophical questioning about being: that sense of the question, according to which being is not exhausted by whatever there is; according to which it refers to and aims at being in its transcendence of what there is and exposes itself to the ambivalence and possible absurdity of the 'and' in "being *and* what there is."

The following remarks on some "ontological" perspectives in Indian thought are as preliminary as they are limited. They are not meant to be an exemplary realization of the preceding programmatic considerations. They are, by and large, not explicitly "comparative" and do not go beyond occasional references to Western concepts. Within the Indian tradition, special attention has been paid to developments in the Vaiśeṣika system, which is certainly not the most inspiring school of thought in India. It might, however, provide some materials for counter-illustrating basic issues of Aristotle's ontological approach, and for reconsidering some of our most familiar ontological concepts. In its very failures and distortions it may help us to keep in mind the challenge of the "and" in our title phrase "being and what there is."

The Indian Tradition in General

In general, we may say that the Indian tradition does not disprove our earlier observation that the question of being, as an explicit theme, assigned to a specific philosophical discipline, is a symptomatically Western phenomenon. The tradition of *sadvidyā* ("knowledge of being") referred to by J.A.B. van Buitenen remains different from that kind of disciplinary tradition which we call ontology. Yet being (*sat*) is thematic in the oldest documents of Indian thought, in the Vedic and upaniṣadic texts (van Buitenen takes such thematization of *sat* as the starting point of Indian "philosophy"), and it remains an important and recurrent topic in later traditions.[6]

In one of the most glorious passages of Indian thought, Uddālaka Āruṇi teaches his son Śvetaketu:

> In the beginning, my dear, this world was just Being (*sat*), one only, without a second. To be sure, some people say: "In the beginning this world was just Non-being (*a-sat*), one only, without a second; from that Non-being Being was produced." But verily, my dear, whence could this be? . . . How from Non-being could Being be produced? On the contrary, my dear, in the beginning this world was just Being, one only, without a second.[7]

The text itself indicates that it is preceded by earlier discussions and speculations about being and non-being. And the theory of the origination of being from non-being, to which it explicitly refers, is, in fact, found not only in the Upaniṣads, but also in the Brāhmaṇas, and even in the Ṛgveda itself.[8]

It would be out of place here to attempt any thorough clarification of the earliest, especially Ṛgvedic uses of *sat* and *asat*, as we find them in the famous hymn X.129, or in X.72.[9] W. Norman Brown has proposed a concrete cosmological interpretation, according to which *sat* would be the realm of men and gods and of the cosmic order (*ṛta*), and *asat* the chaotic underworld of the demons.[10] This interpretation is, no doubt, a significant signpost; its textual basis seems, however, not quite sufficient for a full and definite justification. At any rate, it is obvious that *sat* and *asat* in the Ṛgveda do not mean 'being' versus 'nothing,' or 'existence' and 'non-existence' in any abstract sense.

Discussions of *sat* and *asat* in the Brāhmaṇa texts are usually on the level of mythical and ritualistic identifications and personifications. There are very few philosophically significant occurrences, which, like the equation of what *is* (*asti*) with what is "immortal" in the *Śatapatha Brāhmaṇa* (X.4,2,21), may be taken as corresponding to the upaniṣadic connotations of permanence and self-sufficiency, of unity and identity. Being in this sense becomes a familiar characteristic of *brahman*, and the two terms may even be used as synonyms. The *Kaṭha Upaniṣad* states that there is nothing else to be said or thought about *brahman* than the pure *is* (*asti*) alone (VI.12–13). In this and similar functions, 'being' is not merely, not even primarily, a theoretical and speculative notion. It always designates a soteriological goal; it designates the goal of self-realization: to know being means to coincide with being, which is always present as one's own true potential.[11] A famous passage of the *Bṛhadāraṇyaka Upaniṣad*, which we may call a prayer, says: "From non-being [*asat*] lead me to being [*sat*]; from darkness lead me to light; from death lead me to immortality"; and the text itself goes on to tell us that 'being' in this context is the same as 'light' and 'immortality.'[12] Connotations of truth, purity, and goodness quite naturally accompany such understanding of being.[13]

There is no systematically developed terminology of being in the Upaniṣads, and the applicability of *sat* to *brahman* and to the absolute in its primeval unity remains often ambiguous and is sometimes explicitly disputed, in accordance with the transontological language of Ṛgveda X.129 and with the old dispute over the priority of *sat* or *asat* which was mentioned earlier. It is obvious that in these and similar discussions the question of unity takes precedence over the question of being. The *Bṛhadāraṇyaka Upaniṣad* (II.3, 1 ff.), explaining the "two forms of *brahman*," associates *sat* with that aspect which is "formed," "mortal," and "stationary," and contrasts it with the other aspect of *brahman*, which remains "beyond" (*tyat*). The *Taittirīya Upaniṣad* referring to the same terminology of *sat* and *tyat*, presents *sat* and its separation from *tyat* as a result of *brahman*'s self-procreation, and it puts *sat* on the side of the "defined," "based," "conscious," "real."[14] "As the real [*brahman*] became whatever there is here." Being in these passages appears as a step into diversity; *brahman* is being insofar as it (or "he") coincides with the world, with what there is. But there remains the aspect of transcendence, and *sat* alone falls short of the primeval unity of *brahman*.

In view of such passages on the one hand, and the glorification of *sat* in the *Chāndogya Upaniṣad* on the other, we may say that the upaniṣadic role of *sat* is ambiguous, corresponding to the ambiguity of the relationship between being and what there is. Being is both immanent and transcendent; and such immanence-in-transcendence may have varying facets of identity and difference (a constant theme and stimulus of Indian thought). Being itself is the unity and identity of what there is: in this very function, it may be taken as something over and above the multifarious entities; on the other hand, it may appear as so deeply committed to the actual presence of this world that it cannot also represent its primeval ground and unity. Entities *are*, yet, being alone *is*; being transcends, and it has itself to be transcended. Is there a cleavage in the meaning of 'to be'? Is there a 'higher' and a 'lower' meaning?

The systematic tradition of Advaita Vedānta, basing itself upon the Upaniṣads, reflects and systematically develops these and similar questions and ambiguities. The notion of being no doubt plays an important part in Advaita; yet it is used with caution and reserve. Śaṅkara's references to *brahman* as *sat* or *sanmātra* ("being alone," "pure being") remain somewhat casual; the triad "being, consciousness, bliss" (*saccidānanda*), a standard formula in later Vedānta, is not found in his authentic writings.[15] And the theory of levels of discourse, truth, and reality, which permeates his thought and especially his interpretation of the sacred texts, is not systematically developed in terms of levels of being.[16] Śaṅkara and numerous later Advaitins seem to be more interested in refuting false conceptions of being than in establishing their own view of the absolute in terms of being.

There are Vedāntins, however, who go much further than Śaṅkara in thematizing and explicating being and in using it as a vehicle for the understanding of *brahman*. We hear about a tradition of *sattādvaita*, which identifies *brahman* or the non-dual principle of all reality as *sattā*, "beingness" (a term strictly avoided by Śaṅkara).[17] And Maṇḍanamiśra, the great and influential outsider of classical Advaita, devotes special care to reexamining the notion of being and its applicability to *brahman*. "Pure beingness," *sanmātra*, is, e.g., interpreted as the one and all-pervasive content of immediate, non-relational, pre-predicative perception (*nirvikalpakapratyakṣa*); the supreme unity of all reality is thus presented as a given factor of perception, underlying all conceptualizing, particularizing, predicative perception, imagination, and thought. This is at the same time a rejoinder to the Buddhist theory of innumerable discontinuous and disparate "self-characterizers" (*svalakṣaṇa*) as data of pre-predicative perception, and it is one instance of the far-reaching dialectical relationship between Advaita Vedānta and Buddhism.[18] On the doctrinal and terminological surface it is, of course, one of the most striking differences between Buddhism and Advaita that the Buddhists generally reject, avoid, or ridicule any theorizing in terms of being, with its connotations of self-nature, permanence, and self-sufficiency.[19]

The Vaiśeṣika School

Much of what Vedāntins and Buddhists, as well as representatives of several other systems, have to say about, against, or even in defiance of being is, in some sense, directly or indirectly related to conceptualizations of being as they are found in the Vaiśeṣika system and its sister-system, Nyāya. However narrow and insufficient these conceptualizations may be, they carry out, in a very instructive manner, certain exemplary conceptual procedures. Within the Indian context, they represent an exemplary target of criticism, and we may say that they play a catalytical role in the development of explicit and systematic thought about being in India.

The Vaiśeṣika system is usually labeled a "doctrine of categories," "category" being the traditionally accepted translation of the Sanskrit term *padārtha*. It is, in fact, an attempt to enumerate exhaustively the constituents of our world and to group them in certain highest classes.

In the basic text of the school, the *Vaiśeṣikasūtras* (a text which is somewhat questionable in its present philological status), two terms, *sattā*[20] and *bhāva*, are used to advocate an understanding of being as "highest universal" (*paraṃ sāmānyam*), i.e., the most universal, all-pervasive, common feature, perceivable by all senses, in our world, in its "substances," "qualities," and "motions" (*dravya, guṇa, karman*). It appears likely—there is, indeed, considerable evidence—that at an earlier stage the Vaiśeṣika program of classification did not, at least thematically, go beyond these three "categories" or constituents of reality (*padārtha*). If we accept the testimony of later commentators, especially Vyomaśiva, as valid indication that in the original version of the *Vaiśeṣikasūtras* Kaṇāda announced his philosophy as a program of naming, enumerating whatever "has the character of being" (*bhāvarūpa*), we may assume that he was referring to this group of "categories."[21] We have, of course, insufficient evidence to decide whether being was a really thematic and programmatic concept for Kaṇāda himself, or whether he simply took it for granted in its commonsense connotations.

That the concept of being actually assumes some kind of programmatic and thematic function seems unquestionable. It emerges as the horizon, the framework of Kaṇāda's program of exhaustive enumeration, of classifying the totality of what there is. We have nonetheless no evidence to believe that he ever raised the question of being as an explicit problem and project, or that he designed his system of "categories" as an explicit answer to such a question. Unlike Aristotle's categories, the *padārthas* of classical Vaiśeṣika are never presented as "meanings of being," and there is no Vaiśeṣika science of "being qua being" to which they might be taken as responding. In the *Vaiśeṣikasūtras*, being becomes thematic and problematic in an obviously secondary, derivative, retrospective manner. It emerges in some kind of summarizing reflection upon what seems to be the original and historically earlier stratum of the Vaiśeṣika doctrine of categories—the comprehensive classification of all particular and manifest entities, i.e., "substances," "qualities," and "motions." They all have in common that they are; being (*sattā, bhāva*) is their common denominator, their one and all-pervasive common feature. Being, in this sense, retrospectively circumscribes the realm of thematization. Gradually, however, it manifests itself as an entity of its own: it appears as "something different" (*arthāntara*) from the particular entities in which it is found, and, apart from being the comprehensive nature of the first group and level of "categories," it appears itself as a categorizable entity, an enumerable and juxtaposable world component on the second level of "categories," i.e., "universals," "individualities," "inherence" (*sāmānya, viśeṣa, samavāya*).[22] As "highest," all-pervasive universal, it is itself just one among many other entities, both universals and non-universals. In the *Daśapadārthaśāstra*, a somewhat heretical Vaiśeṣika text of the period around A.D. 500 (?), *sattā* is, in fact, presented as a separate "category," and not as a mere instance of the category or class of Universals.[23]

The familiar rendering of Vaiśeṣika *sattā* (also *bhāva*) as "existence" should, if retained at all, be taken with caution and reserve. It should by no means suggest any contrast to 'essence.' What we are used to calling 'essence' and 'existence' are never explicitly distinguished in Vaiśeṣika. Further, we have to keep in mind that the notion of *sattā* is not meant to establish any confrontation between 'being' and 'nothing' (or 'nothingness'); there is no radical notion of nothingness in Vaiśeṣika or any other Indian system. In its main and basic function, *sattā* is simply the common denominator of what there is; it provides an element of community, a common ground and horizon to what has been thematized by the program of enumerating and classifying all world components. In view of such connotations and non-connotations, *beingness*, though an awkward expression, might be worth considering as a translation of *sattā*. In general, such problems of translation should be taken as welcome opportunities to reexamine our own familiar apparatus of ontological terms and concepts, and to ask ourselves whether we really know what we mean by 'essence' and 'existence,' 'being' and 'nothingness,' 'possibility' and 'actuality,' etc., and how binding this framework really is.

Praśastapāda (sixth century), the most important commentator and reorganizer of classical Vaiśeṣika, follows the usage of *sattā* and *bhāva*, as we find it in the *Vaiśeṣikasūtras*. 'Beingness' is the "highest universal," the most common attribute, and as such, it is not basically different from, only more universal than other common attributes, such as 'blueness' (*nīlatva*). As factors of unity and similarity, as objectively identical correlates of recurrent perception and linguistic repetition, they are on equal terms. In addition, however, Praśastapāda uses a term which symptomatically illustrates his role as reorganizer and definite systematizer of classical Vaiśeṣika: the common abstract attribute 'is-ness' (*astitva*), which, together with 'knowableness' (*jneyatva*) and 'nameableness' (*abhidheyatva*), belongs to all six categories and can therefore be predicated of the universal (*sāmānya*) 'beingness' itself; to attribute 'beingness in the sense of *sattā* to *sattā* or any other universal would, of course, lead to an infinite regress.[24]

Praśastapāda characterizes the first group of "categories" ("substances," "qualities," "motions") as having *sattāsambandha*, "connection with beingness," and the second group ("universals," "individualities," "inherence") as having *svātmasattva*, "beingness, of, or by virtue of, own nature." These terms are found only once in his text, and they are never explicitly defined. Their distinction has, of course, some very obvious commonsense connotations, corresponding to the distinction between the robust reality of causally efficient particulars like cows and horses and the somewhat less tangible being of their universal features, cowness and horseness; cows give milk, cowness obviously doesn't. Such commonsense connotations cannot, however, describe adequately the systematic function of the two concepts.

In the secondary literature, there are a few rather incidental attempts to account for this conceptual structure, but they are far from satisfactory. Leaving aside the full argumentation and textual evidence, let me briefly summarize the following relevant points: *Astitva*, 'is-ness,' appearing side by side with *jñeyatva* and *abhidheyatva*, means the applicability of the word *is*, i.e., the fact that there is an objective basis and condition of saying 'it is,' in the sense of its being identifiable, recognizable, distinguishable from, not reducible to, other entities, and thereby knowable, speakable, suitable as truth-condition for thought and speech.

Astitva, 'is-ness,' in this sense seems to be quite appropriate for Praśastapāda's second group of categories, i.e., "universals," etc. They are what they are, insofar as they are identifiable natures, determinate in themselves, recognizable in thought and speech. It is much less evident how it has to be understood if we try to relate it to the first group of world components, i.e., to the concrete, "manifest" particular entities and processes which we call "substances," "qualities," "motions." In what sense is their being an *astitva* of this sort? In what sense can the 'beingness,' which they have in common, be taken as exemplifying that basic connotation of identifiability which we find in *astitva*, 'is-ness'?

The sense in which we may expect an answer to these questions from Praśastapāda himself has to be qualified; and in order to avoid an entanglement of his conceptual network, we have to keep in mind that there are two different "ontological dichotomies" in his system, which represent, moreover, different levels of thematicity. On the one hand, there is—both basic and somehow in the background—the distinction between *sattā* and *astitva*; on the other hand, there is the subdivision of *astitva* into *sattāsambandha* and *svātmasattva*. In the context under discussion, *sattāsambandha*, 'connection with beingness' (not 'beingness' itself), is referred to and subsumed under *astitva*. In terms of Praśastapāda's conceptual framework, this is not without significance. 'Beingness,' as a real universal, is one of the real, ontologically separable components of the world; but *sattāsambandha*, like *astitva* itself, is not a real universal, is not a separable, juxtaposable world component. It is only a common abstract attribute, a way and aspect of conceptually relating the actual world components, a product of abstraction, and in no way separable from that the attribute of which it is. It is, in Praśastapāda's terminology, a merely abstract "homogeneity," a *sādharmya*. 'Connection with beingness' is the basic condition under which "substances," "qualities," "motions" exist; and this is not the same as the universal 'beingness' itself; *sattā*, as a universal, is eternal and unchangeable. It is potentially omnipresent and can be actually present in, actually exemplified by things which *are*. And *sattāsambandha*, strictly speaking, is this actual presence of *sattā*. It has a much more tangible connotation of temporality than *sattā* itself, which, according to its Prābhākara Mīmāṃsā critics, represents the prototype of a completely atemporal and static understanding of being; this temporal connotation becomes more explicit in later Nyāya and Vaiśeṣika texts.[25]

Sattāsambandha, 'connection with beingness,' thus indicates the condition under which concrete "manifest" entities are what they are, and have that identifiability, recognizability which is the basic meaning of *astitva*; understood as abstract "homogeneity" or as "common abstract attribute" of certain entities, it is a being which falls in no way apart from that the being of which it is.

Recapitulating our interpretation of Praśastapāda's way of dealing with the question of being, we may say there are at least two ways and levels of talking about being. There is being as *sattā*, the most comprehensive real factor of commonness, which is itself a component of the world. It is hypostasized 'somethingness' which has itself become a something, a datum of sense-perception, one factor among others which constitute the world as it is given to us; and there is being as *astitva*, which merely, and in a sense tautologically, states that whatever is, *is* (*asti*), i.e., has a certain character of positivity, identifiability. In accordance with this distinction of levels of discourse, the question what *sattā* and *astitva* have in common, and how they function and cooperate in constituting what occurs to us as the actual concrete reality of entities, remains unasked. And in general, Praśastapāda tends methodically to ignore potentially embarrassing questions. Such questions were, of course, not ignored by the numerous opponents of the Vaiśeṣika system.

I cannot enlarge here upon how the Vaiśeṣika commentators after Praśastapāda—especially Vyomaśiva, Śrīdhara, and Udayana—try to explicate and defend, in sometimes rather desperate conceptual efforts, both *sattā* and *astitva*, how they try to cope with the manifold questions and objections brought forward by Buddhists, Mīmāṃsakas, and Vedāntins, and specifically with that notorious dilemma which is often referred to as *sadasadvikalpa*, i.e., the question whether that in which 'beingness' is said to inhere *is* or *is not* by itself.[26] I can touch only briefly upon one characteristic episode in this development: the way in which the concept of 'own nature' (*svarūpa*) is brought in as a device of ontological discussion and explication.

The Praśastapāda commentators, particularly Śrīdhara and Udayana, not only paraphrase Praśastapāda's *svātmassattva* as *svarūpasattā*, 'own-nature-beingness' (i.e., being which consists in 'own nature'); they also use the term *svarūpa* to explain his *astitva*. Śrīdhara determines: "Whatever is the 'own nature' [*svarūpa*] of an entity [*vastu*], that is its 'is-ness' [*astitva*]," and he explicitly substitutes *svarūpavattva* ("status of something which has its own nature," i.e., its "own nature" itself) for *astitva*.[27] He insists that both *astitva* and *sattā* are necessary to account adequately for our world of experience, and he tells us that while we need *sattā* to explain our awareness of being in its unity and universality, *astitva* or *svarūpavattva* is not superfluous either, because 'beingness' could not be present in what is without a characteristic nature (*svarūpa*) of its own, i.e., in what is not a definite something. It would be utterly wrong to utilize here the Western terminology of essence and existence, as has been attempted, or to refer to the Scholastic idea of an "*esse superadditum essentiae*": *astitva* as *svarūpavattva* is *not* essence without existence, but being without unity and universality.[28]

The word *svarūpa*, which has thus assumed a central role in ontological explication, is one of those highly evasive, allegedly self-evident quasi-terms which philosophers tend to utilize as loopholes whenever their technical terminology and their thematically developed conceptual framework leads them into difficulties.[29] What is obvious is that Śrīdhara wants to elucidate the connotation of identifiability, distinguishability, which we found in Praśastapāda's *astitva*. At the same time, however, he responds to, and tries to neutralize, the criticism of the Vaiśeṣika ontology as we find it in the Prābhākara school of Mīmāṃsa, especially in the writings of Sālikanāthamiśra.[30] The Prābhākaras argue that the assumption of a real universal *sattā*, 'beingness,' is unnecessary, that being, and the reality of our world, has basically to be accounted for in terms of the mere 'own nature' and self-identity of each individual entity (*vastusvarūpa*), and that the alleged common factor, *sattā*, is in reality nothing more than an *upādhi*, a merely accidental and external qualification of what there is. 'Beingness' is reduced to the *upādhi* "suitability for being connected with a means of correct knowledge" (*pramaṇasambandhayogyatā*), i.e., capability to serve as truth-condition. In this interpretation, an entity (*seiendes*) *is*, and it is perfectly real as such and as whatever it may be; its being (*Sein*), however, is nothing but a common aspect, i.e., its knowability, its suitability for being the truth condition of thought and speech.

In a sense the question of being is simply silenced by reverting to the mere fact, somewhat commonsensically accepted, that things *are*, and are *what* they are, as long as they are. However, Sālikanātha gives at least a few hints concerning the context and rationale of his usage of *svarūpa*: "*Svarūpa* as such" (*svarūpamātra*) is the being of each entity in its irreducible, non-relational selfhood and self-identity; it is being without regard to other being or to non-being (*ekāki bhāvaḥ*); and such being as self-identity is claimed as the datum of immediate, non-relational, pre-predicative perception (*nirvikalpakapratyakṣa*).[31] This is obviously a reaction to Buddhist challenges of the notions of 'self-being' and 'own nature' (*svabhāva*; *svarūpa*), as we find them in the doctrines (or anti-doctrines) of "devoidness" (*śūnyatā*) and "negative determination" (*apoha*), and it is a reenactment of an old and traditional association of 'being' and 'own nature.'[32] At the same time, however, it is a reaction to the ontological trend of classical Vaiśeṣika, according to which 'beingness' (*sattā*) appears as some kind of extra, as something added to the 'own nature' of each entity. In its Prābhākara Mīmāṃsā interpretation, being simply coincides with what there is, instead of being presented as a somehow separable factor or component.

What is remarkable about the counter-reaction of such Vaiśeṣika commentators as Śrīdhara is the degree to which they adopt the concept of *svarūpa*, not only in its application to the second group of "categories" but also in accepting *svarūpa* as the underlying condition of *sattā* (which is thus relegated to a secondary and potentially obsolete position), and in using it to describe the basic orientation, the horizon of their understanding of being. However, as the subsequent development shows, this concept is so functional and empty in itself that it is quite inappropriate to vindicate the robust naturalism of ancient Vaiśeṣika and to maintain its realistic conception of being against reductionist and relativistic challenges. Udayana, who even as a Vaiśeṣika commentator leans toward the more epistemologically oriented tradition of Nyāya and its basic notion of *tattva*, truth-conditioning 'thatness' which covers both negative and positive facts, already uses the concept of *svarūpa* not as a device for explicating positive being, but in a sense which comprises both 'being' and 'non-being' (*bhāva* and *abhāva*).[33] Yet *svarūpa* is still meant to include 'non-being' only in the sense of a mere absence of positive entities, thus demarcating it from what will never be actual and real and always remain mere fiction (*tuccha*, *alīka*). It is, of course, very easy for opponents such as the Vedāntic dialectician Śrīharṣa to point out that *svarūpa* is inappropriate for drawing this borderline.[34] In its basic connotation of identifiability and distinguishability, it is applicable to the world of mere fictions, too; it is no problem to distinguish a hare's horn from a sky-flower.

We noticed earlier that being (as *sattā*) seems to become thematic in the *Vaiśeṣikasūtras* in some kind of retrospective manner, in a summarizing reflection upon what has been classified as "substances," "qualities," "motions." Subsequently, this 'beingness,' as one of the universals, becomes itself a quasi-entity, and another concept of being, *astitva*, is introduced to cover the extended field of thematized, hypostasized objects. *Astitva*, however, merely reaffirms whatever may have been objectified (and may thus include what had been *abhāva*, 'non-being,' on another level of objectivication). A concept of being which in such a manner follows the extending horizons of thematization and objectification lends itself to what we may call "semantic evaporation," until it may, in fact, appear as the "last cloudy streak of evaporating reality."[35]

Conclusion

There is, in accordance with my introductory remarks, no explicit question of being and nothing like the Aristotelian project of a science of "being qua being" in Vaiśeṣika; and, of course, the Indian philosophical tradition, at least in classical times, does not favor formulating questions *as* questions, i.e., as open frameworks for future efforts of thought. There is a much more emphatic sense of thematicity in Aristotle's way of dealing with being. It is richer in suggestive ambiguities and its systematic role is much more central. Important areas of Aristotle's philosophy, such as the doctrine of categories, are explicit responses to the question of being. The categories are themselves understood as "meanings of being"; the Vaiśeṣika *padārthas* are not. Being, according to Aristotle, can never be relegated to the role of *summum genus*; in fact, the idea of a *summum genus* as such is rejected.[36]

Aristotle's thought about being is followed by that tradition which in later centuries was called 'ontology.' The Vaiśeṣika conceptualizations of being did not initiate any such tradition of ontology, and they may appear as a mere dead-end road. Yet they remain an honest and respectable attempt in one particular direction, and their very one-sidedness may serve as a catalyst of clarification, and as a basis and vehicle for a more radical questioning. In fact, in the classical Indian tradition, Vaiśeṣika thought about being has served these functions; it has been an exemplary target of criticism, and as such, it may still be instructive today.

Notes

1. *Metaphysics*, 1028b2f; 1003a21ff.; W.D. Ross translates: "science which investigates that which is, as being, and the attributes that belong to it in virtue of its own nature" (*Aristotle's Metaphysics. A Revised Text with Introduction and Commentary*, rpt. [London: Oxford University Press, 1966], vol. 1, p. 251).

2. M. Heidegger, *An introduction to Metaphysics*, trans. R. Manheim (Garden City, N.Y.: Doubleday, 1961), p. 35.

3. Verhaar is editor of the series *The Verb 'Be' and its Synonyms*, Dordrecht-Holland, 1967–; published within the *Supplementary Series* of *Foundations of Language*. The statement quoted from the Editorial Preface is repeated in all volumes so far published.

4. Pt. 5 (1972), p. 225; pt. 1 (1967), p. 1ff.

5. *From a Logical Point of View* (New York: Harper and Row, 1963), p. 1.

6. *Rāmānuja's Vedārthasaṃgraha* (Poona: Deccan College, 1956), pp. 3ff.

7. *Chāndogya Upaniṣad* VI.2,1–2 (trans. R.E. Hume).

8. Cf. *Chāndogya Up.* III.19,1; *Taittirīya Up.* II.7,1; *Bṛhadāraṇyaka Up.* I.2,1; *Śatapatha Brāhmaṇa* VI.1,1,1; *Ṛgveda* X.72,2–3.

9. Especially X.129,1 (*nāsad āsīn no sad āsīt*) and 4 (*sato bandhum asati niravindan*); cf. I.164,46 (*ekaṃ sad viprā bahudhā vadanti*).

10. Cf. *Journal of the American Oriental Society* 61 (1941): 76ff.; 62 (1942), 85ff.; *Man in the Universe* (Berkeley: University of California Press, 1966), pp. 17ff.

11. Cf. *Taittirīya Up.* II.6,1: *asann eva sa bhavati, asad brahmeti veda cet/ asti brahmeti ced veda, santam enaṃ tato viduḥ.*

12. I.3,28 (*asato mā sad gamaya, tamaso mā jyotir gamaya, mṛtyor māmṛtaṃ gamaya*); cf. *Ṛgveda* X.129,2: *na mṛtyur āsīd amṛtaṃ na. . . .*

13. Derivatives like satya and sattva would, of course, also be relevant in this context; cf., e.g., *Taittirīya Up.* II.1,1: *satyaṃ jñānam anantaṃ brahma.*

14. II.6,3. Cf. the use of *bhāva* and *abhāva* in *Śvetāśvatara Up.* V.14.

15. Cf. *Bhāṣya* on *Brahmasūtra* II.3,9: *sanmātraṃ hi brahma*; II.1,16: *ekaṃ ca punaḥ sattvam.* The formula occurs several times in the *Nṛsinhottara-tāpanīya Up.*, which is, however, of uncertain date; cf. P. Deussen, *The System of the Vedānta*, trans. C. Johnston, rpt. (New York: Dover, 1973), p. 212.

16. The distinction of two levels of discourse (cf. *Muṇḍaka Up.* I.1,4, *dve vidye*) is used by Śaṅkara as a basis for reconciling the apparently conflicting upaniṣadic statements about the origin from *sat* or *asat*; of., e.g., *Bhāṣya* on *Brahmasūtra* II.1,17.

17. Cf. B. Gupta, *Die Wahrnehmungslehre in der Nyāyamañjarī* (Walldorf: Verlag für Orientkunde, 1963), p. 21; 81ff.; the conception of *Brahman* as "great universal" (*mahāsāmanya*) *sattā* or *mahāsattā* ("great beingness") is also developed in Bhartṛhari's non-dualistic philosophy of grammar; cf. K.A. Subramania Iyer, *Bhartṛhari* (Poona: Deccan College, 1969), pp. 246ff.; 334ff.

18. Cf. *Brahmasiddhi*, ed. S. Kuppuswami Sastri (Madras: Government Press, 1937), p. 58: *sanmātrarūpe sarvatra pratīyamāne* . . . ; this "mere being" coincides with the mere positivity of the "thing as such" (*vastumātra*; cf., e.g., p. 71).

19. Cf. Nāgārjuna, *Mūlamadhyamakakārikā* XV (*svabhāvaparīkṣā*); also XXI. 12ff.

20. Major parts of my following remarks on classical Vaiśeṣika are a summary or a more philosophically oriented adaptation of my article "Conceptualizations of 'Being' in Classical Vaiśeṣika," *Wiener Zeitschrift für die Kunde Südasiens* 19, 1975. This article gives fuller textual evidence for many of the following statements.

21. See n. 20; cf. especially the fact that *Sūtra* I.1,4 is of very questionable authenticity.

22. *Vaiśeṣikasūtra* I.2,8.

23. Cf. H. Ui, *The Vaiśeshika Philosophy according to the Daśapadārtha-Śāstra* (Varanasi: Chowkhamba, 1962), pp. 99f.; 116.

24. Cf. *Bhāshya of Praśastapāda, together with the Nyāyakandalī of Śrīdhara*, ed. V.P. Dvivedin (Banaras: E.J. Lazarus, 1895), p. 16; cf. pp. 311f.

25. Cf., e.g., *Prakaranapañcikā*, ed. A. Subrahmanya Sastri (Banaras: Banaras Hindu University, 1961), p. 99. See above, n. 20.

26. See the article referred to in n. 20.

27. See *Nyāyakandalī* (edition referred to in n. 24), p. 16.

28. Cf. G. Patti, *Der Samavāya im Nyāya-Vaiçeṣika-System* (Rome: Pontificio Istituto Biblico, 1955), p. 143.

29. The word can be used in a wide variety of contexts and disciplines, with more or less technical or common sense connotations; on the *svaṃ rūpam* reference in Sanskrit grammar, as 'autonymous' use of a word, cf. J. Brough, *Theories of General Linguistics in the Sanskrit Grammarians*, ed. J.F. Staal (Cambridge: M.I.T. Press, 1972), pp. 402ff.

30. Cf. *Prakaranapañcikā*, ed. A. Subrahmanya Sastri (Banaras: Banaras Hindu University, 1961), pp. 97ff.

31. *Prakaranapañcikā*, pp. 289ff.

32. Cf. *Nyāyasūtra* 4.1,38 (*na, svabhāvasiddher bhāvānām*) and *Bhāṣya* (. . . *svena dharmeṇa bhāvā bhavanti* . . .); an investigation of the role of *sva* in Hindu-Buddhist controversies would, no doubt, be worthwhile).

33. Cf. *Nyāyakusumāñjali*, pt. 1, ed. Narendrachandra Vedantatirtha (Calcutta: University of Calcutta, 1954), p. 49 (on Kārīka 1:10); *Kiraṇāvalī*, ed. V. P. Dvivedī (Banaras: Braj Bhushan Das, 1919), p. 6: *abhāvas tu svarūpavān api*. . . .

34. Cf. *Khaṇḍanakhaṇḍakhādya*, ed. Laxmana Sastri Dravida (Banaras: Chowkhamba, 1914), pp. 12ff., 44ff., and esp. 1043ff.

35. This formula from Nietzsche's *Twilight of Idols* is quoted by M. Heidegger, *An Introduction to Metaphysics*, trans. Ralph Manheim (Garden City: Doubleday, 1961), p. 29.

36. Consequently, B.K. Matilal's statement that *sattā*, as "highest *sāmānya*," is "comparable with the notion of highest genus in the Aristotelian system" (*The Navya-Nyāya Doctrine of Negation* [Cambridge: Harvard University Press, 1968], p. 123) is quite unacceptable in terms of Aristotelian thought.

Bibliography

All specific references are given in the notes. For background information, see:

Frauwallner, E., *Geschichte der indischen Philosophie*, vol. 2, Salzburg: Otto Müller Verlag, 1956 (English trans., V. Bedekar, *History of Indian Philosophy*, vol. 2, Delhi: Motilal Banarsidas, 1972).

Halbfass, W., *Remarks on the Vaiśeṣika Concept of Sāmānya*, in *Āñjali . . . A Felicitation Volume to O.H. de A. Wijesekera*, ed. J. Tilakasiri, Peradeniya: University of Ceylon, 1970, pp. 137–151.

Dravid, R.R., *The Problem of Universals in Indian Philosophy*, Delhi: Motilal Banarsidas, 1972.

Gilson, E., *Being and Some Philosophers*. Toronto: Pontifical Institute of Mediaeval Studies, 1952.

J.G. ARAPURA

Some Special Characteristics of *Sat* (Being) in Advaita Vedānta

We must begin with the knowledge that the term *sat* as used in Advaita Vedānta is a genuine verbal and conceptual equivalent of 'being.' The word itself is the present participle of the root *as*, to be. There is another root, *bhū*, with the same meaning, which also yields a variety of nouns and participles, none of which, however, can be translated *Being* with a capital *B*, as befits the need of ontology.[1] *Bhūta* at most means *a being*; and *bhāva* means *becoming* or *coming to be* or, even, *the way something is*.

We restrict our study of *sat* here to the ontological realm, yet in passing we must take note of the manifoldness of meaning the word has in the Indian philosophical tradition; to pursue this, however, would be distracting for our present purpose. No doubt the varieties of meaning the word carries in the religious, ethical, and psycho-metaphysical literature of India must in the last analysis only contribute to a fuller comprehension of ontology itself. The *Bhagavadgītā* tersely condenses this manifoldness, stating "*Aum, That, Being*—this [symbol] is considered to be the threefold recollection device of [i.e., pertaining to] *brahman*" (X.23ab). Afterward, it defines *sat* thus: "The word *sat* is employed in the sense of Reality as well as goodness; [likewise], the word *sat* is used in the sense of praiseworthy action. Steadfastness in sacrifice, austerity, and giving are said to be *sat*, and action aimed at that goal is also called *sat*" (XVII.26–27).

We may briefly trace the history of the word from its beginnings through the later, sustained ontological use of it in the sense of being. A movement in the direction of ontology is met within the uses of the word as early as the *Ṛgveda*. The celebrated *Nāsadīya* hymn (*Ṛgveda* X.129) in its opening refers to a 'then' before all time, when neither *sat* (being) nor *asat* (non-being) existed. However, the hymn is too early for the concept of being in its full-fledged, ontological sense. So it is highly likely that *sat* here stood for something midway between the world and pure being, and *asat*, obviously, for the opposite of it.

Both *sat* and *asat* by themselves, as well as in compound formations, appear many times in the major and minor Upaniṣads. However, following the clue of the *Nāsadīya Sūkta*, perhaps the concept of *asat* is mentioned by the Upaniṣads even prior to that of *sat*. The *Taittirīya Upaniṣad* (II.7.1) declares, "In the beginning this was just non-being; from it being was born. It made itself *ātman*, wherefore it is called well-made."[3] The idea of the priority of being to non-being occurs clearly for the first time in the *Chāndogya Upaniṣad*:

> In the beginning, my dear, this was being itself, one only without a second. Some say that in the beginning this was just non-being, one only without a second; from that non-being being was born. [But] how, indeed, could it be so? said he, how could being arise from non-being? [On the contrary], my dear, this was in the beginning being itself, one only without a second.(VI.2.1–2)

From this we also come to know that the opposite view had already been prevalent in that it is specifically mentioned and refuted.

The Boundaries of the Concept of *Sat* in the Source-Books of the Vedānta

What would appear to an unassisted reader as an equivocation between *sat* and *asat* in the Upaniṣads clearly does not remain so in the interpretations given by the systematic originators of the Vedānta. They entirely subordinate *asat* to *sat*, and the rationale of their whole approach to the problem will become clear to us only if we perceive that the concept of being is set forth in the Upaniṣads in a manner totally unfamiliar to other philosophies and in a manner that would appear, if approached from another philosophical tradition, to be altogether unexpected. Thus, following the lead of the founding philosophers of Vedānta as a *darśana*, some distinguishing characteristics of the Upaniṣads' presentation of *sat* may be outlined.

1. The concept of *sat* comes comprehended in *brahman*, although, no doubt, *sat* is *brahman* and *brahman* is *sat*. Accordingly, when we read about *sat* we are inevitably reading about *brahman*, but, conversely, when we are reading about *brahman* we are not always reading about *sat*. This is not to say that the remotest possibility of disequating the two concepts exists, and that *sat* is only partially identical with *brahman*. Nothing of the kind. Such conjectures must be completely avoided.

It is also true that every important concept in the Upaniṣads likewise appears not only in conjunction with but as inseparably identical with *brahman*, whether language (*vāk*), mind (*manas*), or whatever. But the concept *sat* has a certain priority and uniqueness as the groundwork for all else, as it shares from the start the preeminence of *brahman* or *ātman*, being in most places its equivalent, unlike the other concepts which may start from some other phenomenal ground although reaching their ultimate telos of identity with *brahman*.

2. If *sat* came in most places as the conceptual equivalent of *brahman*, connoting *brahman*, the case was not one of simple or exceptionless identity. As a wide-ranging concept there remained cases—at least apparently—where *sat* stood for phenomenal reality not covered by the concept *brahman*, a possibility eventually resisted and overcome not by reason of the connotation of *sat* but by reason of the denotation of *brahman*. In other words, the concept *sat* was ultimately transvalued and completely comprehended by the implications of being, universal and exceptionless being, which *brahman* was understood to carry. Thus it is *brahman* which put its stamp of character upon *sat* rather than the other way around.

It will help to remember that the word *brahman* originally indicated a unique power of being, known in the phenomenon of growth, expansion. Śaṅkara defines it thus: "[It is called] *brahman* because of the property of growing."[4] It is the power whereby things, the world, and the gods themselves are and also are not. The *Kena Upaniṣad* depicts it effectively as the hidden power of being behind all beings, behind being itself. The allegory in the *Kena Upaniṣad*, III, dramatizes it well. It is introduced by the statement that *brahman* achieved a conquest for the gods and they gloried in it, thinking that the conquest was due to their own power; but when the vainglorious gods Agni and Vāyu were challenged to perform their accustomed function, like burning and blowing, they found that they could not, as the power behind their deeds was an unknown spirit (*yakṣa*), later to be revealed as *brahman*. Finally, when Indra was asked to find out who this spirit was he hastened toward it, but it vanished. This theme, that *brahman* is the deity behind all deities, is well-established also in all Uttara-mīmāṁsā (Vedānta) interpretations of ritualistic texts of the Veda. But strangely enough, as the boundary of language had been reached, the only means by which to further investigate *brahman*, the utterly universal being, was to treat it as if it were a spirit, a god. The *Kena Upaniṣad* had said in a previous passage, "Thither the eye goes not, nor speech, nor mind; we know not, we understand not how we can teach it."[5] Commenting on this, Śaṅkara observes, "Whatever is perceptible to the senses can be taught to others by the particularities of genus, quality and function. But *brahman* has none of these."[6]

In the Upaniṣads we notice further a movement, however implicit, from the unquestioned acceptance—for reasons other than conceptual—of *brahman*'s own being as the primeval ground of all ground (*satyasya satyam*) to the idea of *brahman* as being (*sat*) in the universal and critical sense of the word. This naturally necessitated the arising of the idea of being qua being by reason, essentially, of the juxtaposition and comparison of *brahman*'s being with the problematic existence of the phenomenal world. In this context the word *sat* is used ambiguously, that is to say, sometimes in the sense of *brahman*, with or without the totality of phenomenal things, and sometimes in the sense of the world with or without *brahman* as its tacit source and center. It is the contention of Vedānta, particularly Advaita, that rigorous rules of exegesis required that *sat* be interpreted under the criteriology of *brahman* and not at all independently, as the latter would lend itself to dualism. This is the reason for Śaṅkara's vigorous refutation of the Sāṁkhya doctrine of *pradhāna* (original, independent matter) accounting for the phenomenal world, more especially as carried out in his comments on *Vedānta Sūtra* I.4.1–14.

The incontestable preeminence of *brahman*'s own being compared with the infinitely lower grade—and problematic character—of the being that the world possessed, or seemed to possess, must have contributed to the radical idea that *brahman* is alone being, and that in an absolute sense. In other words the deepening and increasing radicalism of the idea of being came about by way of reflection upon the radical, but conceptually elusive, character of *brahman* (known through scripture) and not the other way around.

3. *Brahman* knowledge is knowledge objectively given, not perfected from an idea originated in the mind by reflection upon the world or human existence. In other words, the Vedānta philosophy of being is the result of drawing the logical conclusions from both the knowledge and the nature of its advent. The idea of being came fundamentally from the objectively given knowledge of *brahman* which came via the word. (Reflection upon the nature of language is a corollary to this.) In countless places in the source literature this is stated in no uncertain terms. Notable among these is *Vedānta Sūtra* I.1.3, *śāstrayonitvāt*. Śaṅkara, in his comment on it, points out two complementary meanings of the text: *brahman* is the source of the scripture; and scripture is the source of the knowledge of *brahman*. In another instance, commenting on the *Kena* passage (I.3) quoted above, which states the total unknowability of *brahman*, he observes, "*āgamena tu śakyatā eva prāpyāyitum* [Only by scripture is it possible to be known]."[7]

This is a central principle not only of Śaṅkara but also of Maṇḍana Miśra, and of all Vedānta writers since their time. Maṇḍana wrote his *Brahmasiddhi* with a view to establishing the authority of the Upaniṣads as the only source of the knowledge of *brahman*. In the second of the two chapters of this work, entitled *Tarkakānda*, the point is especially subjected to critical analysis in the light of the different means of knowledge, and it is pointed out that the knowledge of *brahman* is not something arrived at perceptually or inferentially but by way of direct revelation. This sets an inflexible context for the understanding of the concept of being.

The Problem of Being as It Arose from the Need to Define *Brahman*

The Upaniṣads present *brahman*; hence, in the last analysis, *brahman* is a presentation by the revealing word. The fact that *brahman* is being (rather than its opposite) and is alone being (rather than having any other entity with the ability to share such being) is implicit in that presentation because *brahman* is indicated to be not only a that (*tat*) but a what (*kim*), implied in the question "what is this spirit? [*kim idam yakṣam?*]." The need to interpret *brahman* comes bound up with the presentation itself; in fact, that it does not come totally uninterpreted is obvious from the body of the Upaniṣads. Concrete examples of correlation, for the purpose of interpretation and communication of *brahman*, with even the phenomenal (*vyākṛta*) structures of reality, are abundant in these texts. The most obvious paradigmatic instance is the *Māṇḍūkya Upaniṣad* itself, where we find a four-way correlation of *brahman* with levels of language, with the psychic structure of man, and with the structure of the cosmos. *Brahman* is that; we can even call it "pure" being only by explicitly correlating it with notional being elicited from the being of the world and beings in the world and by way of a negative conceptual act canceling the latter for methodological purposes. Hence it would seem that denial of being to the world and affirmation of being for *brahman* go hand in hand and both are methodological only, occurring in the context where the question as to being is asked. It would even appear that whenever the question is not asked the world is not without being—nor does it possess it except in the most uncritical and conventional way.

The concrete concept of being is an integrative device of the above-depicted type largely because the opposite of being, nothingness, is a conceptual impossibility and, as Śaṅkara and his followers point out, the notion of nothingness conflicts with our experience every moment. In fact, the trinity of basic principles, *sat* (being), *cit* (consciousness), and *ānanda* (bliss) is likewise forged from the necessity of interpretation. But these principles are considered by no means adventitious but essential (*svarūpalakṣaṇa*) to *brahman*.

The problem of being, however, is really a derivative problem in Advaita—as is the rest of metaphysics—but the presentation of *brahman* undoubtedly provokes it. This has required two concurrent procedures: an exegetical integration of texts, and a critical examination of the realms of experience using the canons of human reasoning. The two together respond to the need for interpretation by seeking definitions of *brahman*. They enable the problem of being to be raised in conformity with the known character of *brahman*. (This means, of course, that it is not the case that we meet up with the concept of *brahman* at the conclusion of some presumedly independent investigation of being, but the other way around.)

The ontological inquiry, such as it is, is thus in part acting in compliance with the need for interpretation and definition and in part responding to a demand of the human mind for intelligibility. However, the Vedānta as a whole (not only Advaita), along with the Pūrva-mīmāṁsā, assumes that intelligibility is also impulsive in character. Knowledge must move persons. While expounding the *samanvayādhikaraṇa* (*Vedānta-sūtra* I.1.4), Śaṅkara points out the injunctive (or shall we say imperative?) character of scriptural knowledge pertaining to *brahman*. It is obviously not given in the form of statements of facts like "the earth has seven islands" and "here goes the king." Mere factual statements do not belong to the Vedānta texts, as they are declarations purporting to impel the hearers to a quest, and even an effort *to be* in the spirit of "*brahmavid brahmeti bhavati*" (the knower of *brahman* becomes *brahman*). Also, *sat* has a very definite dynamic character in terms of impelling man toward his supreme end. By making reference to upaniṣadic sentences like "the *ātman* should be seen [*Ātmā va are draṣṭavyaḥ*]" (*Bṛhadāraṇyaka Up.* II.4.5), "he should be investigated, he should be understood [*so ' nveṣṭavyaḥ, so vijijñāsitavyaḥ*]," (*Chāndogya Up.* VIII.7.1), Śaṅkara points out that they undoubtedly contain a certain imperative concerning both our knowing and our *becoming* being. Incidentally, Saṅkara's principal objective in his exegesis in this place is to discourage the belief that there is a valid realm of action for the purpose of achieving man's ultimate goal apart and aside from the realm of knowledge of *brahman*. However, dedication to the latter must absorb into itself the essential properties of action as well as the passion inherent in it.

Brahman as *Sat-cit-ānanda* or *Satyam-jñānam-anantam/ānandam Brahma*

The *Taittirīya Upaniṣad* II.1., presents the basic and the oldest formula for defining *brahman*, that is, as *satyam* (being, truth), *jñānam* (consciousness, knowledge), and *anantam/ānandam* (infinite, bliss). It is the consensus of interpreters that this formula is identical with the later formula *sat cit-ānanda* (being-consciousness-bliss). The latter as a single formula does not, as is well-known, occur in the major Upaniṣads but appears, as is probably not well-known, in a few of the minor ones, the *Vāsudeva Upaniṣad*, the two *Rāma Upaniṣads*, the two *Nṛsiṁha Upaniṣads*, and the *Muktikā Upaniṣad*. However, tradition has invariably regarded the two formulas as identical.

The formula *sat-cit-ānanda*, as Advaita literature has categorized, has come to be accepted as the essential definition (*svarūpalakṣaṇa*) of *brahman*, while another definition, given in terms of the accidental qualities of *brahman*-like activity and relation to the world, constitute the *taṭasthalakṣaṇa*. This distinction between the two is stated in exactly this manner in the *Vedānta Paribhāṣa*.[8]

Śaṅkara, so far as we know, is the first to write that the formula *sat-cit-ānanda* constitutes the essential definition of *brahman*. His *Taittirīya Bhāṣya* II.1.1 expressly puts his stamp of authority on that definition as such, as he declares, "The three words beginning with satya, with qualificatory meanings, are the qualifications of *brahman*."[9] But this effort to define *brahman* thus must face and forestall a possible misunderstanding, especially in view of the definiens-definiendum (*viseṣya-viseṣaṇa*) relation. Advaita should not lend itself to the interpretation such as prevails in realistic systems like *Nyāya-Vaiśeṣika*, which would accept the formula *sat-cit-ānanda* but only as an adjective definition of God the Supreme Being, meaning that *sat*, *cit*, and *ānanda* would be regarded as separate predicates shared, although in a lesser manner, by all beings in their own inherent right. On the grounds of Advaita it can be objected that as defining adjectives are admissible only in order to distinguish an entity from a multitude of other entities of the same nature (*anekāni dravyāni ekajātīyāni*), Advaita would contradict itself if it recognized any other entity to exist in its own right besides *brahman*. Śaṅkara takes full account of this valid objection but argues that there is no scope for such misunderstanding if we understand these words in the defining formula not as actual adjectives but as mere indicators—as that is their meaning—pointing to the invariant entity, *brahman*.[10] The primary import of *viseṣaṇāni* (adjectives) must be sought in their function as *lakṣaṇāni* (indicators), not in their qualifying function.[11] The *Vanamālā* on the *Taittirīya Upaniṣad Bhāṣya* of Śaṅkara, in expounding this point, makes it even clearer that the objective of this threefold definition is not to distinguish *brahman* from any like beings—of which there are none—but to produce grounds for understanding *brahman*'s absoluteness, that is to say, to avoid mistaking *brahman* for any seeming reality (*kalpita-padārtha*) such as space, time, or the *avyakta* (the unmanifest) of the Saṁkhya.

In Advaita there is a call for concrete application of this method of distinguishing *brahman* from seeming entities and to mark it off in this manner. The task is sometimes pursued in the spirit of the *via negativa* (*netivāda*). The most prominent of all concrete instances of this kind of effort is probably in *Vedānta Sūtra* I.4.15, at least in the light of Śaṅkara's commentary. He explains the non-being (*asat*) principle stated in the *Taittirīya* II.7.1, *asadvā idam agra āsīt* ("non-being indeed was this in the beginning"), and in the *Chāndogya* III.19.1, *asadeva idam agra āsīt* ("non-being it is that was in the beginning") thus:

> Considering that the word *sat* is generally known to be used in connection with a thing which has been evolved by name and form, it should be understood that *brahman*, which before creation is of course *sat*,

is here spoken of in a secondary sense, as if it were *asat*, with reference to the fact that before creation there was absence of any differentiation by way of names and forms as is to be seen now in the created world.[12]

With respect to this exegesis of Śaṅkara's—and possibly the *Vedānta Sūtra* which provides the context—we can say only this: the thematization of being as against non-being may not belong to the upaniṣadic texts themselves insofar as there seems to prevail there a total rejection of any such possibility as in the *Kena* passage, I.4a, "other indeed is it than the known as well as the unknown," but there is no point in trying to accomplish here a totally independent exegesis. Even Śaṅkara recognizes that either being or non-being can in principle be assigned to *brahman*, totally depending on with what we first identify being: if it is with the name-form (*nama-rūpa*) phenomena, then *brahman* is to be called non-being. But in any case, it is easy to see that the explicit thematization of being as against non-being arises from Śaṅkara himself.

The course Śaṅkara has adopted has been given greater confirmation by similar exegeses of passages of an opposite kind, as in the context of the *Chāndogya* passage VI.2.1, "Being alone, dear one, was this in the beginning, one without a second." Now that Śaṅkara has been forced to make a choice between being and non-being—which to his own mind could not have been, as observed before, the primary intent of the Vedānta texts—insofar as only one of them can be assigned to *brahman*, he unequivocally makes it in favor of being. He makes the choice because non-being has automatically disqualified itself. Hence being is primarily a category of interpretation-definition; it is also a category of intellectual communication for human beings whose consciousness, phenomenal as it is, is conditioned by the illusion of existence based on awareness of entities that are. In a logical situation of this kind to choose between polar opposites such as being and non-being is inevitable. He obeys the necessity of thematization of the logical opposition between being and non-being and asserts being as the logical principle by means of which one can intellectually grasp the concept *brahman*. He explains the words *sad eva* (being itself) of the text in question as *astitāmātram vastu* ("entity which only exists"). The word *mātram* (only) formally expresses the view that a thing cannot both be and not be, and transcendentally expresses the view that because non-being terminates forever the possibility and worthwhileness of meditating upon *brahman*—the reality which grasps man through the texts and directs him to his goal—such a totally negative concept would do thinking the greatest disservice. Śaṅkara further refers to the notion of pure being which, as a transcendental mental image, responds only to the word *sat* (being).[13]

Śaṅkara further implies another choice imposed by reason of the individuation of the world as well as of oneself in human experience.

Accordingly, one has to make a choice between what is pointed to as 'this' intentionally, as against every 'non-this' in every concrete mode of experience as well as of speaking. So we have to add to the general notion of being the notion of 'this' (*idam*). Thus *brahman* as being also becomes the conceptual object of the word 'this.'[14] In a certain place Śaṅkara even makes the word 'this' in the sentence, "this is *ātman*" (*ayamātmā*), an object of pointing with a gesture of the hand. "The word 'this,' meaning that which appears divided into four quarters, is pointed out as the innermost self with a gesture as in a drama by the statement 'this is *ātman*.'"[15] Śaṅkara does not stop here, however, in the comment referred to above on the *Chāndogya* passage, but goes on, as he must, to explain "one only" (*ekam eva*) and "without a second" (*advītīyam*) so as to disavow any difference in *brahman* of a homogeneous, heterogeneous, or inherent (*sajātīya*, *vijātīya*, *svagata*) kind. This shows that insofar as *brahman* is to be grasped intellectually in a response to man's having been first grasped by *brahman* in the texts, the notion of being as it refers to *brahman* must be regarded in the sense of alone being, without any distinctions within or without.

The foregoing paragraph would lead us to consider the need for the three terms *sat*, *cit*, and *ānanda*, used as the essential definition (*svarūpalakṣaṇa*) of *brahman*. Would not *sat* be enough, for what is more comprehensive than being? It has been suggested that the subject of all definition is one and the same *brahman*; the concept *sat* is not per se the subject of definition, rather it is that by means of which a definition, albeit a necessary and inescapable one, is accomplished. But *sat* also becomes the subject of definition derivatively. It may very well be that this derivative character of *sat* as the subject of definition acts as the ground for the *taṭasthalakṣaṇa* kind of definition of *brahman* which aims at comprehending the structures of the world, time, space, and all possible relativities. The notion of the 'this' is implicit in *brahman*, but not necessarily implicit in *sat*, which could be interpreted as a vague and general concept of being.

The concept of being needs to be bounded if it is to serve as a definition of *brahman*—the possibility of all kinds of differences must be removed and oneness asserted. Further it has to be explicitly pointed out as 'this.' In order to do that, the further concepts of *cit* and *ānanda* become necessary. Obviously they are not artificial contrivances, not even the result of any elaborate methodological introspection. So *cit* is just that without which being cannot be present—in fact it is that through which being is always present. The famous dialogue between Yājñavalkya and Janaka (*Bṛhadāraṇyaka Upaniṣad* IV.3.1–6) enunciates it so powerfully, concluding thus: "When the sun has set, Yājñavalkya, and the moon has set, and the fire has gone out and speech has stopped, what light does a person here have? The self, indeed, is his light, said he, for with the self indeed as light, one sits, moves about, does one's work and returns."[16]

And further, *cit*, the Vedānta understands, leads to *ānanda*; *brahman* is *ānanda*.[17] Again, how *cit* implies *ānanda* must not be misunderstood in the sense that the concept of *cit* formally entails the concept of *ānanda*. Rather, *ānanda* should be undertood as a presence in *cit*, but insofar as its presence is not a mere fortuitous occurrence in any localized, fortuitous consciousness it must straightway be called *brahman*.

The 'this'-ness of *sat* is deepened, in fact made concrete, by means of *cit* and *ānanda*. There have been differences of opinion in the traditional literature as to whether the three words provide three individual and separate definitions or one single definition, although, according to both, of the same subject (*brahman*).[18] These discussions are somewhat hair-splitting and must not occupy us. There is agreement, as spelled out by Madhusūdana Sarasvatī, that through their *lakṣaṇaśakti* (power of signification) the three words refer to the one object *brahman*, though through *abhidhā* (analytic presentation of that which qualifies and that which is qualified separately) each denotes a different conceptual entity: reality as marked by the absence of falsity (*sat*), ignorance (*cit*), limitation/sorrow (*ānanda*), respectively. Madhusūdana and his predecessor Citsukha have forged this theory under the caption of their comprehensive theory of *akhaṇḍārtha* (indivisible meaning of statements).[19] But these technical elaborations are not apposite here. The important thing is to see how a formula like *satyam-jñānam-anantam brahma* (or its variant as we more frequently have been using) explicates the implicit 'this'-ness. This formula (like some other sentences) yields an *akhaṇḍārtha*, which must be appropriated by another paradigm formula *tat tvam asi* (that thou art). What is already implicitly present as the meaning of the first formula—the 'this'-ness of being—is made absolutely explicit and concrete by means of the second utterance. 'That' and 'thou' are considered, respectively, to carry the *akhaṇḍārtha* of the two formulas: *satyam-jñānam-anantam/ānandam* and *tat tvam asi*. Obviously, the latter is considered a more inclusive one as far as completing the process of pointing out to man that 'that' is 'this,' and thereby announcing the presence of being. According to Madhusūdana at least, the first is an elaboration of the word-meaning (*padārtha*) of 'that,' while the latter is a sentence-meaning (*vākyārtha*) and hence that which completes the former. The pertinent thing to be noted here is that the 'this' of being has become as concrete and as definite as it can be because it is pointed to as 'thou.'

Some Concluding Observations

A discerning study of Advaita literature will bring home the truth that the pursuit of being was undertaken in the form of two dominant inquiries, centered around, respectively, the problem of the meaning of linguistic expressions and statements and the problem of the real, of being (*satya*) versus the false (*mithyā*). This is even more true of the post-Śaṅkara dialecticians, as they are sometimes called, than of the earlier literature.

As we have seen something of the meaning problem, we must at least take a quick glance at the even more agonizing problem of reality versus falsity, just in order to see what effect it had on ontology. Here we see a tremendous shift in the burden of the whole problem of being, which we see moving in a particular path. No doubt it could not have been otherwise for Advaita as we know it. The great preoccupation with this can be gauged only by the varieties of clever dialectical arguments advanced in support of it. Even the question of the real (*satya*), in a sense, moves into the shadow, and the issue of falsity (*mithyātva*) and how to define it adequately occupies the center of the philosophical stage. To be sure, this problem was taken up with vigor and passion not for its own sake but indirectly in the interests of the real—being. When the false is negated the real shines by itself.

In fact that which complements the question of being or the real is not the question of non-being. Probably partly because the word *satya* often serves for both being and the real, any thought of non-being cannot arise as distinct from the unreal. The unreal has been ruled out as mere logical contradiction like "the son of a barren woman."

There has seldom been in Vedānta a problem of non-being as such, as the possibility of non-being having any depth has not been entertained. In truth, *asat* seems to be a mere nullity, and one is not encouraged to waste one's thought on a nullity. The case is clearly different in Buddhism where *śūnya* (nothingness), which comprehends all existences, inevitably has depth.

The formal opposition in Advaita is no longer between *sat* and *asat* but between *satya* and *mithyā*. The care invested in unraveling the character of *mithyā* as that which is neither *sat* nor *asat* through some very skillful definitions is indeed impressive. *Mithyā*, as a third category apart from being and non-being, takes the center of the philosophical stage for several later advaitins.

Five definitions of falsity (*mithyātva*) are usually listed:[20]

1. As that which is not the locus of either *sat* or *asat* (*sadasattvānadhikaraṇatvam vā mithyātvam*). Here the false is distinguished from both of them. *Sat* implies non-contradictability or irremovability, which in turn implies non-temporality. *Asat* cannot appear at all. But something (which we call the world) appears, which is also temporal. Hence what appears is neither *sat* nor *asat*. This is the definition of Padmapāda in the *Pancapādika*.

2. As that which is eternally negated in the same locus where it is

cognized (*pratipannopādhau traikālikaniṣedhapratiyogitvam vā mithyātvam*). For example, when a man mistakes a rope for a snake, he first perceives the snake in the rope, but when he comes closer he perceives the rope for what it is. The false snake appears in the rope temporarily but cannot persist through the three tenses of time. This is given by Prakāśātman in the *Pancapādikavivaraṇa*.

3. Another definition is given by Prakāśātman, viz., as that which is dissolved by knowledge (*jñānanivartakam*). It means that what appears as the content of illusion-induced cognition and ceases with the cognition of the real content is false.

4. That whose locus is equally the locus of its eternal negation (*svāśrayaniṣṭhātyantābhāvapratiyogitvam*). This, given by Citsukha in the *Tattvapradīpikā*, appears to be the same as Prakāsātman's first definition.

5. As simply other than *sat* (*sadviviktatvam*) it is given by Anandabodha in the *Nyāyaratnadīpavalī*. Obviously, it does not recognize non-being at all.

It may be observed that although the problem of being has been pursued in Advaita in this particular form, sometimes to the exclusion of other possibilities, and although non-being has been literally consigned to itself, that is to say, to the state of a non-problem, there is no doubt that the depth of being (as *satcitānanda*) has continued to be a source of infinite challenge and infinite fascination for Advaita. Here, too, thought is the extension of being, and this guarantees the continued existence of Advaita as a philosophy. It may even be believed, certainly from the Vedānta point of view, that the possibility of philosophy itself rests in the infinite challenge and fascination of being.

This calls for some very general reflections, which, seen in the right perspective, will not appear as intrusions. First, it may be observed that despite all the great depth of thought on the question characteristic of Advaita, to the extent that it chose to focus a great part of it on the *mithyātva* problem, it might appear that the general existential condition which initially called forth the particular resolution that *mithyātva* itself is, viz., the collision between being and non-being and the shock it produces, felt as existence, may have been pushed into the shadow. The threat of the impending victory of non-being and the fear that it may prevail, both in terms of personal and universal life, has not a little to do with man's turning his attention to the question of being. The shock-waves produced by this collision and the inevitable pervasion of being by non-being and non-being by being, is, it was understood by the ancient thinkers, including the Buddha, what constitutes what is known as *saṁsāra*. As *saṁsāra* is, in this way at least, dynamic in that it is the realm generated by the shock-waves from the collision of being and non-being, there is a call for a philosophy of the world different from that which has been registered by the doctrine of *mithyātva*. This suggestion is perhaps not out of place here as it concerns one of the outstanding issues arising from Advaita ontology. On the other side of the ledger, it is certain that, in spite of the inhibition with regard to a philosophy of the world, Advaita, insofar as it dwells on *brahman* as it does, unveils the possibility of standing steadfastly in being.

The reason for this particular turn—toward *mithyātva* as the central problem governing being, with all that it entails—may be stated briefly as a second general observation. The esoteric-exoteric distinction is an old one in the Vedānta, as we know it in the two forms of knowledge, *parāvidyā* and *aparāvidyā*. But that is not what we have in mind when we say that the esoteric as a dimension of thought, particularly pertaining to being, as against the exoteric, seems to have been pushed into the shadow. The debates of philosophy (or dialectics, as some Indian writers nowadays call it), through which not only Advaita but all *darśanas* grew, seem to typify rather the exoteric character of thought in spite of the unmistakable skill and subtlety which pervade it. The esoteric no doubt lives, but more as part of the various *vidyās* of mysticism rather than philosophic thought itself. No doubt the exoteric *tarka* philosophy is well balanced, even in Advaita, with an ample mystical literature. In the ancient times this was true, even in the Upaniṣads, but mystically oriented rituals mediated with thought, even acting as signposts of thought. That, no doubt, we can only try to re-live today by understanding, not by actually duplicating. The question is, having been reduced to thinking of being—the alternative is not to think of it at all—without the traditional signposts, is it not possible for Advaita to show the way to incorporate the symbols of its mysticism—not as realization techniques (*sādhanā*), which is what they are—but as signposts also for thought? That may be one way of avoiding the typical bifurcation of our striving after being into the exotericism of *mithyāvāda* and its attendant *vādas* and the esotericism of ritual mysticism. At this point this is no more than a question, perhaps even an idle question.

Notes

1. Caroline Rhys Davids in a treatise, *To Become or Not to Become* (London: Luzac, 1937) examines the problem posed by the two roots, *as* and *bhū*. Much of her discussion is very useful, although her main argument seems to be erroneous. In reference to the famous statement of the *Chāndogya Upaniṣad*, *tat tvam asi* (that thou

art), she argues that the original verb must have been the dynamic *bhavasi* (from *bhū*), meaning "becomes," and some later editor changed it into *asi*. From there she draws the implausible conclusion that the statement as it originally was, in form, in part, or both, "fails to give any support to that sanctity of Being (*Sat*) on which Vedantist teaching has leaned so heavily," p. 43.

2. Sources of quotations are given in the text. Translations are my own unless otherwise indicated.

3. R.D. Ranade observes: "Commentators on this passage who do not want a privative conception like not-Being to be the 'arche' of all things, rightly understand this passage to signify that at the very beginning of things it was 'as if' nothing existed and not that not-Being was verily the first concrete existent, and that it was from such a semblance of non-existence that Being was created. We could very well conceive how philosophers like Śaṅkarācharya who believe in an ultimate Being would explain such a passage. . . ." *A Constructive Survey of Upanishadic Philosophy* (Poona: Oriental Book Agency, 1926), p. 81.

4. *bṛhattamatvat brahma,* Śaṅkara's *Commentary on the Taittirīya Upaniṣad* (II.1), Sanskrit text, ed. V.G. Apte (Poona: Anandasrama, 1929), p. 45.

5. *Kena Upaniṣad* I.3. trans. S. Radhakrishnan, *The Principal Upaniṣads* (London: Allen & Unwin, 1953), p. 582.

6. *yad dhi karaṇagocaram tad anyasmā upadeṣṭum śakyam jātiguṇakrīyāviśeṣaṇaiḥ. na tajjātyādi viśeṣaṇavad brahma,* Śaṅkara's Commentary on the *Kena Upaniṣad*, Sanskrit text, ed. V.G. Apte (Poona: Anandasrama, 1934), p. 9.

7. Śaṅkara's Commentary on the *Kena Upaniṣad*, p. 9.

8. *svarūpameva lakṣaṇam svarūpalakṣaṇam.* Also, *yāvallaksyakālam anavasthitatve sati lakṣaṇatvam taṭasthalakṣaṇam iti. The Vedānta Paribhāṣā,* ed. Anantakrishna Sastri (Calcutta: University of Calcutta Press, 1930), p. 281, cf. p. 278.

9. *satyādini trīni viśeṣaṇārdhāni padāni viśeṣasyaḥ brahmaṇaḥ,* Śaṅkara's *Commentary on the Taittirīya Upaniṣad,* p. 47.

10. *lakṣaṇārthatvāt viśeṣāṇānam,* ibid., p. 48.

11. *lakṣaṇapradhānāni viśeṣaṇāni naviśeṣaṇapradhānāni,* ibid.

12. *Brahma-Sūtra Shānkara-Bhāshya,* trans. V.M. Apte, (Bombay: Popular Book Depot, 1960), p. 253.

13. *sat kevala, sac cabdabuddhimātra gamyameva.* Cf. Ganganath Jha's translation of the *Chāndogya Upaniṣad* with the *Commentary of Śaṅkara,* (Poona: Oriental Book Agency, 1942), p. 296. He uses the word "responsible" instead of "responds" as I do, which is incorrect.

14. *idam śabdabuddhiviṣayaḥ.* Cf. Jha, ibid.

15. *abhinayena nirdiśati āyam ātmeti,* Śaṅkara's *Commentary on the Māṇḍūkya Upaniṣad,* Sanskrit text, ed. V.G. Apte, with Gauḍapāda's *Māṇḍūkya kārikā* (Poona: Anandasrama, 1936), p. 13. Cf. The *Māṇḍūkya Upaniṣad with Śaṅkara's Commentary and Gaudapāda kārikā,* trans. Swami Nikhilananda (Mysore: Sri Ramakrishna Ashram, 1955), p. 12.

16. The *Bṛhadāraṇyaka Upaniṣad* IV.3–6, trans. S. Radhakrishnan, *The Principal Upaniṣads,* p. 256.

17. *ānando brahmeti,* The *Taittirīya Upaniṣad* III.6.1.

18. Brahmānanda Sarasvatī's gloss on the *Siddhāntabindu,* called the *Ratnāvalī,* takes the view that the three constitute essentially a single definition, as otherwise

there is a risk of three reals being implied. The *Vedānta Paribhāṣā* refutes this view that they are three separate definitions and that the danger envisaged by the author of the gloss on the *Siddhāntabindu* (*purvamuktam bindutīkānusārena*) does not arise (*pratyekalakṣaṇam api na dosāyeti*), *Vedānta Paribhāṣā*, pp. 278–79.

19. The *akhaṇḍārtha* theory is propounded and elaborately discussed in Citsukha's *Tattvapradīpīkā* and Madhusūdana Sarasvatī's *Advaita Siddhi*. For a cursory acquaintance with this, see Sanjukta Gupta, *Studies in the Philosophy of Madhusudana Sarasvati* (Calcutta: Sanskrit Pustak Bhandar, 1966), pp. 159–69. There is much stake on the concept of *akhaṇḍa* (impartite) in Advaita. Vidyāranya (*Pancadaśī* II.20), speaks of three kinds of difference: (1) between the roots, trunk, leaves, and fruits of the self-same tree; (2) between one tree and another; (3) between a tree and a stone. See *Pancadaśī*, trans. H.P. Sastri (London: Shanti Sodan, 1954). Cf. Nṛsimhasarasvati's definition of *akhaṇḍa*, along the same lines, for which see *The Philosophy of the Vedānta* and the *Vedānta Sāra*, P. Deussen and G.A. Jacob (Calcutta: Susil Gupta, 1957), p. 33.

20. For a comprehensive view of this, see Nirod Baran Chakraborty, *The Advaita Concept of Falsity* (Calcutta: Sanskrit College, 1967), pp. 48–78.

Recommended Reading in English

Texts

Brahma-Sūtra Shānkara-Bhāshya: Bādarayana's Brahma-Sūtras with Shankarāchar-ya's commentary. Bombay: Popular Book Depot, 1960, or *The Vedānta Sūtras of Bādarāyana with the Commentary by Śaṅkara*, pts. 1 and 2 trans. George Thibaut. New York: Dover, 1962.

The Bṛhadāraṇyaka Upaniṣad, with the Commentary of Śaṅkarācārya, trans. Swami Madhavananda. Mayavati, Almora: Advaita Ashrama, 1950.

The Māṇḍūkya Upaniṣad, with Śaṅkara's commentary and Gaudapāda's *Māndūkya Kārikā*, trans. Swami Nikhilananda. Mysore: Sri Ramakrishna Ashram, 1955.

The Chāndogya Upaniṣad, with the *Commentary of Śaṅkara*, trans. Ganganath Jha. Poona: Oriental Book Agency, 1942.

The Pancapādika of Padmapāda (Gaekwad Oriental Series), trans. and ed. D. Venketaramaiah. Baroda: Oriental Institute, 1948.

The Vedānta Paribhāṣā of Dharmrāja Adhvarindra, trans. and annot. Swami Madhavananda. Calcutta: Ramakrishna Mission, 1963.

The Saṁkṣapasārīraka of Sarvajnātman, Introduction, English translation, and notes by N. Veezhinathan. Madras: University of Madras, 1972.

The Sambandha-Vārtika of Sureśvara. Edited with English translation, introduction, and notes, by T.M.P. Mahadevan. Madras: University of Madras, 1972.

The Siddhāntaleśasangraha of Appayya Dikṣita, vol. 1. English translation by S.S. Suryanarayana Sastri. Madras: University of Madras, 1935.

Advaita Siddhi of Madhusūdana Sarasvatī, trans. Ganganath Jha, ed. G. Jha and G. Thibaut. Serialized in *Indian Thought Series*, Allahabad, vols. 6–9, 1914–17.

Secondary Literature

Mahadevan, T.M.P. *The Philosophy of Advaita*. Madras: Ganesh, 1969.

Warrier, A.G. Krishna. *The Concept of Mukti in Advaita Vedānta*. Madras: University of Madras, 1961.

Sundaram, P.K. *Advaita Epistemology*, with special reference to *Iṣṭasiddhi*. Madras: University of Madras, 1968.

Sastri, Ashutosh Bhattacharyya. *Studies in Post-Śaṅkara Dialectics*. Calcutta: University of Calcutta, 1942.

Chakraborty, Nirod Baran. *The Advaita Concept of Falsity: A Critical Study*. Calcutta: Sanskrit College, 1967.

Gupta, Sanjukta. *Studies in the Philosophy of Madhusūdana Sarasvatī*. Calcutta: Sanskrit Pustak Bhandar, 1966.

MERVYN SPRUNG

Being and the Middle Way

The Problem

"What is one the wise call by many names." *To ontōs on*, *ousia*, *brahman*, *nirvāṇa*, *sat*, *tao*, *Sein*, being, god, are some of the many names. Whatever the range of difference among them, the many names are one in this sense: they stand for what the proponent thinker is in search of, for what is wanting in his thought. In these ways each names what the thinker wants to know; what, knowing, he can rest in, or what, knowing, he knows everything; not everything as in omniscience, but the truth of everything; he knows what, on being known, leaves nothing further to be known. The end of the philosopher's thought, so he understands himself, with only few exceptions, is something that can be thought. It is, in some sense, an object of thought, though, of course, an object unique in that it does not permit itself to be further thought about. This may disqualify it as an object in the plain sense, yet the end of thought yields knowledge, we commonly think. Thought must end in knowledge, for the alternatives are not acceptable: feeling (poetry, religion) on the one extreme; action (politics, engineering) on the other. If not these, what else but knowledge is yielded in philosophical thinking?

The functions—cosmological, ontological, redemptive—which the end of thought, variously named being, *sat*, *Sein*, and so on, serves, vary by philosopher, though some are commoner than others. It is often understood as cause or source of everything that is other than itself; sometimes as the most universal, irreducible fact; sometimes as what makes saving, redemptive sense out of a senseless, ulcerous existence; sometimes as immanent spirit, *telos*. It usually serves a fusion of functions: it is fact, cause, saving sense, in varying ways. Commonly it must function as ground—a strong blend of logical rigor and source: the ground of things allows us to understand them as we think they must be.

The end of thought, however it is understood to be related to everyday things, must, by its purpose, be:

1. Invariant. Should the end of philosophic thought prove to be changeable, philosophic thought would know that it was not the end: it would persist relentlessly, hopefully, assuming that there must be a

cause or ground or source of such change—and that *that* would be the end.

2. Not itself caused by or grounded in anything else.

3. The preferred way of understanding ourselves and the everyday world.

4. Most important, and the precise launching point of this paper, accessible to thought, discovered by thought, as understood by thought and so must count as known, thus is an object of knowledge (however carefully we disqualify most of, or all, everyday kinds of knowing from the philosophic enterprise).

The ability of any of the natural languages available to us to carry the weight of investigations such as these is of course a question which cannot go unmentioned. When we have said everything we can say grammatically and etymologically about the focal words, 'being,' '*Sein*,' '*sat*,' '*einai*,' and so on, and are alive to the varieties of literal, metaphorical, analogical meanings they have in our philosophies, then the problem of the philosopher's distinctive object of knowledge has not been reduced to a flagrant case of the misuse of words. Is it not rather that such words, however sensitively used, or clumsily misused, are the philosopher's way of living with the necessities of thought; that these necessities generate his use of words as much as the available words form or constrain his understanding? In dogmatic brevity: the philosopher's effort to think his way to the end is, as undeniably as it is understood in each case *through* language, just as undeniably not a problem *of* language; it is a problem of what, in spite of misuse, language is capable of yielding to thought in the way of meaning. Let it be agreed that these focal terms are monuments to the crippled struggle of the philosopher to grasp what they point his thinking toward. They are indeed language stoppages; they mark failure in a sense. But if they are stoppages, it is not because they stop thought, but because thought stops in them. And if they fail to express and to convince, it is not because thinking has gone astray, but because what they are about does not relate to language by means of more language. They are end terms.

That the philosopher's object of knowledge may be different from our everyday understanding of an object of knowledge has occurred to most. That it may be an object of knowledge only by a convention of speech has only recently become openly propounded. Among those who consider philosophy to be more than "talk about talk" most still understand the implicit purpose of what they are doing to be some form or mode of knowing—however knowing may be understood. Whatever philosophy is, it is at least not poetry, or histrionics, or manipulation. It has not often occurred to philosophers that the end of philosophy may be *mis*understood as knowing; that it may not be a mode of knowing in any sense; that the end of philosophy may, indeed, be just that: its ending, its termination, conceivably as the transmutation of knowing into something else.

The Mādhyamika School of Buddhism

Such is my understanding of what those philosophers who have written about the problem of being have thought they were doing. This paper attempts to close with a philosophy which is certainly no less earnest than those I have had in mind so far, but which understands the capability of thought, the end of thought, in a radically other way. It is a philosophy which winds its way as a continuous thread through centuries of Indian intellectual history but takes its clearest and final form in the Mādhyamika school of Indian Buddhism. This is the school of the so-called Middle Way—strictly, the school of the 'middlers' or 'middlemosters,' which derives from one Nāgārjuna, of the second century A.D. The text I shall be working from primarily is a commentary on Nāgārjuna's *Middle Way Stanzas* by Candrakīrti, of the seventh century A.D., called by him the serene or clear-worded, the *Prasannapadā*.[1] There are other schools of Buddhist philosophy—some pluralist, some realist, some idealist—and their thought about being is greatly different from Nāgārjuna's. His, however, is the most extreme and somehow the most contemporaneous.

Now Nāgārjuna, a true Buddhist and Indian, understood himself not to be working out a novel philosophy—though he was—but to be returning faithfully to the words and intentions of Buddha with a view to making them intelligible to his own time by removing erroneous interpretations.

His philosophy of the middle way (*madhyamā pratipad*) is not intelligible abstracted from the tradition of Buddhist thought, which had its source in the discourses, conversations, and sayings of Buddha as preserved in the Buddhist canon. Vast as that is, the thread which leads directly to Nāgārjuna, which he followed on his return to the sources, can be singled out readily. I must try to interpret the Four Aryan Truths as I believe Nāgārjuna must have understood them, and I wish to go to one of the many passages in which Buddha speaks of the middle way—a passage to which Nāgārjuna refers explicitly; this is the brief exchange known as the *Kātyāyana Sūtra*. From such beginnings I hope to show how it came about that the Mādhyamika school knowingly, radically, audaciously attempted to deny the term 'being' any philosophical content, putting in its place the non-cognitive term 'middle way.'

Buddhist Beginnings

It is universally recognized that Buddhist thought from the beginning was modal, non-substantive. All things, inner and outer, are seen as kaleidoscopic complexes of simple qualities—and nothing more. But by far the full weight of the original Buddhist grasp of existence is not given in this way.

In the Buddha's first discourse—which concerns the so-called Four Aryan Truths—all the truths are expressed in terms of *duḥkha*.[2] All the factors composing a personal world (*skandhas*) are *duḥkha*. All process in time—origination, decay, cessation—is *duḥkha*. To be deprived of the desired while bonded to the undesired is *duḥkha*. This is the first truth. *Duḥkha* is here not an adjective describing "life" or "existence" as sorrowful. It is the nature of existence, of unregenerate, afflicted, everyday existence. It is the name for such existence—a name created, clearly, by one standing outside of it.

The second truth is that *duḥkha* arises from a cause or, as the Buddhists have it, "in dependence on something"; this cause is given as *taṅhā*. *Taṅhā* appears to be the underived, unaccountable hunger of all beings for existence and more existence—for rebirth. It expresses itself in the pursuit of and attachment to pleasurable experiences and objects. *Duḥkha*, accordingly, is not the nature of an immutable reality autonomously imposed upon men. *Duḥkha* arises from an identifiable cause—hunger for pleasurable existence—which lies in men themselves.

And, the third truth is that *duḥkha* can be brought to an end by removing the cause. The everyday world of persons—*duḥkha*—will cease, will no longer arise when *taṅhā* ceases.

The last of the four truths, that there is a path (*mārga*), a life discipline leading to the cessation of *duḥkha*, strengthens the point I am making—the world is not a reality apart from men—but adds nothing new. This path is not synonomous with the middle way (*madhyamā pratipad*), the key notion of the Mādhyamika school, as I shall attempt to make very clear.[3]

These four truths are not a tactic for happiness: they are philosophically radical. They do not invoke the notion of a reality standing over against men and indifferent to the human presence; they give us to understand existence as mutable; they reveal the everyday world as a summons to action—the action of remaking it. Buddhism, in its beginning, issued from a total posture which did not ask "What is?" or "What can I know?" but rather, "How is freedom from *duḥkha* achieved?" The questions "What is?" and "What can I know?" are subordinated to the question "What must I do?" Thus far the Four Aryan Truths.

Before taking up the arguments of the Mādhyamika school, there is a second element in early Buddhism which should be recalled. Nāgārjuna mentions in one of his verses (unusual for him) an early *sūtra*, the *Kātyāyana*.[4] In it Buddha repudiates the two dogmas: (1) what is is perishable and (2) what is is imperishable. Candrakīrti enlarges on this text by quoting from another: "What avoids these two dogmas is said to be without a specific nature, beyond proof, not dependent, unmanifest, without an abode, not to be known conceptually. It is, Kāśyapa, the middle way: it is the right way of regarding the true nature of things."[5] To regard what arises as neither existing nor as not existing is to see it truly (*yathābhūtam*). This insight is then said to be "not dependent on anything other than itself." These early, trenchant, seminal thoughts echo and mature into philosophic self-awareness in the Mādhyamika school several hundred years after they were presumably spoken.

Investigation into *Svabhāva*

From the wealth of Nāgārjuna's *Madhyamaka Kārikās* and Candrakīrti's serene commentary, the *Prasannapadā*, it may perhaps be helpful to single out one investigation, that of 'self-existence' (*svabhāva*), in order to approach an understanding of the middle way, the term which in my view takes the place of the concepts being and non-being in Mādhyamika thought.[6] *Svabhāva* can with equal etymological right be given in English as 'self-being.' 'Self-existence' is preferred because the term 'being,' with its Western ontological overtones, is less appropriate to Buddhist thinking. In any case the term embraces, but does not distinguish, both what we call essence or nature and being or existence.

The analysis of *svabhāva* begins with an attack on prevailing Buddhist metaphysics, which commonly held that the elements of existence (*dharmas*), which arise and perish in the temporal flux, are self-existent. A seed, which is self-existent, gives rise to a seedling, likewise self-existent; the self-existent factor of ignorance in a personal destiny gives rise to self-existent character dispositions. Thus the prevailing view. Yet it is universally agreed that self-existence means "to be itself in and through itself."[7] This, however, is incompatible with the self-existence of particular elements, and for two reasons. All particular elements arise from causes; what arises from causes is created; what is created does not exist "in and through itself." Again, all particular elements are dependent on what is other than themselves. 'Long,' 'short,' 'this side,' 'other side' are examples. But what is dependent cannot be "in and through itself." Clearly the concepts 'self-existence' and 'particular element' are incompatible and one or the other must be given up. It is unintelligible to say that anything which can be constitutive of perishable things or situations can be self-existent. As we will see, Mādhyamika gives up the notion of the self-existent particular and retains the notion of self-existence for other purposes.

A word of caution: our accustomed distinction between particulars and universals is here not decisive. Both are thought to enter into things and situations which perish. Therefore both are perishable. Neither is conceded self-existence. The distinction here is between whatever enters into things and situations as nameable constituents, and that embraces both particulars and universals (I use the term 'ontic' to name such constituents) and what does not so enter, namely, the self-existent. Whether this enters into things and situations in any way has not yet been made clear.

At this point in the exposition an imaginary opponent accuses the Mādhyamika of being nihilist, that is, of holding that the elements in the temporal flux are *not* self-existent. Paraphrased, this seems to mean that elements must be non-existent. Candrakīrti repudiates this charge, which brings the reader up short. Has he not been arguing that elements cannot be said to exist in any clear sense? Yet Candrakīrti denies that, having shown that we cannot hold that particulars are self-existent, we are therefore committed to the view that they are *not* self-existent.

This is the first hint of the paradox which lies at the heart of the Mādhyamika position. In response to the direct question, "Is there a self-existent nature in particular things?" the answer, equally direct, is given, "The heat of fire neither exists nor does not exist as an inherent nature"; this may be paraphrased: "Particular things (ontic elements) neither exist nor do they not exist."[8] This is not a double negative, but the assertion that it is equally false to say that ontic elements are self-existent, and that ontic elements are not self-existent. This is of course puzzling or worse but we are not ready yet to ask for the resolution of the puzzlement.

We have seen up to this point that the Mādhyamika refuses to take the things of the everyday world as either truly existing or truly not existing. But how does the common misprehension arise according to which the things we live with—inner and outer—are 'real,' as we say? It arises, Candrakīrti explains, because men would be afraid of the truth. They can endure only a reassuring world. To this end, men project into, superimpose upon, impute to the seeming things around them, gratuitously but not arbitrarily, the notion of self-existence, and this gives rise to the reassuring everyday world. This projection, superimposition, or imputation arises from the dynamic of human needs and ignorance.

The imaginary opponent, not yet silenced, might still ask, "Well, but what does this notion 'self-existence' which, you say, is not *in* things but is imputed *to* them, have as a meaning?" This is a fair question and a momentous one. The Mādhyamika is ready, contrary to his reputation, to give an answer.

Candrakīrti says that self-existence is the quintessential nature of all things; and that is their devoidness of particular, ontic character (*śūnyatā*); and that is the way things really are (*tattvam*)—invariable through all time.[9] "Whatever it is in fire and other things which does not come into existence at any point in time, because it is not created, *that* is said to be its self-existent nature."[10]

Candrakīrti tells us here that the self-existence *of* things is their not existing as things. The demon of Mādhyamika, *śūnyatā*—the illusoriness of particular being—is unleashed at this point to transmute a logically difficult question. And *śūnyatā* is said to be *tattvam*—the way things truly are. Elsewhere Nāgārjuna develops the notion *tattvam*. "Not dependent on anything other than itself, at peace, not manifested as named-thing, beyond thought construction, not of varying form—this is *tattvam*—the way things are truly."[11]

The Mādhyamika Problem

This would seem to be the end of the matter: self-existence has been defined. Indeed, it is only the beginning. How can Nāgārjuna so crudely contradict himself as to define the indefinable, what he says is "beyond thought construction"? The commentary says, somewhat laconically, "Even though what language is to name comes to an end, nonetheless the way things truly are must be spoken of in terms drawn from the transactional realm accepting the everyday judgments, 'this is real,' 'that is unreal,' and so on." How can language from a transactional realm serve in speaking of what is essentially other than transaction? How can such an attempt, on the face of it ill-fated, be understood with credit? My understanding of the attempt is the central concern of this paper.

The notion I wish to work with is, as I have said, 'way'—or, 'middle way'—but the technical term which will point us in that direction is *prajñapti*. Much has been said about this term, but, in my view, not enough. *Prajñapti* has, in Mādhyamika usage, two meanings, a general and a peculiar one. In general all words which would name anything are *prajñaptis*: that is, nothing is found in the object to which they point, which corresponds uniquely to the putative name. For example, the name 'chariot' corresponds to no ontic element over and above the components of a chariot. In its peculiar sense a *prajñapti* is only such a name as leads, via the Buddhist discipline, to the Buddhist truth. The term *svabhāva*, for example, which was analytically nonsense, yet led, by some hidden connection, unerringly to the truth of things. That other names, e.g., matter, atom, self, do not have this odd power sets the problem. How is it that a *prajñapti* can guide or conduct, without giving knowledge in the ordinary sense?

How will the Mādhyamika justify using ordinary language—the only language there is—to speak of the way things are really? In fact, at this point in his exposition, Candrakīrti, apparently not knowing how else to proceed—having denied himself the right to define self-existence—has recourse to the Buddhist wise man—the *yogī*. Candrakīrti does not have the *yogī* say anything: the wise man does not inform us how things are, really. Candrakīrti adopts what may be called a functional approach; he refers to a certain context—the *yogī*'s world—and says that what is present there is self-existent; the way things are for the *yogī* is the way they truly are. What the ordinary man misapprehends as a world of things "that and nothing else as it is realized in their singular way of seeing by the wise ones who are rid of the defect of ignorance, has self-existence."[12] The wise one, it is said further, taking things neither as existent nor as non-existent, proceeds on his way. In short, the way the wise man takes things is the only permissible understanding of the formulation concerning *tattvam*, the way things truly are: "Not dependent on anything other than itself . . ." and so on.

It will surely occur to one that seeming things, which neither exist nor do not exist, must be chimeras; but it is not so. Their nature is as they give themselves to the wise man or as he takes them. Up to this point we have been following an exposition of the text. There now arise some special questions which will demand interpretation beyond the text.

The problem left us by Nāgārjuna and Candrakīrti is this: How can a term 'self-existence,' which has been discredited in its everyday use, serve, nonetheless, to understand the truth? Self-existence, as *śūnyatā*, has been declared a *prajñapti*. *Prajñapti* is frequently translated as 'metaphor.' But this does not help here, because the primary meaning of self-existence, i.e., the self-existence of things, has been shown to be nonsensical. Nonsense can hardly be transferred, as such, to the truth; so there can be no metaphor. And in fact the Mādhyamika has argued that the truth is not to be understood as self-existent *things* are understood. Such repudiation is hardly a basis for metaphor. I find the same difficulty in taking the Mādhyamika's understanding of the truth as self-existent to be an analogy. How can an analogy hold between what, at the one pole (the everyday) does not exist, and what, at the other (*tattvam*), rejects this misconception as inapplicable?

Perhaps Kant's *transcendentaler Schein* comes closer; I think it does, though, of course, the differences between Kant and the Buddhist are vast and numerous. Still, Kant's ideas of reason give themselves as objects to be known, but are not such. Self-existence appears, at first, to be an equally incorrigible assumption about the way things must be, yet it too proves to be an imputation, not a cognition. Ideas of reason and *prajñaptis* are, however, not arbitrary fictions but apparently indefeasible ways of orienting and understanding ourselves. They are both guiding, conductal notions. That is, their relation to the way things are is not a cognitive one. It is, in a sense, 'practical,' but this should not be pushed very far, for *prajñaptis* are effective at a level beyond the everyday. One difference between Kant and Nāgārjuna is this: Kant held ideas to be inseparable from the faculty of reason; Nāgārjuna held *prajñaptis* to be eradicable through Buddhist discipline.

This places us, I hope, squarely in front of the problem I wish to raise. Nāgārjuna says, in perhaps the most pregnant of all his verses: "That all things arise in dependence is what we mean by devoidness of being [*śūnyatā*]. Now devoidness of being is a guiding, conductal expression based on transactional language [*prajñapti upādāya*]. It is itself the middle way."[13] If the way things are is to be understood neither as existent nor as non-existent, then the very notion of 'is-ing' or 'be-ing' has to be given up. Thought no longer has an assured basis: it lacks the one idea which alone allows thought to be what it takes itself to be: it lacks the possibility of assertion. If nothing 'ises' or 'bes' then there is nothing of which assertions hold good. Thought ceases to achieve knowledge and becomes an internal movement of the mind which realizes another concern and another purpose. In short, the cognition model, the subject-object, I-and-the-world way of orienting ourselves must be given up. This means giving up mystical intuition and other similar explanations of Buddhist insight (*prajñā*) which retain the cognition model. In their place I suggest we consider the merits (and the problems) of another understanding of what it is the Mādhyamika is trying to do.

The Middle Way

This is, as indicated earlier, the notion of 'way,' in Mādhyamika, the 'middle way.' It is decisive to remember that there is here no unbalanced negation of the everyday world. On this way everyday things are neither illusory and so ignored or disdained, nor are they real in themselves and so cherished. What third modus which would be neither affirmative nor negative do we impute to them, then? There is no third modus of 'is-ing.' The truth of all things is given to the wise man in the middle way. And that 'way' is not midway between 'is' and 'not is.' It is to be grasped in non-ontic terms. In the middle way there are no causes or effects, actions or consequences, before and after. The Mādhyamika cannot say *what* things are in this way, for to do so would be to fall back into the illusion of is and not-is. He can say only that *as* they are in this way, so they are in truth, such is *tattvam*.

But, then, is or is not this *tattvam*? The question is inapposite. The vocabulary of 'is' and 'is not' and all its variants does not apply; it has lost its validity. To use it is to distort, to draw down into the everyday what is of another nature. *Existence* and *non-existence* are quite legitimate terms in the realm of cause and effect, action and consequence, explanation and proof, but are not to be used in the realm where causes, actions, and explanations have come to an end. The *prajñapti* 'way' has replaced the *prajñapti* 'existence.' To confuse or interchange the two is to misunderstand the level of truth on which one is thinking. Bluntly, 'existence' is not a legitimate philosophical concept.

At this point a few possible misconceptions should, I think, be considered. It must be understood at once that this is not the philosophy of the '*als ob*,' of the 'as if.' The *yogī* does not orient to things 'as if' they neither were nor were not. He orients, understanding that it is the nature of things neither to be nor not to be. He takes things in their truth. *We* may describe his way of taking things as 'as if,' but that is for our purposes, not his; the everyday for the *yogī* could not be 'as if,' because there is nothing outside the middle way for it to be as, for it, that is, to be compared with.

I need hardly stress now that a 'way' is not composed of a subject and a world. There is no dichotomy of subject and object, inner and outer. It is the cloven everyday, based on such dichotomy that demands and nourishes the notions of person, things, and reality. The middle way is the end of such a cleft and restless world.

It follows that the middle way is not a means to some final truth; it is not a path leading to knowledge. Whatever it is, it is the end of socratizing, of theory, and of knowing. It is the practice of wisdom, not a means to it. It embodies knowledge but is not a knowing.

Again, the middle way is not a means to some goal or end beyond itself. It is not a course of conduct undertaken with a view to attaining some result—perhaps enlightenment. It has often been so understood, but my interpretation of Mādhyamika turns on what I am saying about the middle way. The Mādhyamika philosophers understood themselves to have rediscovered the original Buddhist truth as the truth of the middle way, with the consequences which I am trying to unravel.

The middle way is not knowledge but it is not a practical undertaking either. It renders the dichotomy of theory and practice inapposite. There is no inner or outer here. There are no subjects, no doers, set against a world of objects to be manipulated in doing. The 'way' invalidates such opposition. It is not that the wise man has the approved way of dealing *with* things. There are no things on the middle way; they disappear into the way itself. The 'way *things* really are' (*tattvam*) is the way of the *wise man*. To adapt what Candrakīrti says about *nirvāṇa*, the way supervenes when perception no longer functions as the interpretation of signs, when the manifold of named-things comes to rest, when discursive thought ceases. What this may imply about *praxis*, about the nature of reflective thought, about the value of this preferred mode of human orientation, must remain implication to be drawn out at another time. I believe I have recounted as much as the Mādhyamikas have committed themselves to expressly, and perhaps a little more.

But, again, and for the last time: Is or is not the middle way? The question is inapposite; it neither is nor is not; it is itself a *prajñapti.*

A Final Doubt

A final doubt and suspicion: Does the Mādhyamika not abandon philosophical thought in favor of a religious goal perhaps because he found no tenable conclusions? And is this not cowardly and defeatist? If he had, it would be and we would lose interest in his thought.

Nāgārjuna is, I find, determined to stay with reason as long as it makes sense to do so. His concern as a philosopher is to bind all things together in sense. He tests all theories known to him, and in the end he rejects ontological categories as ways of making sense. Only the devoidness of being (*śūnyatā*), he says, binds all things together in sense. But *śūnyatā* is not another ontology, it is the middle way.

Now the vital point here is the relation of the middle way to the theoretical questions which terminate in it. If this relation is arbitrary it can have little interest for the philosopher. But could it be that Nāgārjuna has pushed ontological thinking to its limit in such a way that he forces us to reexamine the sense of the ontological question we have been asking? Does he force us to ask what the ultimate nature of the ontological problem is? To ask ourselves what we are *doing* when we ask questions about being?

Is he telling us that the end of philosophical thought is not the answer to a question with which it began nor even the end of a quest, but the transmutation of 'thought' into what is more than thought: into a 'way,' which is what it is, which binds together in sense, only because it has taken up into itself all that thought can do—and so is not like other cessations of thought: passion, trance, ecstasy? Does the middle way not supervene at precisely the point where thought is driven beyond itself, having failed to achieve its aim—that of making sense out of all matters brought before it? Is the end of philosophy to discover that philosophical questions, all along, were not in the service of philosophical answers?

Notes

1. The standard text from which all quotations are taken is Louis de le Vallée Poussin, *Mūlamadhyamakakārikās de Nāgārjuna avec la Prasannapadā Commentaire de Candrakīrti* (St. Petersburg: Bibliotheca Buddhica, 1913). Referred to as *Prasan-*

napadā. Nāgārjuna's verses are referred to as MK. See Bibliography for translations available.

2. Max Müller, ed., *Sacred Books of the East*, vol. 13, Vinaya texts, pt. 1 (Delhi: (Motilal Banarsidas, 1965), pp. 94–96.

3. The terms *mārga* and *pratipad* frequently are interchanged in the early *sūtras*, but the Mādhyamika school gave *pratipad* a unique philosophical significance.

4. MK. XV.7. The *sūtra* is found in *The Book of the Kindred Sayings*, trans. Caroline Rhys Dayids (London: Luzac, 1952), vol. 2, pp. 12–13.

5. The *Ratnakūṭa Sūtra*. For an account of this work see A.K. Warder, *Indian Buddhism* (Delhi: Motilal Banarsidas, 1970), pp. 356–59.

6. Chapter 15. An English translation was published in *Ānvīksikī* (Banaras: Banaras Hindu University) by M. Sprung and U.S. Vyas. A German translation is available in Schayer *Ausgewählte Kapitel*. See Bibliography.

7. *Prasannapadā*, 260.4–5.

8. Ibid., 264.3.

9. Ibid., 264.12–265.1. The key passage in the entire chapter because it gives devoidness of particular being (*śūnyatā*) and the way things truly are (*tattvam*) as synonyms of self-existence. *Śūnyatā* is the term around which Mādhyamika thought revolves. A compressed account of its many facets would be worthless. For present purposes one can bear in mind that *śūnyatā* is itself the middle way.

10. Ibid., 265.1–2.

11. MK. XVIII.9.

12. *Prasannapadā* 265.3–5.

13. MK. XXIV.18.

Bibliography

Texts

de la Vallée Poussin, Louis. *Mūlamadhyamakakārikās de Nāgārjuna avec la Prasannapadā Commentaire de Candrakīrti*. St. Petersburg: Bibliotheca Buddhica, 1913.

Translations of the Prasannapadā *(into European Languages)*

de Jong, J.W. *Cinq Chapitres de la Prasannapadā*. Paris: Paul Geuthner, 1949. Chaps. 18–22.

Lamotte, E. *Le Traite de l'acte de Vasubandhu*. Appendix, chap. 17.

May, Jacques. *Candrakīrti Prasannapadā Madhyamakavṛtti*. Paris: Adrien Maisonneure, 1959. Chaps. 2, 3, 4, 6, 8, 9, 11, 23, 24, 26, 28.

Schayer, S. *Ausgewählte Kapitel aus der Prasannapadā.* Cracow: Polish Academy of Sciences, 1931. Chaps. 5, 12, 13, 14, 15, 16.
Schayer, S. *Feuer und Brennstoff*, Rocznik Orientalistyczny, vol. 7 (1931). Chap. 10, pp. 26–51.
Stcherbatsky, Th. *The Conception of Buddhist Nirvāṇa.* Leningrad: 1927. Reprint: The Hague: Mouton, 1965. Chaps. 1 and 25.

Translations of Nāgārjuna's Madhyamakakārikās (into English)

Streng, Fred J. *Emptiness* (Appendix). Nashville: Abingdon Press, 1967.
Inada, Kenneth K. *Nāgārjuna.* Tokyo: Hokuscido Press, 1970.

Other Major Texts

Conze, Edward. *The Perfection of Wisdom in Eight Thousand Lines and Its Verse Summary.* Berkeley: The Four Seasons Foundation, 1970.
Matics, Marion L. trans. *Entering the Path of Enlightenment* (*Bodhicaryāvatara of Śāntideva*). London: MacMillan, 1970.

Secondary Literature

Inada, Kenneth K. *Nāgārjuna*, Tokyo: Hokuscido Press, 1970.
Murti, T.R.V. *The Central Philosophy of Buddhism.* London: Allen and Unwin, 1955.
Robinson, R. *Early Mādhyamika in India and China.* Madison: University of Wisconsin Press, 1967.
Sprung, Mervyn, ed. *The Problem of Two Truths in Buddhism and Vedānta.* Dordrecht: Reidel, 1973.
Streng, Frederic J. *Emptiness.* Nashville: Abingdon Press, 1967.

J.N. MOHANTY

Some Aspects of Indian Thinking on Being

The three Sanskrit words, crucial for any thinking about being, are: the verb *asti* (exists), having for its root *as*; the abstract noun *sattā* (being); and *bhāva*, which is derived from the root *bhū*.

The root *as* has among its meanings to be, to live, to exist, to be present, to take place or happen, to abide, dwell, or stay, and also to become. Grassman's *Wörterbuch zum Rig Veda* singles out as its primary meaning "Sich regen, leben"—out of which the concept of being is said to have developed. As should be obvious, the root verb denotes to be present, to happen, as well as to become. *Astitā*, or existence, is then that which is common to them all, existence in a sense which applies both to that which is present, to a happening or occurrence, and to becoming. They all are.

The word *sat* is more commonly used in philosophical literature; while it retains the ontologically and valuationally 'neutral' meaning of *astitā*, it goes beyond that in its connotation, so that besides meaning being, existing, occurring, happening, being present, living, and enduring, it also comes to mean the true, good, and right. Both these aspects together lead to the idea of essence, the true being. We have here the origins, or perhaps the traces, of a sort of coexistence of what may be called the phenomenological and metaphysical strands in Indian thought on being. Being or existence—unqualified by the modifiers 'real' or 'true'—is a phenomenological concept. Among the meanings of *sat* which Grassman lists, there is also *tüchtig*, *wirksam*—a meaning which was developed by some of the Buddhist philosophers.

The word *sat*, as well as its abstract derivative, *sattā*, is closely related to the word *satya* which, besides meaning true, real, also has valuational meanings such as genuine, sincere, honest, truthful, pure, virtuous, good, successful, effectual. Attempts to give *satya* a metaphysical meaning are already found in the *Bṛhadāraṇyaka Upaniṣad* (V.5.1), where the three syllables constituting the word (*sa* + *ti* + *yam*) are interpreted as standing, respectively, for the real, the unreal, and the real—so that the word is made to refer to the fact that unreality is enclosed on both sides by reality. *Taittirīya Upaniṣad* (II.6.1) does the same with the concepts of the "formed" and the "formless," whereby the word *satya* is interpreted as meaning the unity of both.

The word *bhāva*, along with its root *bhū*, is more unambiguously a becoming word; it means to become, to arise, to come into being, but also to live, stay, abide, and exist, and, also, to happen and to occur. By implication, it comes to mean the place of coming into being, i.e., space, world, or universe—the place, spot, piece of ground, the earth. The root has two derivative abstract nouns: *bhava*, which predominantly expresses the sense of becoming, continuity of becoming, in Buddhist writings; and *bhāva*, where the sense of what has been comes to the fore. *Bhāva*, as the state of being of anything, also means the essence of a thing, but essence in the sense in which, according to Hegel, the German term *Wesen* points to what has been, or *gewesen*.[1] There is a narrower sense of *bhāva*, to be distinguished from this, where, as in later philosophical literature, it came to qualify *padārtha* or entity, to mean positive entity as contrasted with *a-bhava padārtha* or negative entity. It was neither meant that an *abhāva padārtha* or negative entity has no nature of its own, nor was it intended that it, the negative entity, does not possess being in some sense or other. Thus when Yāska, the author of *Nirukta*, refers to the view of Vārsyāyani that there are six modes of *bhāva*—is born, is, undergoes change, grows, decays, and perishes—he is evidently referring to positive and non-eternal entities.[2]

The uses of the three words, *sattā*, *astitā*, and *bhāva* have been specified as follows:

1. *Astitā*, or "existence," belongs to all entities, positive and negative, particular and universal, permanent and changing.
2. *Bhāva* belongs to all entities which, contrasted with the negative entities, have a positive nature of their own.
3. *Sattā* belongs to all positive entities excepting universals and certain other entities in which a universal cannot be said to inhere.

It was this scheme which determined the Nyāya-Vaiśeṣika attitude toward the problem of being, to which I shall now turn, and which was opposed by both the Buddhists and the Vedāntins.

Is 'existence' a *real* predicate? That is to say, in the words of Kant, does 'exist' or 'is' add anything to the concept of the subject and enlarge it?[3] The Nyāya school answers this question in the affirmative; both the Buddhists and the Vedānta deny it, but on very different grounds. The Buddhists deny it, for they think that of something that exists, affirmation of existence must be tautologous and denial must be self-contradictory. The Vedāntins deny it, for 'existence' designates for them not a predicate but the ultimate substance, and thus the subject of which the grammatical subject of an existential proposition is a predicate. But to begin with, let me turn to the Nyāya view.

To recall some familiar Nyāya doctrines: while proper names denote individuals, class-names denote individuals as qualified by class-properties. The reference to a commonly shared class-property is implied in any use of a class-name; of these class-properties only those that are not further analyzable, i.e., are simple, and that are instantiated in more than one individual, and which fulfill several other technical requirements are granted the ontological status of being real universals. Consider then the following judgments:

This jar is blue (1)

and

This jar exists (2)

Judgment (1) is roughly analyzed as a certainty (*niścaya*) whose content is the fact that 'blue,' as determined by blueness, serves as a qualifier (*prakāra*) of the 'jar,' as determined by jarness and thisness. This analysis is provisional and needs expansion in the light of further details of the Navya-Nyāya theory, for which reference may be made to B.K. Matilal's *The Navya-Nyāya Doctrine of Negation* and my *Gangeśa's Theory of Truth*.[4] What is important for our present purpose is that nowhere in this analysis does 'existence' enter as a component of the fully analyzed expression—so that one may say that existence of the jar, as also the existence of blueness in it, are "presupposed" rather than asserted when one asserts the content. The Sanskrit linguistic form *ghato nilaḥ* correctly reflects the situation by letting the copula 'is' remain unsaid, and even when it is explicitly there, it stands not for assertion of existence, but either for the relation obtaining between the epistemic contents, or for the subjective certainty about it. It is also worth noticing that in the analysis of the judgment (1), as in all Nyāya epistemic analysis, the term that is directly designated by the word actually used is to be taken as qualified by the class-property designated by the corresponding "unsaid" abstract noun. Though the name for blueness will be 'blueness,' the word 'blue' does the job of invoking blueness as the unspoken-of (*anullikhita*) qualifier of the blue color; it is the same as in the cases of 'this' and 'jar.'

Judgment (2), however, is an existential judgment in which, instead of 'blue,' 'existence' is predicated of 'this jar'; and likewise the particular existence of this jar is to be taken as determined by the universal generic property of "existence in general" or *sattā*. Here, it seems to me, the Nyāya analysis of (2), if construed in parallel terms with that of (1), runs into difficulties, for one then has to distinguish between the particular existence of this jar and existence in general—which the Nyāya does not want to do in accordance with its principle that qualified being (*viśiṣtasattā*) and pure being (*suddhasattā*) are identical.[5] But then one has to say that the predicate 'exists' directly attributes the universal *sattā* (and not an instance of it) to the subject term 'this jar.' Judgment (2), then, expresses the certainty about the inherence of the universal *sattā* in the particular entity referred to by 'this jar.'

Of course, the Nyāya took care to see that there is no infinite regress in speaking of existence as a universal, for if universals are real entities, then they too may be said to exist, so that existence may be predicated of existence itself. To avoid this infinite regress and self-predication they restricted the domain of meaningful ascription of existence to the first three types of entities recognized in their ontology: substance (*dravya*), quality (*guṇa*), and action (*karma*). This restriction, though saving the theory from logical puzzles, has been a source of a major philosophical difficulty for the system—for now the problem is one of inevitably distinguishing between, and also relating, two senses of 'existence': one applying to substances, qualities, and actions, and the other applying to universals, negative entities, and the other two types of entities recognized, inherence (*samavāya*) and individuality (*viśeṣa*).

One way out of this difficulty is to suggest that only substances, their qualities, and actions *are*, i.e., exist, in the primary and the stronger sense; while the other sorts of entities (universals, negative entities, etc.) exist in a weaker sense, i.e., as in some way or other related to one or more of those that exist in the stronger sense. This is a plausible thesis, except that the Nyāya did hold a sort of universal realism according to which a universal *is*, irrespective of whether its instances are real or not.

Another way of avoiding the difficulty is to give 'existence,' in its stronger sense, the meaning of spatio-temporal location, and 'existence,' in its weaker sense, the meaning of 'subsistence' in the once fashionable Russellian sense. Though universals may be said to 'subsist' in the sense of having their *original* (uninstantiated) being outside of space and time, to say the same of negative entities would seem to be counter-intuitive. Furthermore, among substances which are said to exist in the stronger sense of having spatio-temporal location are included space, time, and self. The Nyāya, of course, locates self in space by regarding it as all-pervading (some even do the same with regard to universals), but what is spatially all-pervading, just for that reason, may be said to be located in space only in a very special sense. Leaving this aside, what do we do with space and time themselves? Do they exist in the strong sense?

A third answer is to distinguish between the two senses of 'exist' thus: in the case of substances, their properties and actions, 'to exist' means to be the locus of a relation of inherence with the universal 'existence.' A jar exists in the sense that the universal 'existence' inheres in it, i.e., the relation of inherence (*samavāya*) holds good between 'existence' and the jar. 'To exist,' in the weak sense, then would mean to be 'intrinsically existent' (i.e., to have *svarūpasattā*). Negatively, what this means is that even without being the locus of a relation of inherence to 'existence,' a universal like blueness *is*. But what this concept of intrinsic existence (*svarūpasattā*) could positively mean is difficult to ascertain.

It seems then, that it might be wiser, in the absence of a satisfying way of distinguishing between the two senses of 'exist,' to retain only one sense applicable to all sorts of entities that are admitted in the system.[6] Raghunātha Śiromaṇi seeks to do just that in his *Padārthatattvanirūpaṇam* by identifying *sattā* and *bhāva*. We are still left with a sense of 'being' that would apply, in the same sense, to negative entities as well; and in each case, saying that something exists would then mean, following Raghunātha, not relatedness to a universal 'existence' (for that would not allow extension to universals) but relatedness to *time* in the mode of presence: *ghatādau sadvyavahāraśca vartamānatvanibandhanaḥ*. This would be virtually retracting the Nyāya theory that 'existence' designates a real universal and is a real predicate—as Ingalls rightly suspects.[7] One consequence of this sense of 'existence' is a need to mellow down the realism, with regard to universals, to a kind of Aristotelianism; another—and a more revolutionary consequence—is the need of taking time out of the list of real entities, for if existence be relatedness to time (*kālasambandhitvam*), then time itself would have to have an altogether different status.

For the Buddhist thesis that existence is not a real predicate, I will quote the following statement from Vasubandhu's *Abhidharmakoṣa*, book IX: "We say matter 'is produced,' 'it exists,' but there is no difference between existence and the element which does exist."[8] The point of the argument is thus developed by Vācaspati Miśra in his *Nyāyavārttikatātparyaṭīkā*: Consider the existential affirmative judment 'Cow exists' and the existential negative judgment 'Cow does not exist.' In both, the predicate is 'existence.' But of what is 'existence' predicated? If the word 'cow' designated a real existent, then affirmation of existence would be pointless and denial of existence self-contradictory. Therefore 'existence' is not a predicate of a real; it is affirmed or denied only of a concept. Of what is real, 'existence' need not be affirmed and cannot be denied. In fact, it and its existence are one and inseparable. As Vasubandhu said, "there is no difference between existence and the element which does exist."

This argument, though not the Buddhist's use of it, is precisely that which Russell advanced to prove that existence is not a predicate. As he put it, in "Lions exist," 'existence' is predicated not of things designated by 'lion,' but of the concept 'lion' or the propositional function '*x* is lion'

—so that to say that lions exist is to say that this function is true for some values of *x*. Russell, like the Buddhists, also held that if "Socrates" were a proper name and not a concept or a description, then "Socrates exists" would be tautologous and "Socrates does not exist" would be self-contradictory. This is precisely what he meant by his denial of the thesis that 'existence' is a predicate.

So for the Buddhist, when 'existence' is being predicated—affirmed or denied—it is predicated of what does not exist, namely, of a concept, a *vikalpa*. Of what does exist, 'existence' is not a possible predicate at all. But the Buddhist thesis is stronger than Russell's: in fact, nothing is a predicate of the real, as the real is ineffable.

Vacaspati goes on to ask: What then is the similarity between that which is pure existence (*sattāmātra*) and the universal 'cow' which can be affirmed or denied? He formulates the Buddhist answer thus: "It is the fact that both are not *non-cows*. If the constructed object (*vikalpaviṣaya*) 'cow' is nothing beyond its contrast with non-cows, the similarity (with the point of reality expressed in the element 'This') becomes possible and explains the possibility of the existential judgment 'This is a cow.'"[9] This position is necessitated by the fact that though 'existence' is predicated only of the concept, there is nevertheless a real existent underlying the true judgment: Both the concept and the real that underlies it have only this much in common, that they both exclude non-cows (in accordance with the Buddhist *apohavāda*), so that a *true* judgment of the form "This cow exists" is possible. This should not give the impression that, according to the Buddhist view I am expounding, the real, like the concept, is also *anyāpoha*, or negation of the other. On the contrary, the real is purely positive, *bhāvasvarūpa*, or even *vidhisvarūpa*.[10] What is excluded from it is "all that we can alternately affirm *and* deny." The concept, on the other hand, is constituted by negativity, by differentiation from others (*anyāpoha*). The real underlies the concept, renders the differentiation through concepts possible, but it is not itself conceptualizable: it is *vikalpa-jñānapratibhā-sāyogya*; it is its own nature (*svalakṣaṇa*); it cannot even be named; names are as much constructions (*vikalpa*) as concepts; there are no Russellian proper names which merely denote but do not describe; even 'this' ascribes the property of 'thisness.'

If the Buddhist had completely separated the two realms, the existent and the construct, his position would have been simpler, but only at the cost of overlooking the complexity of phenomena. However, he realized that mental constructions cannot hang in the air, and that there is a sense in which some judgments are true and some false. Furthermore, even if the criterion of truth within empirical discourse be pragmatic success, one would expect that success to be rooted at some point in the real. With a view to taking care of these considerations, the Buddhists nevertheless made the ineffable, unutterable, unconceptualizable real the underlying support of mental constructions, and also made pure perception, in which such a real is encountered, the *basis* of perceptual judgments. To that extent, and only to that extent, is the real, though transcendental, also immanent in ordinary experience: hence also the source of the otherwise misleading ascription of 'existence' to what are mental constructs!

It is now understandable why the Buddhist should admit the possibility of making significant statements about what are empty subject terms. The context in which this issue has generally been introduced is, of course, the Buddhist statement, "Whatever is non-momentary is non-existent," to which the Nyāya objection, based on the theory that the subject term of any significant statement must be referring, is obvious: "How can you talk about the non-momentary when no such thing exists, according to you?" I do not intend to discuss how the Buddhist defends such talk, or how the Naiyāyika would paraphrase such sentences to dispense with the non-referring expressions. What I wish to point out is simply this: Given the philosophical situation to the effect that the existent is unspeakable, unconceptualizable, indescribable, and that what we in fact talk about are mental constructions, it follows that all that we do talk about are fictions (though in a rather attenuated sense of 'about' our talk is about existents). Though within mental constructs we have to distinguish between those that have empirical reality (cows) and those that do not have it (dragons), yet the fundamental situation is the same; and it is only natural that the Buddhist has to defend the possibility of talk about fictions—for, after all, what else is any talk about?

I should also add that when the Buddhist defines existence as causal efficiency (*arthakriyākāritva*), he should *not* be interpreted as ascribing to the existent particular any "capacity" or "power" in the sense in which Hume has criticized these concepts. To ascribe to the existent any such "power" would be to ascribe to it an "essence," a *svabhāva*, an inner nature, which would be inconsistent with its characterization as *sva-lakṣaṇa*, i.e., with the Buddhist's denial of unactualized potentialities. To say that existence is characterized by causal efficiency is but to say that all that exists is causally efficient, i.e., produces an effect, or is replaced by a next member, also that whatever is not is not-existent. Both statements as statements are about mental constructs: the former about constructs that are relatively valid, the latter about constructs that are complete fictions (the non-efficient, the non-existent).

Whatever else the Buddhist real may be, it certainly is not a substance, for *dravya* is one of the five types of conceptual constructions mentioned by Dignāga.[11] It has to be a simple, but surely not a physical atom. To be consistent with the thesis of utter ineffability and the instantaneousness of the real, it should be an event. Other terms used are "point-instants," "exclusive particulars" (Matilal), "momentary bursts of energy" (Sharma), "quanta of energy" (McDermott). The event may be construed either as extra-mental, or as a flash of cognition—depending upon whether one is a *sautrāntika* or a *yogācāra*; in the former case, the objective event occurs simultaneously with the flashing of consciousness, both being independent and there being a coordination (*sādrśya*) between them.[12] In the latter case, the one flash of cognition bifurcates itself into act and content.

My purpose is not to enter into the details of Buddhist metaphysics or even to survey, in barest outlines, the major Buddhist theories. What I have tried to do is to highlight one dominant Buddhist concept of being. According to this view, then, 'being' or 'existence' or *sattā*, taken as universal terms, designate mental constructions (like all general terms); as logical predicates of the form 'exists' and 'does not exist,' they are predicated only of other mental constructs (cow, dragon). What is real is the existent which is non-different from its existence. The picture of the existent as a substance possessing properties, or even as an aggregate of properties, of which 'existence' is one, is misleading. Each is a unique occurrence. Such a series of unique occurrences underlies and supports mental constructions, and lends whatever plausibility there is in talking of truth and validity with regard to these mental constructions.

If, for the Nyāya, 'existence' is the most general predicate, the highest universal, and according to the Buddhists there is no existence as such, but only the uniquely existing occurrence, then the Advaita Vedānta regards 'existence' not as a predicate, but as the ultimate subject of all predication—the enduring 'substratum' of all qualifications. This agrees with the Nyāya that existence (*sattā*) is the highest generality, but it differs in regarding it not as a universal but as a substance (*dravya*); it agrees with the Buddhist that it is not a predicate, but differs in regarding it not as instantaneous occurrence but as a timeless, simple substance underlying all things and permitting them to borrow their existence-claim from their "association" with it. Again, another of its affinities to the Buddhist thesis is apparent: just as, according to the Buddhist, any empirical judgment derives its validity from the uniquely existing occurrence that underlies and supports the mental constructions constituting the judgment, so also for Advaita Vedānta, any existential judgment, in fact any judgment, presupposes the self-manifesting being as the ground of its possibility.

Thus runs a well-known Advaita couplet:

> Astibhāti priyam rūpam nāma ca iti aṁśapañcakam
> ādyatrayam brahmarūpam jagadrūpamatodvayam

Of the five "parts"—'exists,' 'appears,' 'pleases,' 'form,' and 'name'—the first three are of the nature of *brahman*, and the remaining two of the nature of the world. In other words, according to the Advaita thesis, whenever we assert of anything that it exists, its existence is of the nature of *brahman*, but only as limited by the content of "it." Likewise, whenever we say of anything that it appears, the bare element of manifestation as abstracted from the content that is manifested is the *brahman*. It is also the same in the case of value judgments. This shows, according to Advaita Vedānta, that being is as much immanent as transcendent with regard to ordinary experience; it is immanent as the indwelling condition of its possibility, it is transcendent inasmuch as in its purity it is beyond the limitations of content encountered in ordinary experience.

In saying that Advaita construes being in the manner of a substance, I am aware that my contention is liable to serious objections and disclaimers. I will therefore adduce two evidences in support of my contention, and then proceed to subject it to an important qualification. First, let us recall the famous statement of the *Chāndogya Upaniṣad*, of which Śaṅkara makes much use: "Just as, good Sir, when the one lump of clay is known, all things made of clay are known, so all formations are merely differences of name, the clay alone is the truth."[13] The priority of substance in Śaṅkara's ontology is most clearly stated in his commentary on *Brahma-sūtra* II.2.17:

> We ascertain the difference of smoke and fire from the fact of their being apperceived in separation. Substance and quality, on the other hand, are not so apperceived; for when we are conscious of a white blanket, or a red cow, or a blue lotus, the substance is in each case cognised by means of the quality; the latter therefore has its Self in the substance. The same reasoning applies to action, generality, particularity, and inherence.[14]

It would then seem that, according to Śaṅkara, the one being is the one universal substance; it is different from the finite substances qua substance in that the finite substances have qualities, whereas the one being has no distinguishable quality; furthermore, of a finite substance, existence appears to be a predicate, whereas this one being is the existence to which all finite substantial contents are, in reality, predicates. The qualification, then, to my contention that Śaṅkara regards being as a substance, is this: Of all finite ontological categories, the category of "substance," being the most fundamental of them, comes closest to a true understanding of the nature of being; where this cateogry fails, none other can do the job any better.

Unlike the Nyāya-Vaiśeṣika, for whom everything whatsoever *is* (whether by relatedness to the universal *sattā*, or "intrinsically"), the Advaita Vedānta operates with a criterion of being, and in this it shares a common mode of thinking with the Buddhist who also has his criterion of causal efficiency to begin with. The criterion with which Advaita Vedānta operates—the criterion both of being and reality, for the two are identical in it, as in Buddhism—is non-contradiction. Now there would seem to be two ways of formulating the criterion of non-contradiction, one logical, the other experiential. The former is employed by Nāgārjuna and F.H. Bradley: That is real which is free from logical self-contradiction. It seems to me that the philosophers who apply the logical criterion are primarily metaphysicians; even if they seek to demolish metaphysics, they do so through metaphysical thinking. Their concern is *reality*. Śaṅkara's criterion is experiential: Being must be that which admits of no experiential contradiction, it must be that whose negation is not possible, for it must be the all-pervasive, ever-present support of all that appears to be. If the illusory snake is, upon correction of the illusion, negated as non-existent, the being of the snake-phenomenon is not. Of no empirical *content* as such can we say that it cannot possibly be negated by subsequent empirical evidence. There is only one thing which, with absolute certainty, precludes the possibility of experiential contradiction, and that is consciousness. For the absence of consciousness, to be a possibility, must be established by and testified to by consciousness. To say that an entity is, but cannot be proved, perceived, or otherwise known, talked about, etc., is to be inconsistent. If there were absence of consciousness, such absence must be an object of consciousness, which would be a manifest absurdity. Consciousness alone can posit its own absence; hence, although absence of this or that modality of consciousness, this or that content of consciousness, is well conceivable, absence of consciousness *as such* is inconceivable. Being is consciousness. Any content whatsoever *appears to be*, because consciousness *is*. As the *Vedāntaparibhāṣā* puts it: "*Brahmasattayā eva sarveṣām sattāvyavahāraḥ*."

Consciousness alone does not appear to be; it *is*. For, in the case of consciousness, appearance and reality coincide; it is fully transparent, its being is manifestation, *prakāśa eka rasa*. Whatever is an object of consciousness may be negated; consciousness, not being an object of consciousness, cannot be negated, for any such negation would be a negating consciousness.

From this thesis that consciousness is not a possible counter-positive (*pratiyogi*) of negation, the Advaita philosophers proceed to deduce various propositions about consciousness. Negation is either difference or absence. Difference is either homogenous (as of one cow from another), heterogenous (as of a cow from a horse), or internal (as of parts of a whole). Absence is either absence antecedent to origination, absence consequent upon destruction, or absence of a thing at one place or time while it is present at another place or another time. Now if none of these modes of difference, as well as none of these modes of absence, are applicable to consciousness,

consciousness becomes one being, undifferentiated, eternal, changeless. All differences and absences are its objects, none belongs to its nature.

In this conclusion, phenomenology and metaphysics get blended together. Here, as in Buddhism, the link between the two is provided by a most elusive concept, the concept of ignorance or *avidyā*. If being is consciousness, and if, as being, consciousness provides the foundation and the support for all beings and makes possible ascription of existence to any object whatsoever; if, that is to say, any ascription of existence as a predicate is, in fact, an ascription of a predicate *to* existence or being, then why is it that this *inversion* takes place? Why is it that what is, in itself, appears as attaching predicatively to what is in reality not a substantive? Why is it that consciousness seems to be my state when in fact it is my being, and 'I' am its modification? Why is it that consciousness—self-shining and autonomous in its self-concern—should come to exhibit that intentionality, or being-toward-the-world, which characterizes ordinary experience? The answer is *avidyā* or "ignorance"; but even the being of ignorance is the same self-shining consciousness. *Avidyā* both rests on it and seeks to conceal it, i.e., to conceal that which lends it its own being; in this consists the paradoxical nature of *avidyā*. *Avidyā* conceals being but insofar as it itself is experienced, as in the judgment "I am ignorant," being is not totally concealed. For were it in total concealment, *avidyā* itself would not be manifested, in fact, there would be, as some Vedānta authors put it, utter darkness (*jagadāndhyaprasaṅga*). Experience is the chiaroscuro of light and darkness; neither complete, unhindered illumination, nor all-enveloping darkness, but darkness resting on, concealing, and yet revealed by, light.

But darkness is not sheer non-being. *Avidyā* is a positive being, a beginningless power which is conceived as of having the two functions of *concealment* of being and *projection* of empirical forms on the formless being. In order not to appear to be identifying the world of entities with sheer non-being, some Vedānta authors distinguish between three orders of being: *pāramarthika* or transcendental being; *vyavahārika* or empirical being; and *prātibhāsika* or apparent being. These three are ordered in such a manner that the third form of being derives its being from the second, while its content is its own; and the second, likewise, derives its being from the first, while its content is its own. The first is contentless being, the mere 'that' without any 'what.' In fact, all 'that,' the 'that' of an empirical object or even of a hallucinatory object, derives from it. When an apparent being is negated with cancelation of an illusion, what is canceled is the content, not the fact of its appearing. The same holds good, when—as in spiritual knowledge—the reality of the empirical being is canceled. The unnegatable, uncanceled abstraction of mere "appearing," "manifestation," "awareness"—abstracted from all contents that appear—is being.

It is time now to tie together some of the loose ends in the exposition given above, and to use this for throwing light on some fresh aspects of the problems concerned.

We began by asking whether 'being' is a real predicate. To this the Nyāya offered an affirmative answer, but its answer ran into difficulties owing to its exclusion of all entities other than substances, qualities, and actions from existing in the primary sense: It had to search for a common and generic sense in which all its entities (*padārthas*) might be said to exist, and that led Raghunātha Śiromaṇi to the conception of relatedness to time in the mode of presence. We pointed out some likely consequences of such a theory. The Buddhist rejected the theory that existence is a real predicate of existing particulars, for such existents are unique and ineffable; he admitted, however, that it is a logical predicate of *concepts*, which are but logical constructions. To exist, in the primary sense, then—for the Buddhist view expounded—is to be a member of a series of instantaneous occurrences; to exist, in this sense is for a mental construct to be related to such a primary construct by the relation of coordination or *sārūpya*. The Advaita Vedānta understands being as that which is in principle unnegatable, that which is the principle of manifestation, the self-manifesting and other-manifesting awareness abstracted from all contents, to be understood on the analogy of the most universal substance, but again, as Hegel said, substance understood as subjectivity. To be, in the primary sense, is to be self-manifest*ing*; to be, in the derived sense, is to be manifest*ed* by consciousness.

How are these three concepts of being reflected in the respective ontologies and also in their epistemologies? The following points are worth recalling. In the Nyāya ontology, since all entities possess being, in some sense or other, each has a being of its own, so that there is a resulting pluralism of entities. But at the same time, substances, qualities, and actions have being in a preeminent sense, requiring thereby that all other entities must inhere in, be residing in, some entity belonging to one or other of these three types. Particularities (*viśeṣa*) must inhere in, by its very conception, an ultimate, indivisible substance; and absence must 'reside in' an entity of some such kind. Consequently the Nyāya needs a relation which is both adequate to tie such diverse types of entities together and compatible with their type-differences. Of the three basic types, substance, quality, and action, again qualities and actions must belong to substances by the same sort of relation which would "tolerate" their type-differences, and yet bind them inalienably. Such a relation is *samavāya*, by which the Nyāya succeeds in reconciling a pluralistic ontology required by its concept of being with a systematically structured conception of the world in which the category of substance and the relation of *samavāya* occupy an especially basic status.

Advaita Vedānta denies the legitimacy of a relation that would inseparably bind entities and yet tolerate their type-differences. Either deny inseparability or deny difference. Śaṅkara chooses the latter. He writes in his commentary on *Brahma-sūtra* II.2.17: "Or else let the qualities, etc., depend on substance; then it follows that, as they are present where substance is present, and absent where it is absent, substance only exists, and according to its various forms, becomes the object of different forms and conceptions (such as quality, action, etc.); just as Devadatta, for instance, according to the conditions in which he finds himself, is the object of various conceptions and names." The relation, then, between the blue of the blue lotus and the lotus is not inherence of a quality in a substance, but *tādātmya*, which is not mere identity, but "the relation of having that (*tat*) as one's own self (*ātman*)."[15] The Self is the being. Substance is the being of qualities, etc., and of empirical substances. Being is the unnegatable principle of manifestation. Thus it follows from the Advaita Vedānta concept of being that such a relation should be fundamental to its ontology. But note that this relation is not one of undifferentiated identity, for that would not be a relation at all. *Tādātmya* is that identity which "tolerates" differences (*bhedasahiṣṇu*), but here it is not the difference between two types of reals, but between the real and its appearances.

For the Buddhist, the real is the instantaneous event; the only relation that such a concept allows is one of succession. But, with only the instant being real, there is no real relation that could relate the successor to the predecessor; moreover, the relation itself would tend to be a recurrent relation and so could not be real. It is a mental construction. But that which "connects" a mental construct, like a concept, to its founding instant is not causation, not correspondence, but "co-ordination" (*sārūpya*). Most nominalistic ontologies, of course, recognize resemblance as a basic relation, but for the Buddhists *sārūpya*, though literally meaning "resemblance," is to be understood as "similarity between two things absolutely dissimilar" (*atyantavilakṣaṇānām sālakṣaṇyam*), a "similarity" produced either by non-apprehension of difference (*bhedāgraha*) or a common exclusion (*apoha*).[16]

How is being known, apprehended? It seems to me that, in general, consistent with the thesis of the *priority* of perception common to most systems, to every concept of being there is a correlative mode of perception in which it is given. Even in their theory of perception all three theories distinguish between a primary, "non-qualificative" (*nirvikalpaka*) pre-predicative, non-judgmental perception, and a subsequent, qualificative, predicative, judgmental perception. This distinction, as is well known, is made in different ways. It seems, however, that in each system being is apprehended in non-judgmental perception. This contention should be immediately accepted in the case of the Buddhist and the Advaita Vedānta systems. For the Buddhist, perception, in the strict sense, is but the pure sensation in which a unique, ineffable particular is apprehended; even for the Advaita Vedānta, the primary, pre-predicative encounter with any object presents us with the mere that, *sanmātram*, which subsequent predicative perception characterizes with a what. But I would even ascribe a type of the same thesis to the Nyāya. What I mean is this: If the Nyāya had only the theory of judgmental perception which it has, knowledge would always apprehend, e.g., the jar as qualified by jarness and as possessing the blue which itself is qualified by blueness. But, in that theory, there would have been no way for validating, even in principle, its basic pluralism, i.e., the separate being of each term of this predicative complex. This latter is validated by the primary non-qualificative perception, wherein there is no relational complex, no epistemic entities or relations (*viṣayatā*, *prakāratā*, or *saṁsargatā*, etc.), which apprehends, as Matilal puts it, "the Thing."[17] But the domain of the object of such a pre-predicative perception ranges over all types of entities: substances, qualities, actions, etc., which is in accord with the thesis that they all have being.

It is indeed difficult to decide whether in each of these cases the conception of being determines or is determined by the epistemological thesis. It seems to me plausible that in all these cases the epistemological thesis is a consequence of, a necessary concession to, the ontological thesis. Neither the Buddhist's pure sensation in which an instantaneous event flashes forth, nor the Advaita Vedānta's pre-predicative perception of the mere that, seems to me to be phenomenologically self-evidencing; the Nyāya non-qualificative perception, on the Nyāya admission itself, is not self-evidencing, but is rather inferred.

Another way of looking at the three theories is to note that for the Nyāya, the concept of being, in the widest sense, is the concept of an *indifference*. To be is extrinsic to the intrinsic nature of an entity. There is a sense, as was pointed out, in which all entities *are*. Let me call it *being as indifference*. This being is not exhausted by being an object of an act of consciousness, for a being may as well not be such an object. And even in the case of an entity that is *also* an object, being-object is not the same as mere being. Further, in the later systems of Navya-Nyāya such epistemic entities as object-ness (*viṣayatā*) are also entities and have being; just as an act of consciousness also *is*. An act of consciousness is, of course, directed to an object, but its being is not other than that of any other entity. In this widest sense there are types of entities, but there are no types of being. Again, just as all entities may be objects of knowledge, but the being is in no case exhausted by being-an-object, so also every entity may be named (*vācya*) but the property of being nameable (*vācyatva*) does not define being.

To be contrasted with this concept of being as indifference are the more *restricted* concepts of being, which allow distinction between entities qua entities, not all of which have being in any commonly ascribable sense. Such are the Buddhist and the Advaita Vedānta theories. As pointed out earlier, Advaita Vedānta distinguishes between three orders of being, so that illusory objects and empirically real objects have being in different senses from that in which *brahman*, or pure consciousness, has being. The same holds good of the Buddhist view expounded. Particularly in Advaita Vedānta, then, we have the overarching contrast between consciousness and the world: the former self-revealing, the latter not self-revealing but manifested only by being an object of consciousness; the former, independent and self-supporting, the latter dependent upon—in the sense of being an object of—the latter. To be sure, the being of the world does not consist in its being perceived; the world certainly—unlike the hallucinatory object—possesses *ajñātasattā*, unknown existence. But even as unknown, it is an object of consciousness. As the author of the *Vivaraṇaprameyasaṁgraha* expresses it: All things whatsoever are objects of pure consciousness, either as known or as unknown. Thus we can say the following:

1. The existence of hallucinatory objects consists in their being perceived.
2. The existence of the empirical world consists in its being object of consciousness—either in the mode of knowledge or in the mode of ignorance.
3. The being of consciousness is precisely its self-manifesting nature.

However, there is no Husserlian doctrine of constitution of the world in consciousness, for, first, consciousness is understood here as pure transparence, but not as intentionality; second, being simply the principle of manifestation, consciousness has no content of its own. Thus empty of all contents, consciousness more resembles the Sartrean "nothingness"; the world is given to it as an inexplicable absurdity, *anirvacanīya*, whose sense cannot, in principle, be entirely explicated.

How is the thought of being related to thought on time? It seems to me that, generally speaking, no Indian philosopher accorded to time that central place in ontology which modern Western philosophy has. But there were certainly tendencies which could have led in that direction. What I have in mind are the following:

1. The *Maitri Upaniṣad* (VI.15) says there are two forms of *brahman*: time and timeless (*kālaścākālaḥ*), and then goes on to add: "Time cooks all things [*kālaḥ pacati bhūtāni*]." "He who knows in what time is cooked, he is the knower of the Vedas."

But this primacy of time was never fully developed.

2. The Nyāya, as hinted above, did *come to hold* being as relatedness to time in the mode of presence. But this, as also was pointed out, would have required taking time out of the list of entities and giving it a primacy in speculations about being. That this turn of thought, namely, founding the concept of being on that of time, did not take place is partly due to a strong tendency in the opposite direction which is anticipated very early by Vātsāyana's commentary on the *Nyāya Sūtras* (II.1.41–43).[18] Vātsāyana argues that the present time is apprehended in two ways: first, as dissociated from the past and the future, and second, as associated with them. The first kind of apprehension is made possible by the *being* of an object, the second by a series of actions, such as "cooking" or "cutting." This analysis suggests that instead of the concept of being being rooted in the temporal mode of presence, the present is apprehended through the *being* of an object. The priority of time is replaced by the priority of the concept of being.

Nor does time play any role in the Advaita Vedānta thoughts on being, for it belongs to the world and consciousness is not characterized by temporality. The contents of consciousness are temporal, but they are in the world.

The Buddhist view of the real as the instantaneous occurrence has no more place for time, for temporality involves the notion of either a series or a specious present; it needs the idea of duration, and the Buddhists' pure particular has no duration. It is as much outside of time as is the Advaita Vedānta's pure consciousness.

Time is an entity for the realist. It is mundane for the Advaita Vedānta, and so has empirical being. It is a construction according to the Buddhist; it has no privileged role in thought on being. The notion of the historicity of being is alien to Indian thought; that entities are historical is a commonplace. But to locate and characterize the precise Indian attitude toward history is another matter.[19]

Notes

1. Thus Yāska, in *Nirukta* 1.1 distinguishes between nouns and verbs by saying that while nouns have being (*sattva*) for their predominant notion, verbs have becoming (*bhāva*) as the predominant notion. He then adds that the embodiment of the whole process from the beginning to the end which has taken up the character

of *being* is denoted by a noun such as 'going' or 'cooking.' This leads him to question whether all nouns are derived from verbs, which seems to have been the view of Sakatāyana. Yāska contends, as against this, that though surely some names derive from verbs, this is not always the case, for in general becoming is preceded by being. This lays the basis for most Hindu philosophical thought, which Buddhist philosophy opposed.

2. *Nirukta* I.2.

3. Immanuel Kant, *Kritik der reinen Vernunft*, A 598, B 626.

4. Bimal K. Matilal, *The Navya Nyāya Doctrine of Negation* (Cambridge: Harvard University Press, 1968), esp. pt. 1; J.N. Mohanty, *Gangeśa's Theory of Truth* (Śantiniketan: Center for Advanced Study in Philosophy, 1966), esp. pp. 32–37.

5. D.H. Ingalls, *Materials for the Study of Navya-Nyāya Logic* (Cambridge: Harvard University Press, 1951), p. 69.

6. K.H. Potter, *Presuppositions of India's Philosophies* (New York: Prentice-Hall, 1963), p. 69.

7. Ingalls, *Materials*, p. 54.

8. Th. Stcherbatsky, *Buddhist Logic* (New York: Dover Paperback), vol. 2, p. 347.

9. Ibid., p. 417.

10. Ibid., p. 416, n. 4.

11. M. Hattori, *Digñāga, on Perception* (Cambridge: Harvard University Press, 1968), p. 25.

12. Stcherbatsky, *Buddhist Logic*, vol. 2, p. 347, n. 1.

13. *Chāndogya Upaniṣad* VI.1.4.

14. Thibaut's English translation of Śaṅkara's *Brahmasûtrabhaṣyam*. Cf. *The Vedānta sûtras of Bādarāyaṇa with the commentary of Śaṅkara*, trans. George Thibaut (New York: Dover Paperback), pt. 1, p. 395.

15. Cf. R.V. De Smet, "Patterns and Theories of Causality," in *Essays in Philosophy Presented to T.M.P. Mahadevan*, ed. C.T.K. Chari et al. (Madras: Ganesh, 1962), pp. 347–67; esp. p. 366.

16. Stcherbatsky, *Buddhist Logic*, vol. 1, p. 213.

17. Bimal K. Matilal, *Epistemology, Logic and Grammar in Indian Philosophical Analysis* (The Hague: Mouton, 1971), esp. p. 90.

18. See M. Hiriyanna, *Indian Philosophical Studies* (Mysore: Kavyalaya, 1957), esp. pp. 121–26.

19. Cf. J.N. Mohanty, "Indian Thought and Philosophy of History," to appear in Grace E. Cairns and T.M.P. Mahadevan, eds., *Indian Philosophies of History*.

Selected Bibliography

Source Material

Rg.Veda X.129
Chāndogya Upaniṣad 1.4
Maitrî Upaniṣad VI.15
Yaska. *Nirukta* 1.1–1.2
Kaṇāda, *Vaiśeṣika Sûtras* 1.2.7–17; *Upaskara* and *Vivrti* on 7.2.27
Śaṅkara, *Bhāṣyam* on *Brahmasūtra* II.1.14 and II.2.17
Rāmānuja. Śrî Bhāṣyam, section "Mahāpûrvapakṣam"
Vallabha, *Nyāyalîlavatî* (Chowkhamba ed.), pp. 778–801
Prabhācandra. *Prameyakamalamārtanda.* Bombay: Nirnayasagara Press, 1941, pp. 531–34
Śāntarakṣîta. *Tattvasaṁgraha*, edited by Swami Dvarakadasasastri. Banares: Bauddha Bharali, 1968, section on "Sthirabhāvaparikṣā," verses 350–475, with Kamalāsīla's *Pañjikā*

Secondary Literature

Hiriyanna, M. *Indian Philosophical Studies.* Mysore: Kavyalaya, 1957
Matilal, Bimal K. *Epistemology, Logic and Grammar in Indian Philosophical Analysis.* The Hague: Mouton, 1971
Mookerjee, Satkari. "The Absolutist Standpoint in Logic," in S. Mookerjee, ed., *The Nava-Nalanda-Mahavihara Research Publication*, vol. 1. Nalanda: Navanalandamahavihara, 1957
Potter, Karl H. "Reality and Dependence in the Indian Darshanas," in *Essays in Philosophy Presented to T.M.P. Mahadevan*, edited by C.T.K. Chari et al. Madras: Ganesh, 1962, pp. 155–62.
Sastri, D.N. *Critique of Indian Realism.* Agra: Agra University Press, 1964
De Smet, R.V. "Patterns and Theories of Causality," in *Essays in Philosophy Presented to T.M.P. Mahadevan*, edited by C.T.K. Charietal. Madras: Ganesh, 1962
Stcherbatsky, Th. *Buddhist Logic*, 2 vols. New York: Dover, 1962.

Index